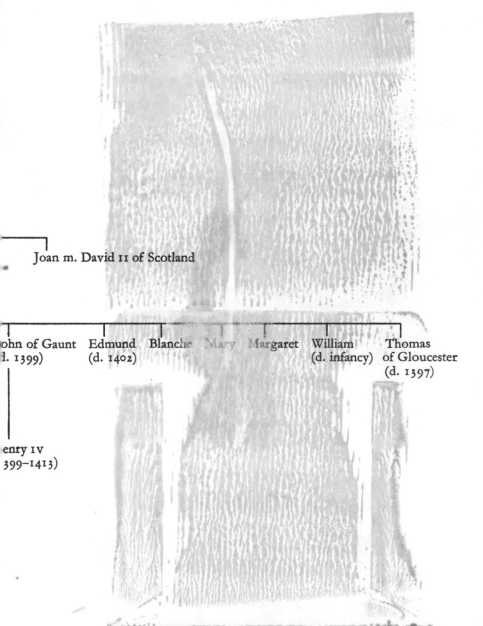

Joan m. David II of Scotland

ohn of Gaunt   Edmund   Blanche   Mary   Margaret   William   Thomas
l. 1399)   (d. 1402)   (d. infancy) of Gloucester
                                                 (d. 1397)

enry IV
399–1413)

War in Medieval
English Society

War in Medieval English Society

Social Values in the Hundred Years War 1337-99

John Barnie

Cornell University Press

Ithaca, New York

First published 1974 by Cornell University Press.

This book is published in the United Kingdom and
British Commonwealth under the title *War in Medieval
Society*.

International Standard Book Number 0-8014-0865-2
Library of Congress Catalog Card Number 74-2687

Printed in Great Britain by
REDWOOD BURN LIMITED
Trowbridge & Esher

To my Father and Mother

Contents

Acknowledgements

Professor Geoffrey Shepherd, who suggested this field of study to me, read and discussed the first draft of the book. I owe much to his wide and humane learning. My greatest debt is to Heather Barnie whose knowledge of medieval social history was always at my disposal, and whose help and encouragement during a difficult period were invaluable. I would also like to thank Professor R. H. Hilton for reading the book in its first draft; and Museumsinspektør J. Steen Jensen for help with the gold coinage of the reign of Edward iii. Needless to say, any remaining errors are my own.

The cost of typing the manuscript and compiling the index was defrayed by a generous grant from Statens Humanistiske Forskningsråd, Copenhagen.

I am grateful to the following for permission to quote from books copyrighted by them: The Council of the Early English Text Society (*Mum and the Sothsegger*, ed. M. Day and R. Steele); Manchester University Press (*Anonimalle Chronicle*, ed. V. H. Galbraith); Liverpool University Press (Bonet, *The Tree of Battles*, ed. G. W. Coopland); The Clarendon Press, Oxford (*The Life of the Black Prince by the Herald of Sir John Chandos*, ed. Mildred K. Pope and Eleanor C. Lodge); University of Washington Press (*The Major Latin Works of John Gower*, ed. and trans. E. W. Stockton).

Introduction

For three generations from 1337 to 99 England was either at war or in a state of preparedness for war with France and her allies. The effects of this on the kingdom's economy, and on its social and political institutions have been studied in some detail; but its influence on the thoughts and feelings of Englishmen has been largely neglected. This neglect may in part be due to the distrust which many historians feel for studies based on qualitative rather than quantitative evidence, but it also results from ignorance as to the exact nature and extent of available sources. In his valuable book *The Organization of War under Edward III*,[1] H. J. Hewitt has a chapter on 'Mind and Outlook' which attempts a study of this aspect of the war. Dr Hewitt's main sources are the Parliamentary Rolls, the Close and Patent Rolls, and Rymer's *Foedera*. Evidence from the chronicles is cited, but that which may be obtained from contemporary literature hardly at all.

It is unfortunate that historians' just suspicions of the value of chronicles to the study of certain aspects of political and social history should have led to a more general neglect of the genre. Particularly in the history of social and moral ideas and attitudes the evidence of the chronicles is often invaluable.

The literature of the fourteenth century is evidently a *terra incognita* for many historians. Dr Hewitt, for example, writes of 'the dearth of literary sources' for the Hundred Years War, and claims that although Chaucer, Langland and Gower 'reveal phases of the outlook of the English people . . . their references to the war are of the slightest'. In the same way he dismisses romance as reflecting the aristocratic conception of war as a 'gallant adventure'.[2] Dr Hewitt appears to be unaware of such Middle English romances as the alliterative *Morte Arthure* which describes the processes of contemporary warfare in some detail; or of the poems of Laurence Minot which are invaluable as a guide to popular responses to the war in its early stages. Likewise he ignores the considerable body of Latin literature devoted to the war: the prophecies attributed to John of Bridlington, for example, or the poems written in celebration of the battle of Neville's Cross and against the truce of 1347.

War in Medieval Society is an attempt to extend the study of the 'mind and outlook' of the English during the first sixty years of the Hundred Years War with the aid of sources partially or totally neglected by historians of the period. Its conclusions are of necessity qualitative and not quantitative, and more is revealed about the attitudes and ideas of some social groups than of others. Dr Hewitt is largely correct when he claims that the literature does not necessarily reflect the response of 'the people at large'; but it does reflect the emotions and thoughts which the war provoked in a surprisingly wide range of social groups. The response of the court and the military élite is well documented in the works of Froissart, the Chandos Herald, and to some extent Chaucer; a wide range of opinion amongst the regular and secular clergy is reflected in the monastic chronicles, vernacular and Latin sermons, the pamphlets of the Wyclifites, and a number of occasional poems; the poetry of Gower and Hoccleve presents the views of educated professional men on the periphery of court circles; and a unique insight into the mentality and outlook of a *miles strenuus* is provided by Sir Thomas Gray's *Scalacronica*. Even the views of 'the people at large' can be pieced together in general terms. The poetry of Minot, for example, clearly reflects the enthusiastic response of an unsophisticated audience; while the chronicles provide much incidental information about popular reaction to particular events, and at times attempt to characterize the general mood of the populace. It is even possible to trace differences in regional reactions to the war, for a number of chroniclers and poets writing in the northern counties have left impressions of the war with Scotland, while a chronicler like Thomas Walsingham was well placed to observe popular reaction in London and the south-east.

The aim of the present study is twofold. It attempts to trace in as great a detail as possible the changing responses of Englishmen to the Hundred Years War from the heyday of Crécy and Poitiers to the collapse of the kingdom's military fortunes in the

1370s and 1380s. More particularly, it examines the extent to which two important aspects of the social and moral consciousness of the age, chivalry and nationalism, were influenced by six decades of almost continuous warfare with France and Scotland.

I

Aspects of the War 1337-99[1]

When Edward III succeeded to the throne in 1327 England's prestige was at its lowest for many years. His father, Edward II, had failed miserably to give the kingdom good government, a failure made worse in contemporary eyes by comparison with the achievements of his predecessor, Edward I. Summing up the difference between the two kings the chronicler, Jean Froissart, observed that 'his son, Edward II, was by no means so valiant, nor so renowned, nor so full of prudence as the king his father had been.'[2] Shortly after his death there was a movement amongst the common people to sanctify the murdered king, but most informed men of the age saw little that was saintly or commendable in his life.[3] Edward II was renowned for his delight 'in the vice of sodomy'; he surrounded himself with players and buffoons; and took no pleasure in the royal pastimes of hawking and hunting, indulging instead an unforgivably rustic taste for swimming, and hedging and ditching.[4]

As a military commander Edward II was a failure. The only large-scale expedition to be mounted against the Scots during his reign ended in 1314 at the battle of Bannockburn. Here the English chivalry suffered an unparalleled defeat at the hands of Robert Bruce which dictated Anglo-Scottish relations for the rest of the reign.[5] Years later it was still remembered with shame. The Leicester chronicler, Henry Knighton, recalled that never before had a Scottish king inflicted such damage on the English. Indeed at that time, due to lack of good governance, 'two Englishmen were hardly worth one feeble Scot.'[6]

The assumption of the throne by Edward III at the age of fourteen did not seem to offer hope for an improvement in England's fortunes. Ranulph Higden, writing with hindsight, might praise his accession as marking a new era in the prosperity of the realm, but there was little indication of this in 1327. Edward was obliged to do homage to the king of France for the duchy of Gascony in 1325 and again in 1329, to the disgust of many Englishmen. More damaging still to the young king's reputation was his first expedition against the Scots (the Weardale campaign of 1327) which proved as humiliating if not as disastrous as his father's in 1314. According to the chroniclers Edward was deeply affected by the failure. Adam Murimuth, who wrote in the 1340s but was a contemporary of the events he describes, says that after the campaign the king returned 'mortified and without honour' to York; Knighton states that he returned 'in great desolation and sorrow that the beginning of his reign had not turned out better for him and, affected deeply by a sense of shame, he grieved much.'[7] Even more humiliating was the *turpis pax*, the 'shameful peace' of 1328. This was negotiated in Edward's name by Mortimer and Isabella, its main term being the renunciation by the English crown of all claims to the overlordship of Scotland. This more than anything outraged public opinion, for it was popularly held that Scotland had been an appanage of the English crown from the time of its conquest by the legendary Brutus.[8]

Nevertheless Edward himself remained free from censure. The chronicler, Geoffrey Baker, says that he was 'led by traitors', and popular blame fell upon Mortimer and Isabella who were thought to have favoured the Scots 'to the great derogation and dishonour of the king and the kingdom of England'.[9] One of the charges preferred against Mortimer in 1330 was that 'having received a large sum of money, he impeded the honour of the king at Stanhope Park.'[10] In their triumph the Scots nicknamed the English 'Jane make peace' and derided them in doggerel verse:*

> Long beerdys hartles,*   *cowardly
> Paynted hoodys wytles,
> Gay cotis graceles
> Makyth Englande thryfteles.*[11]   *unsuccessful

The probable effect of these humiliations on Edward has been summarized by Ranald Nicholson:

At the age of twenty Edward III had survived many a lurid or humiliating experience. His natural reaction was a lifelong pursuit of

*Quotations in Middle English have been partially modernized.

personal prestige and urbane conventionality. If, by contemporary standards, Edward II had been an arrant failure, his son was determined by the same standards to be an outstanding success. Only in the triumphs of a warlike king would England and Edward himself forget the recent past.[12]

The first of the triumphs needed to restore England's military prestige came with the renewal of the Anglo-Scots conflict. In 1332, with the unofficial support of the English king, the pretender to the throne, Edward Balliol, invaded Scotland and routed his opponents at the battle of Dupplin Moor.[13] The victory was short-lived for in the same year a nationalist uprising forced Balliol to take refuge in England. But in response to this Edward III finally repudiated the 'shameful peace' – according to Murimuth on the grounds that it was 'entered upon through treachery' while he was a minor in the charge of his mother.[14]

The parliament summoned by Edward to meet at York on 20 January 1333 was against intervention in Scottish affairs, however. Something of its apprehension in view of England's recent defeats may be glimpsed in the lines on the battle of Halidon Hill (1333) by the patriotic versifier Laurence Minot, who tells us that his heart had 'grete care' for England 'when Edward founded first to were [war]'.[15] Such concern was probably widespread, but in the north, where hatred of the Scots was always more bitter than elsewhere, Balliol's cause attracted popular support. According to the Lanercost chronicler the pretender was showered with gifts by the sympathetic citizens of Carlisle after his flight from Annandale in 1332: 'indeed, the community greatly esteemed him and his on account of the great confusion which he made amongst the Scots after he entered that land, even though at that very time that misfortune had befallen him.'[16] The chronicler repeats propagandist tales of a miracle at Balliol's coronation and of divine revelation of the Scots' defeat at Halidon Hill. In a similar vein, John Erghome, the Yorkshire compiler of *The Prophecy of John of Bridlington*, upholds Balliol as 'the true heir' to the Scottish crown.[17]

The victory at Halidon Hill over the Scots army sent to relieve Berwick did much to dispel the doubts expressed by the parliament at York and must have encouraged Balliol's English sympathizers. Minot's poem on the battle reveals something of the jubilation which Englishmen felt on hearing news of the victory:

Whare er ye, Skottes of Saint Iohnes toune?
The boste of yowre baner es betin* all doune;   *beaten
When ye bosting will bede* sir Edward es bounet†
                                          *offer †ready
For to kindel yow care and crak yowre crowne.

The Scots, he declares, were too bold when they slew innocent men at Bannockburn 'and now has king Edward wroken [avenged] it, I wene [suppose]'. Murimuth recalls that it was declared 'universally' that the war with Scotland was over for good 'because no one remained of that nation who either wanted to or had the power or the skill to assemble men for battle, or to lead them once assembled.' In Scotland itself the defeat was seen as divine punishment for the pride of the Scots.[18]

The rumour reported by Murimuth proved to be over-optimistic, but the campaign of 1333 gave England its first military success in years and proved Edward's qualities as a general. More importantly it betrayed something of the identity of royal and national interest which was to be such a remarkable feature of the early years of the war with France.

Modern historians seek the origin of the Hundred Years War in the conflict between Edward III and Philip VI over the duchy of Guienne, an essentially feudal struggle between a lord and an over-mighty vassal. It is the fashion to minimize the importance and seriousness of Edward's pretensions to the crown of France itself – the dynastic issue.[19] Contemporary opinion certainly recognized the importance of the quarrel over the duchy. Edward's homage to the French king aroused bitter comment and disapproval. Froissart, who follows the negotiations in some detail, notes the opposition of the populace to Edward's homage in 1329: 'for indeed many in England murmured that their lord was nearer to the inheritance of France than King Philip.' A sense of humiliation at the king's submission was accompanied by widespread resentment at the support given by Philip to the hated Scots. In 1334 he gave shelter to David Bruce and was instrumental in persuading the Scots to continue the war in the following year. Knighton saw a connection between Philip's interference in Anglo-Scottish affairs and French aggression in Aquitaine in 1337. He repeats rumours that this was part of the French king's plan to destroy England utterly 'and all this because King Edward had laboured so much to humble the Scots.' According to Knighton, further attacks in 1339 are due to Philip's frustrations at the failure of a Scottish invasion of the north of England which had been instigated by the French.[20]

In all this the English are consistently represented as the victims of French aggression, reluctantly forced into a war they do not want. John Erghome, interpreting one of the Bridlington 'prophecies', says that the war was caused by the pride of the French and by their desire to subjugate territory belonging to England. He writes of the 'blamelessness of the English in the face of all these evils', and adds significantly that they wished to avoid war because the regular and secular clergy and many of the lords 'feared the might of France which was reputed one of the most powerful kingdoms in the world'.[21]

Philip VI becomes a particular object of hatred and fear. Murimuth remembers that he was the son of Charles of Valois who always hated the English, and Baker, who insists on styling him *tyranus Francorum*, says that it was through his pride and madness that the French were incited against the English 'whence a terrible war was set in motion'.[22] In contrast to the malicious and aggressive French king, Edward is without exception presented as the man of peace who wishes to avoid war if an honourable settlement may be reached, 'being averse to war with the said Philip'. He makes 'many humble offers' in an attempt to regain the Gascon territories which Philip has wrongly appropriated. Amongst these he proposes a marriage alliance between the Black Prince and a French princess; offers Philip all the advantages of Gascony for seven years after which they are to revert to the English crown; and suggests a joint crusade against the Saracens. But Philip, 'like one proud and covetous', refuses and Edward is eventually forced into war because the king of France 'did not wish to have peace and reasonable accord in any honest form'.[23] Froissart, who is sympathetic to the English cause in the early years of the war, gives an imaginative reconstruction of the council in which the young king asks what is best 'for his honour and that of his kingdom'. The reply reveals the great restraint and forbearance which Froissart thought Edward had shown in the face of Philip's intransigence:

Wherefore those who were judged the wisest replied and said that on considering the requests, the proposals, the offers, the concessions, the negotiations, and the conferences which the king had made and suggested, of which the French took no account, he could not delay in withdrawing his homage from the king of France and in defying him and all his supporters (11, 418).

Philip's provocative policy in Aquitaine, his support of the rebel Scots, and the French coastal raids of 1338-9 helped predispose the English in favour of war, but such acts of aggression were never thought of as constituting the underlying cause of the conflict. There was no doubt in the minds of contemporaries that the kingdom was at war for one reason: the prosecution of Edward's right to the crown of France which peaceful negotiation had failed to secure.

It is difficult to decide how far Edward III was serious in upholding his claim, and how far it was a mere pawn in a war waged to recover an independent Aquitaine, as most modern historians insist. It is true that Edward was an opportunist. In the disputed succession to the dukedom of Brittany he did not scruple to support John de Montfort whose claim was dependent on the exclusion of women from the succession, while his own claim to the crown of France rested on the very opposite principle.[24] Furthermore, in 1360 he was prepared to abjure his claim in return for an independent Aquitaine. Yet it may be objected that this was after the failure of the great *chevauchée* of 1359-60 when it had become clear that the crown was beyond his reach.[25] On the whole there seems no reason to doubt the seriousness with which he urged his claim in the early years of the war, especially when one considers the belief that it was a duty to prosecute an inherited right. Edward makes the point himself in a manifesto published in 1340. He states that since the kingdom fell to him by divine disposition it is his duty to put forward his claim, 'lest we should seem to neglect our right and the gift of divine grace, or be unwilling to submit the direction of our will to the divine pleasure'.[26]

Nevertheless the chroniclers maintain the tradition, fostered by royal propaganda, that Edward went to war only when all attempts at negotiation and conciliation had failed. According to them he was even reluctant to assume the title and arms of France until urged to do so by his Flemish allies in 1340 in order to circumvent the delicate problem of their allegiance to the king of France.[27] Continental writers sympathetic to the French cause saw the insidious influence of the banished Robert of Artois behind Edward's final decision. Froissart says that Robert 'did not cease night or day in unfolding the right he had to the crown of France, and the king listened willingly.' Later he adds that it was Robert who 'first set in motion the war between the king of France and the king of England'.[28]

Even if Edward was not entirely serious in urging his claim, its importance in other ways should not be underestimated. The concept of the 'just war' was so widely disseminated in fourteenth-century Europe that, if not essential, it was at least desirable for a monarch to convince his peers and subjects of the righteousness of his cause.[29] Edward was well aware of this and went to great lengths to justify himself at home and abroad. The manifesto supporting his assumption of the title and arms of France in 1340 was published in England, Flanders, Aquitaine, and France.[30] He particularly sought papal recognition of his rights, submitting a letter of justification to the College of Cardinals in 1339, and dispatching an embassy under Henry of Grosmont to argue his case at the papal court in 1344.[31] At home he used the machinery of local government as well as the Church to popularize his claim and to justify the ensuing war. Froissart makes clear how important this was thought to be by Philip VI as well as by Edward:

> To tell the truth, since they wished to make war, both kings found it necessary to make known to their people and to set before them the nature of their dispute, so that each would be the more eager to support their lord. And by this means they [the people] were aroused in each kingdom. [32]

In England Edward's propaganda was remarkably successful. The letters and proclamations with which he urged his claim were highly regarded as a source of information, frequently finding their way into the chronicles,[33] and since contemporary historians rarely examined them critically the official version of events passed into history. Nor was such government propaganda accepted passively. Edward's cause was championed by many of the chroniclers and expounded in some detail.[34] The most comprehensive account is that of Adam Murimuth, whose training in civil law and long experience as a Church and government diplomat may explain the remarkable objectivity with which he approaches the subject. He alone amongst English historians gives a coherent analysis of the objections to Edward's claim which were current in France.[35]

But the chronicles, written for the most part by regular and secular clerics, merely indicate that Edward's cause was strongly supported in some of the more conservative circles of the Church. Literary evidence suggests that support was in fact more widespread, though careful explanation gives way to unreasoned affirmation in the patriotic and propagandist verse of the day. In Minot's poems, clearly written for a sympathetic but unsophisticated audience, the king's right is made a focal point for the author's patriotic fervour, in prayers for Edward's success, and in his explanation of the king's purpose in going to war. The references are frequent, always favourable, and always allusive – 'Now God help Edward in his right', 'For he defendes fast his right' – which suggests not only that Minot could presume upon some knowledge of Edward's dynastic pretensions on the part of his audience (an indication of the effectiveness of government propaganda) but also that such pretensions were considered seriously and could even be manipulated by a patriotic writer to encourage support for the war. The anonymous author of *An Invective Against France* plays upon contemporary sympathy for Edward's cause in this way. It was probably composed after the battle of Crécy in the autumn of 1346 with the aim of encouraging the continuation of the war. Written in Latin verse, the *Invective* was never intended for as wide an audience as Minot's poems, but it survives in three manuscripts, which suggests that it enjoyed a certain vogue, and may have been known in clerical and even government circles. The author observes bitterly that the young king was 'prevailed upon by traitors' to do homage to Philip VI, homage which he later renounced 'with my whole-hearted approval'. He repeats the usual arguments in justification of Edward's claim to the throne, producing in confutation of the Salic Law an ingenious parallel between Edward and Christ:

Christ is the king of the Jews by right of his mother,
Therefore let the boar [Edward] be made king over the French by
right of his mother.[36]

English victories in the early years of the war gave weight to
Edward's claim in contemporary eyes. As the propagandists were
quick to point out, the military triumphs of Crécy and Poitiers
were clear indications of divine sanction for the royal cause.
Erghome observes that 'the Lord God ordains the English to
have strength in arms and battles against the French on account
of the right which they have in the kingdom of France.' Years
later John Lydgate was to claim that King John's defeat at
Poitiers was

> An heuenli signe be influent purueiaunce*
> > *shaping providence
> Sent from aboue to shewe Edwardis riht.[37]

The course of the Hundred Years War in the 1340s and 50s so
favoured the English that it is easy to forget that for most of the
fourteenth century England regarded France with apprehension.
In the years before the war the dominant position of France in
European politics, her wealth and military prestige, caused many
to doubt the wisdom of Edward's aggressive policy in his quarrel
with the house of Valois. A French invasion and even conquest of
England seemed a more likely outcome of hostilities than a
successful offensive on the part of the English; and yet for a decade
and a half, from 1345–60, England consistently carried the war
into France.

Contemporaries were naturally most impressed by the spectacu-
lar victories at Crécy and Poitiers, but pitched battles of this sort
were in fact untypical of the war as a whole. English armies were
almost always numerically inferior to those of France, and
Edward's commanders wisely tended to avoid direct confrontation. Only on two occasions did England put an army of more
than 10,000 in the field: during the siege of Calais in 1347 and
during Edward's last campaign of 1359–60. An army of 5–6,000
was considered substantial, and it has been estimated that during
the campaign in Guienne in 1355 the Black Prince had a mere
2,600 at his command.[38]

Pitched battle was accepted only when there was no alternative. The typical campaign consisted of a *chevauchée* or cavalry raid, the aim of which was to inflict as much damage as possible on the enemy through the destruction of his resources. Such raids were ruthlessly efficient. Unprotected towns and villages were pillaged and then burnt to the ground, while the surrounding countryside was systematically devastated. The after-effects are described by the Carmelite friar, Jean de Venette, in his account of the devastation in the region of his native village in 1359. The description is rhetorically structured to emphasize the general rather than the particular, but it is based on Venette's personal observation. He describes how after the raid the fields were unsown and the vines left to rot:

There were no cattle or fowl in the fields. No cock crowed in the depths of the night to tell the hours. . . . At this time rabbits and hares played freely about in the deserted fields with no fear of hunting dogs, for no-one dared go coursing through the pleasant woods and fields. . . . No wayfarers went along the roads, carrying their best cheese and dairy produce to market. . . . Houses and churches no longer presented a smiling appearance with newly repaired roofs but rather the lamentable spectacle of scattered, smoking ruins to which they had been reduced by devouring flames. The eye of man was no longer rejoiced by the accustomed sight of green pastures and fields charmingly coloured by the growing grain, but rather saddened by the looks of the nettles and thistles springing up on every side. The pleasant sound of bells was heard indeed, not as a summons to divine worship, but as a warning of hostile incursions, in order that men might seek out hiding places while the enemy were yet on the way.[39]

During the early years of the war the chances of such devastation occurring on English rather than on French soil must have seemed high. Yet – unbelievably, as it must have seemed to many contemporaries – France failed to carry the war into England, while year after year Edward III and his captains launched successful *chevauchées* deep into French territory from Calais and their bases in Brittany and Gascony. This fact had a profound effect on English responses to the war in the 1340s and 50s. Deep-rooted feelings of inferiority and insecurity with respect to France were replaced by an overwhelming self-confidence and optimism. The much-vaunted chivalry of France, accounted the finest in Europe and feared as such by the English in the early years of the war, was thought by many to have been annihilated at Crécy and Poitiers. Referring to Crécy, Minot rejoiced that

> The best of France and of Artayse
> War al to-dongyn* in that daunce.   *vanquished

Even as late as 1367 it was possible for an ardent patriot like Walter of Peterborough to look back on Poitiers as a crushing blow to the French after which they abandoned the struggle. Walter's panegyric on the Black Prince reflects the confidence of the English in the years following the Treaty of Bretigny (1360). Surveying the Europe of his day it seemed to him as if all nations bowed beneath the English yoke:

> England is gladdened, Gascony now under control;
> France is grieved, Spain brought to justice;
> Scotland grows weak, and false Flanders is fearful;
> Dacia diminishes, conquered Ireland remains quiet.

He was not alone in this belief. In a poem on the taking of Guines in January 1352 Minot confidently predicted that the war would be over by the summer; while Walter's contemporary, John Erghome, prophesied that the Black Prince would complete the conquest of France by 1405.[40]

The war must have seemed at an end to many who witnessed the triumphant entry of the prince into London in 1357. Jubilant citizens so packed the streets that he processed with great difficulty from London Bridge to the Palace of Westminster; and knights and squires who were lucky enough to have fought at Poitiers were feted on their return 'and honoured more than the rest'. As part of the celebrations Edward III held a feast so lavish that its like 'had never before been seen in England'. Here his greatest enemies, the kings of France and Scotland – 'both formerly great monarchs and at that time fellow-captives of the king of England' – sat to the right and left of their conqueror.[41]

After the battles of Sluys (1340) and Les Espagnols-sur-Mer (1350) the struggle for control of the Channel also seemed decided in England's favour. This is reflected in the verse of Minot. He rejoices that the men of Calais, who often harmed the English through their piracy, have been humbled by Edward; in a poem celebrating Les Espagnols-sur-Mer he boasts of England's ability to defend her coasts and to maintain the high seas; and elsewhere he points out that while France has been devastated by Edward, England remains unscathed.[42]

During these years the English learned to despise rather than fear the fighting abilities of their opponents. Higden gives an account of the weaknesses of the French which he learnedly but falsely ascribes to Eutropius. They are, he says, greater than most men in stature but 'just as the courage of the French is greater than other men's in the first assault, so afterwards is it weaker than that of women.' They are like the Alps in stature, but they are like the snow on the Alps with regard to endurance; for as the snow breaks out in sweat and melts in the sun, so do they in the heat of battle. To Higden's contemporary, Richard de Bury, the pursuit of arms shared in what he saw as a general decline in French civilization.[43]

The French king, Philip vi, was held in especial contempt. To Minot he is the 'vnkind coward' who will never offer battle but always flees in fear – 'God giff him care'; and in English eyes his cowardice was matched only by his treachery:

> In the chambers you're an ornament, in battle almost a virgin;
> Trusting in a tower of deceit, you seek means of defence.[44]

Inevitably the English saw the hand of divine providence in their victories, and if Knighton is to be believed, so did many foreigners. He says that during the siege of Calais men from Flanders, Brabant, Hainault, Germany and even France came over to Edward's side 'because of the divine favour which they saw in him'. He also repeats a joke current after Poitiers which cynically exploits the same belief at the expense of the pope:

> And because the pope always favoured the French and aided them as much as he could against the English, and because of the miracle in which God had bestowed victory on so small a force against such a great multitude of the French, it had been written in many places in Vienne and in many other places: 'Now the pope has become French and Jesus has become English; now it will be seen who will do more, the pope or Jesus.' And this was written in mockery.[45]

In these circumstances it is not surprising that there was strong opposition to any proposal for peace with France. To the professional soldier it meant the end of all opportunity for personal enrichment, unless he decided to join one of the free companies.

When the siege of Tournai was raised in 1340 the English forces 'raised a great cry of lament' because they had hoped to make their fortunes from the war, 'and then everything was lost'. Even more unpopular was the withdrawal of troops after the Treaty of Bretigny in 1360. Froissart says that the English captains were 'very angry' when they received orders to evacuate certain territories in accordance with the treaty, 'but they could do nothing about it'. They salvaged what they could, however, by selling their castles to the French.[46]

There was also a real fear that the French, aided by the papacy, would capitalize on any truce or peace to the disadvantage of the English. The Lanercost chronicler thought that the truce of Malestroit, which temporarily halted the war in Brittany in 1343, had greatly favoured the French who would otherwise have lost the city of Vannes. Significantly enough, in his eyes, the truce had been negotiated by papal legates – 'which truce was more of a betrayal than a settlement' (p. 335). Opposition was even greater to the truce negotiated after the fall of Calais in 1347. At least two poems, *An Invective Against France* and *On the Truce of 1347*, were written specifically to arouse opposition to the negotiations.[47] Both poems exploit contemporary fears of French duplicity should a truce be agreed upon. In an apostrophe to the king the author of the *Invective* warns, 'King, beware of truces lest you be destroyed by them.' The warning is made more explicit still in *On the Truce*: 'Through warfare you will be conqueror; accept truces and you will be cheated.' The poet turns to his advantage a popular saying that Edward has good weather on his outward voyages to France but bad weather on his return. This, he explains, is because God favours the war and disapproves of its cessation.[48]

But to those who supported war the ultimate act of betrayal was the Treaty of Bretigny. England had not suffered a defeat in the field for a decade and a half, and France was thought to have avoided conquest only by the use of the deceitful diplomacy for which she was renowned. The *Anonimalle* chronicler expresses the chagrin felt by many at the news of a treaty which was made

to the great loss and harm of the king of England and his heirs for ever, for nearly the whole of the community of France was in subjection and ransom to them; and within a brief period the said captains and their men could easily have conquered the kingdom of France to the advantage of the king of England and his heirs, if he had allowed them.[49]

During the troubled decades of the 1370s and 80s the views expressed here were to harden into the myth 'that England, undefeated in the field, had been betrayed at the negotiating table and cheated of victory.

Despite a succession of brilliant campaigns and unprecedented victories, England's success in the early years of the Hundred Years War was short-lived. By 1360 it was clear that the king was unable to make good his claim to the crown of France, and by the end of the decade, notwithstanding the Treaty of Bretigny, he had even lost the greater part of his Gascon fiefs. The causes of this reversal in England's fortunes are complex. After 1369 there is a distinct decline in the qualities of the armies, and especially of the commanders, which Edward III and later Richard II were able to put into the field, but in any case the conditions in France which had favoured the English in earlier years no longer prevailed. The exhaustion of that kingdom – a direct result of England's war effort – meant that it was less easy than formerly to live off the land, and at the same time the reorganization of its defences by Charles V proved an effective foil to English strategy based on the *chevauchée*. At home the false sense of prosperity created by the boom in ransoms and the spoils of war during the 1340s and 50s was beginning to have its inevitable consequence. M. M. Postan has demonstrated how the great expense of the war in terms of payments for alliances, the maintenance of garrisons and the wages of troops placed an intolerable strain on the nation's resources at a time when national production and income were falling. Edward III's war taxes and levies in kind had a serious adverse effect on the all-important wool industry, while the practice of purveyance may have 'extended the depressing effects of war economy to agricultural production as a whole'.[50] Such far-reaching economic consequences of the war affected all classes in society and were an important factor in the crisis facing England at the end of the fourteenth century.

The renewal of the war in 1369 found the English far from sanguine.[51] For some time rumours had been circulating about the machinations of Charles V, and these must have seemed confirmed by the events of 1368–9. While the French, 'always full of fraud and deceit', broke the peace in Aquitaine, the cunning and crafty

Charles sent envoys to England 'to entrap the innocence of the king of England'. The Black Prince is said to have warned his father of the king's perfidy from Bordeaux, but the ageing monarch was persuaded by his counsellors that the prince was 'unadvised' and that his love of war prompted him to defame his cousin of France. When he finally learned the truth Edward dismissed the envoys with some sharp words, but by then he had already lost the initiative.[52]

The uncertain events of these years gave added impetus to the invasion scares which were endemic in England. John of Reading has a curious tale about a raid by a Danish fleet in 1366 and reports plans for a combined attack on England in the following year by the Danes, Norwegians and Scots. Such scaremongering, which had little basis in fact, suggests the growing sense of uncertainty and alarm in the country. The very real threat of an invasion from France prompted some response from the government. A fleet was sent to patrol the approaches to the south coast, but no one knew where to expect the attack, 'wherefore [says Froissart] I tell you that the English were really dumbfounded then.' When more certain news reached England of the French plans, 'all the realm of England was warned and strengthened to oppose the French if they came.'[53]

At the same time Edward belatedly attempted to revive his traditional alliance with the princes of the Low Countries. But times had changed; he had already been anticipated by Charles v who had negotiated favourable treaties with them three years previously, 'and he knew well that he had good friends in Hainault and Brabant'. Of Edward's old allies only the dukes of Guelders and Juliers saw fit to send their defiance to the French king.[54]

Edward's inept diplomacy was paralleled by his failure to make sufficient military preparations. On the outbreak of war an expedition was despatched to Calais under John of Gaunt and Humphrey de Bohun, but it lacked sufficient strength and failed to engage the enemy. A scapegoat was needed and in some quarters Gaunt and de Bohun came under severe criticism. As the hostile Thomas Walsingham bitterly observed:

Yet the aforesaid dukes, who were very faint-hearted and witless, would not consent to a plan of this kind [i.e. confrontation with the enemy] on the pretext that they did not have sufficient force to engage such a large army – when to speak the truth, it was not strength in numbers they lacked but a bold spirit.[55]

The failure of two further *chevauchées*, led by Knolles in 1370 and Gaunt in 1373, caused similar outbursts from Walsingham. The Saint Albans chronicler was not alone in his poor estimate of Gaunt's performance in 1373. The author of the *Chronique des Règnes de Jean II et de Charles V* believed that Edward III and the Black Prince were greatly displeased with him on his return from Bordeaux in 1374. According to the French chronicler the duke had lost three hundred horses and a third of his men during the *chevauchée*.[56]

But these expeditions drew attention away from the main theatre of war which centred on the struggle for control of Gascony. It was here that the gravity of England's predicament was most clearly revealed. Edward III's hold on his fief had always been precarious, but when large sectors of the population became disaffected the duchy was at last ripe for plucking by the king of France. Charles V was well aware of this. For some time he had been urged by his counsellors to renew the war on the pretext that the English had failed to abide by the articles of the Treaty of Bretigny; but also because the Gascons held their overlords 'in great scorn and contempt'. The French were further encouraged by the crippling illness of the Black Prince and by the death of Sir John Chandos, the foremost English captain then in Aquitaine. 'All will be ours, as true as is the paternoster' was the popular cry when news of Chandos's death reached France in 1370, and this note of confidence was reflected in the renewed activity of the French military. The Chandos Herald reports the duke of Anjou's hopes for the future in a supposed conversation with du Guesclin who had returned from Spain at the urgent summons of the king:

We have great need of you, for if you are with us we shall conquer Aquitaine; for this is a very certain matter, Audeley and Chandos are dead, who have wrought so much mischief, and the Prince lies abed ill, with but scant cheer, so that if you counsel it we are all prepared to override the land.[57]

The duke's confidence was fully justified. When he invaded Guienne in 1370 many towns and castles surrendered without

resistance, while the position of those which remained loyal to
Edward worsened from day to day. Something of their predicament may be glimpsed in the dilemma facing the loyal defenders
of Thouars during the siege of 1372. Without reinforcements they
could not hope to survive a prolonged siege and were forced as a
consequence to agree to surrender if Edward failed to send a relief
force by an agreed date:

> ... for we are not at all strong enough in ourselves to resist and
> fight against the power of the king of France. For we see in this
> country that cities, towns, strongholds, and castles, together with
> prelates, barons, knights, ladies, and communities are turning French
> every day and make war on us ...

The final blow to England's hopes came with the defeat of the
fleet under Pembroke at La Rochelle in 1372. Thereafter, those
who had remained loyal to the English king were left to shift for
themselves. Many made their peace with Charles, but it was a
bitter blow to men like the Captal de Buch who had risked everything in the service of the English cause in Gascony. The *Quatre
Premiers Valois* represents him as sunk in gloom after his capture
in 1372: 'Ah! Ah! Guienne, you are truly lost!' But Edward and
his lieutenants could do no more. The Black Prince lay on his sick
bed making vain plans for revenge, while his father, enfeebled
with age, grew querulous at a situation beyond his grasp: 'God
help us and St George! There never has been so wicked a king in
France as the present one; and there never has been a king who
gave me so much to do as he does.'[58]

England, outmanoeuvred at every stage since the renewal of the
war, was ready to come to terms. Pope Gregory XI had been
seeking a negotiated settlement since 1372, and his efforts at last
seemed rewarded when the peace conference at Bruges agreed to a
general truce in 1375. In the event this lasted for two years, but in
1377 the war was resumed. It had proved impossible to find a basis
for a permanent settlement acceptable to both sides.[59]

Walsingham, one of the most outspoken critics of royal policy
at the time, considered the truce detrimental to England's interests.
He believed that the French were using it to stockpile arms while
the English, lulled into a false sense of security, indulged in feasts
and sports. The St Albans chronicler was partially correct.
Between 1375-7 the English government, overburdened with so

many other problems, neglected to negotiate new alliances or even to secure the country's defences against the resumption of the war. In France, on the other hand, the navy had been reorganized by the energetic Jean de Vienne and offensive alliances confirmed with Castile and Scotland. England paid for the government's negligence. Four days after the death of Edward III a French fleet harried the south coast from Rye to Plymouth, meeting with little organized resistance. The Isle of Wight was overrun and the inhabitants forced to buy the enemy off. In the opinion of Walsingham this would never have happened if the defences had been in order.[60]

The times demanded strong leadership, but in the ageing Edward the English found only a shadow of their former king. The encroachment of senility together with his infatuation for Alice Perrers left him incapable of government, so that to many the corruption which they saw in society generally was merely a reflection of the corruption at court. Edward's declining health was observed with concern. In 1376 he had the strength and presence of mind to summon the barons to Westminster to gain from them a promise of allegiance to the young Richard, but after that 'the stout-hearted king declined into a feebleness' from which he died the following year. During this period he was so ill that he was unable to attend to the government in person and confided more and more in John of Gaunt. Meanwhile, abroad, the French took advantage of the old king's critical condition to plan raids on the Channel Islands and the Isle of Wight.[61]

After 1369 there was a growing dissatisfaction with the war effort in England. To many it seemed that the government was incapable of defending its own coastline, let alone of taking the war into France, and there were persistent rumours that funds voted for the defence of the realm were being misappropriated by royal officials. The author of the *Brut*, following Walsingham, notes the failure of Knolle's *chevauchée* in 1370 and comments that:

King Edward, with owne-wise counceyll and vndescret, borwed a gret summe of gold of the prelatis and lordes, Marchauntes and other riche men of the reaume, saynge that hit sholde be spende in deffendyng of holy cherche & of his reaume; but neuer the latter hit profited hit not.[62]

The peace conferences of these years were particularly galling. Memories of Crécy, Poiters, and Nájera were far from dead, and the people wanted a successful prosecution of the war, not a humiliating peace. Besides, the old suspicion still prevailed that the French were insincere in their protestations of peace. The English, it was feared, were being duped and, worst of all, were paying for the privilege as well. An anonymous continuator of the *Eulogium Historiarum* grumbles about the vast expense of the fruitless talks held in 1372, and his complaints are repeated by the *Anonimalle* chronicler with regard to the prolonged negotiations at Bruges in 1375. The English delegation was led by Gaunt who roused hostile criticism for the irresponsible way in which he conducted the talks. In particular he was blamed for the costly entertainments he provided each day for the duke of Anjou and the French party which did nothing to further the English cause. Walsingham also complains of the 'astonishing and unbelievable expenses' of the conference from which the English gained no benefit whatsoever, for under cover of the negotiations the treacherous French were preparing for a renewal of the war. The English, he says, put their faith in the duke's ability to negotiate a settlement, but the truth was that they were caught unawares by the enemy.[63]

These grievances found expression in the petitions of the Good Parliament of 1376. The day after the opening session the Commons met in the chapter house of Westminster Abbey, ostensibly to discuss the chancellor's demand for a levy for the defence of the realm. But the ensuing debate turned into an attack on the corruption and incompetence of royal officials in which the mishandling of the war played a prominent part. A knight 'from the south' who addressed the assembly, spoke for all when he claimed that the commons could not possibly meet the chancellor's demand since they were already enfeebled and impoverished by previous taxation. He urged the king to govern the realm and pay for the war from the revenues of his demesne lands, and suggested a number of reforms which would enable him to do so. It was well known that 'we have lost all that we have given for the war for a long time because it has been wickedly wasted and falsely spent.' This, the knight asserted, was due to the corruption of officials who had embezzled royal funds to the detriment of the king and his subjects. At the next full session of parliament, de la Mare openly accused Lord Latimer, the chamberlain, and Richard Lyons, a prominent London merchant, of misappropriating government funds. Latimer was further accused of misconduct as viceroy in Brittany, of selling the castle of St Sauveur-le-Vicomte to the enemy, and of impeding the relief of Becherel which was lost to the king as a result. How far the accused were guilty is a matter of doubt, but the accusations underline the Commons' lack of faith in the authorities generally, and in their conduct of the war in particular.[64]

The one prominent member of the king's council to retain popular support was the Black Prince. He was revered for the part he had played in the heyday of England's military triumphs, and despite his disastrous rule in Aquitaine, was still generally above reproach. The prince's reputation was further enhanced by the belief that he stood for good government and, rightly or wrongly, he was thought by many to support the reforms advocated by the Commons during the Good Parliament. Rumour was rife. He was said to have refused contemptuously bribes sent him by Lyons, and some believed that de la Mare was only able to speak so openly because he was 'trustyng mych forto be supported & maynteyned in this mater by help & fauour of the Pryns'. Perhaps this supposititious support for the Commons explains another persistent rumour, that the prince's illness was the result of poisoning by his enemies. In the circumstances his accession to the throne was eagerly anticipated. Erghome confidently predicted the prince's reign as one of outstanding achievement at home and abroad, culminating in the occupation of Paris. His untimely death in 1376 was consequently a great blow, and Capgrave was hardly exaggerating when he wrote that his death 'bare awey al the sickirnes of this lond'. The hopes of the English have died with him, laments Walsingham, for while he lived they feared no enemy, but now it is a different matter. He reproves death for taking off the chosen successor to the throne. It was, he says, the desire of all England as well as of the ageing monarch, that the Black Prince should rule after him. Deprived of their prince the English must place their trust in God alone: 'Arise Lord; aid us and protect us in your name !'[65]

This atmosphere of despondency and defeatism was hardly alleviated by the death of Edward III in the following year. There were many who, like Erghome, lamented the misgovernment of his last years, but he was still revered as the king who had led England to victory, and his death, following closely on that of the

prince, was felt to mark the end of an era. This is the theme of an
elegy composed shortly after the accession of the young Richard.[66]
In it the unknown poet contrasts the glories of the past with the
failures of the present and hints at his fears for England's future.
He expresses perfectly the mingled regret and apprehension which
characterized much of the political literature of the late 1370s.

The elegiac mood of the poem is established by a lament on the
transience of the world and this leads naturally to the poet's
particular theme, the fickleness of friendship and the lack of
constancy in popular gratitude. There follows an examination of
the causes of England's former greatness, but the theme of in-
constancy and ingratitude is sustained by variations on the idea of
'out of sight, out of mind' in the refrain.

The poet recognizes that the immediate cause of Edward's
military success lay in the quality of his commanders and the
prowess of the English military, but he urges that without the co-
operation of all three estates this alone would have been insufficient. To demonstrate this he adopts the allegory of the ship of
state. The ship itself represents the chivalry of England which
once 'counted not a bean' for all the power of France; the rudder
is the king; the helm the Black Prince 'who was never defeated in
battle'; and the ship's barge Henry, duke of Lancaster, whose
loyalty was tested in 'many a fierce onslaught'. A ship, however,
depends on a stout mast and a fair wind, and so the military
depend on the goods of the commons and the prayers of the
devout:

> This gode comunes, bi the rode,*   *cross
> I likne hem* to the schipes mast;   *them
> That with heore* catel† & heore goode   *their †chattels
> Mayntened the werre both furst and last.
> The wynd that bleuw the schip with Blast,
> Hit was gode preyers, I sei hit a-trete.*   *plainly

Recollection of past glories inevitably invites comparison with
the present. Devoutness, the poet laments, is cast out; the achievements of the past are forgotten; and the lords who once led
England's armies to victory are 'layed full low'. Worst of all at a
time of crisis, the crown has devolved upon an inexperienced boy.

Yet despite these reverses the poet is not entirely without hope.
As he expresses it, 'the stem is of the same root', and if Richard

takes after his father and grandfather he may still triumph over the enemy. But until the young king comes of age it is the duty of every Englishman to 'up with the head' and stand firm against the French. The poet's attempt to rally his audience is hardly convincing, however, and this he seems to acknowledge in the concluding lines where his pessimism reasserts itself in a return to his initial theme. It will be hard, he reflects, to find the like on earth of King Edward and his son the prince:

> And nou heore los* biginneth to swage,†   *fame
>   †grow less
> That selde I-seye* is sone forgete.   *seen

Yet if the anonymous poet was far from optimistic with regard to England's future, he was at least well disposed towards the young king. In fact Richard inherited a wealth of popular good will when he came to the throne – a circumstance sometimes forgotten in the retrospect of later events. Dissatisfaction with the government continued, but allowances were made for the king's youthful inexperience and as with his grandfather fifty years before, blame fell on Richard's counsellors. As John Gower puts it in the earliest recension of *Vox Clamantis*: 'The boy is free of blame, but those who have instrumented this boyish reign shall not endure without a fall. So not the king but his council is the cause of our sorrow, for which the land grieves as if with a general murmur.'[67]

In particular the cost of the war continued to give rise to complaint. By 1377 funds were again urgently needed for the defence of the realm and in the first parliament of the new reign the Commons were once more being urged to make a grant, payable within the year, 'or otherwise the realm could be lost'. The perennial fear of a French invasion together with a sense of good will towards the young king led the Commons to make a liberal grant of two-tenths and two-fifteenths on this occasion. But such generosity was short-lived. The Commons expected some return for their money in the form of a successful prosecution of the war. All they got were delays, the misappropriation of war funds, and the imposition of a new and extremely unpopular poll tax which was, according to Walsingham, the cause of 'unheard of evils in the land'.[68]

The belief persisted that funds raised for the war never reached their destination because of the corruption of royal officials and the military. The compiler of the *Brut* tells of one John Munsterworth who made a small fortune by defaulting on indentures negotiated with the king. In this case justice was done, for Munsterworth was eventually hanged, drawn and quartered for his crimes. But others were too powerful to be dealt with so easily, and there was mounting frustration at the rumoured embezzlement of war funds by royal favourites and officials. The king himself was no longer exempt from criticism. It was believed that Richard connived at the misappropriations committed by his favourites, and this seemed confirmed by the dismissal of Sir Richard Scrope from the office of chancellor in 1382. Scrope had strenuously opposed the king's extravagance and there was widespread indignation at his dismissal. 'He had governed in a praiseworthy manner and prudently', observed Walsingham.[69]

The resumption of hostilities in 1377 brought with it the usual crop of invasion scares, especially in the southern counties where recent French raids had demonstrated the inadequacy of the coastal defences.[70] As a result there was even less confidence than before in the government's conduct of the war. Dissatisfaction seems to have reached a climax during the parliament of 1386. A major invasion by the French seemed imminent and Richard was forced to summon parliament to obtain a grant for the defence of the realm. But despite the seriousness of the situation the Commons made a grant dependent on a number of reforms. These Richard refused outright and there followed an incredible exchange in which the king is said to have threatened to seek aid from his cousin of France rather than submit. The duke of Gloucester, acting in the name of the Lords and Commons, countered by intimating that if the king of France set foot in England they would labour to destroy the realm. More harsh words followed. The king was reminded of the days when his father and grandfather had laboured so tirelessly 'for the conquest of France'. Even then the people had endured untold hardships, but in the present reign they were taxed beyond endurance while the realm was being impoverished by evil counsellors. Moreover 'the kingdom of England, so honourable and in all the world by far the most renowned for war above other kingdoms in the time of your father, is now indeed in your days shamefully abandoned through the division caused by bad government.' But, it was hinted, there was a remedy: a king who governed badly could be deposed. The spectre of Edward II was raised before Richard and in the circumstances he had no alternative but to submit to the Commons' demands. Only then was he granted the necessary subsidy for the war.[71]

In the seventeen months that elapsed before the next parliament was called, however, there was no improvement in England's military fortunes. During the Merciless Parliament, therefore, the same issues were raised, this time by the Lords Appellant in their accusations against individual members of Richard's coterie.[72] A petition presented by the Commons complained amongst other things of the lamentable decay of the coastal defences: 'Along the coast in divers parts of your realm the houses of the poor commons have been burnt, villages and individuals put to ransom, and the fleet utterly destroyed, and the land altogether abandoned.' The only remedy, they urged, was the removal from office of those members of the king's council who were responsible and who were 'traitors to you and to the realm as men who know neither good nor reason'. Inevitably the continued expense of the war was criticized, together with the burdensome taxation which threatened to destroy the realm. If the king would only right this wrong, the petitioners humbly continued, it would be an act pleasing to God as well as adding to the renown of Richard's 'good' government. Consequently they pressed for a commission to carry out relief measures which would ensure good government and would leave 'all the people in peace'.[73]

During the later 1380s and 1390s the desire to remain 'in peace' was to be strengthened by a growing conviction that prosperity depended on an end to the war with France; but in the early years of the reign many still looked for a military solution to England's declining fortunes. The reversals of recent years were keenly felt by those who remembered the triumphs of Edward's reign. Since the renewal of the war there had been no English victory of any significance; on the contrary, the enemy had harried the south coast with impunity and in 1385–6 there had been alarming news of French plans for a massive invasion of England. A scapegoat was needed and, although the government was censured for its lack of initiative and organization, blame fell with some justification on those aristocrats and knights who commanded in the field. The exasperation felt by many with the ineptness of the military is conveyed by Froissart in an imagined speech which he puts in the mouths of the populace at large in 1387:

What has become of the great undertakings, the proud deeds, and all the brave men of the kingdom of England? When King Edward was alive and his son the prince, we used to enter France and repel our enemies in such a manner that none dared engage us in battle, and if any did, they were utterly routed. . . . Where are the knights and all their offspring who perform similar feats of arms now? . . . In those days the English nation was wondrously feared and we were talked about throughout the world and the good chivalry which issued from us. But now one can and must keep silent for they don't know how to make war, except on the purses of poor folk – all our lords are ready for that. (XII, 145f.)

It is a remarkable fact that by the end of Edward's reign nearly all the captains who had fought at Crécy, Poitiers, and Nájera were either dead or in captivity. The list is impressive. Apart from the Black Prince, the following had died by 1377: Henry of Grosmont, Humphrey de Bohun, Thomas Beauchamp, James Audley, John Chandos, and Walter Manny. Of those who had been taken prisoner, Jean de Grailly, Captal de Buch, died in captivity in 1377; while Sir Thomas Felton, taken in 1377 and released in 1380, died the following year. Such men were widely lamented, the more so because there were few commanders of any worth to take their place. The compiler of the *Brut* regretted the death of Thomas Beauchamp, earl of Warwick, 'nowt lewyng behynde him, after his dayes, non so noble a knight, ne so orpid [brave] of armes' (p. 322). Behind the conventional epithets one glimpses the truth – the war had drained England of its manpower as well as its wealth.

Those who succeeded the great captains of Edward's day showed little aptitude for war. Richard himself was no general – the expedition he led in person in 1385 ended in ignominious retreat. As Henry of Derby is said to have taunted him in 1399, he had never behaved like the son of the Black Prince and it was widely held that he must be a changeling, the son of some clerk or canon.[74] Even the great lords of the realm revealed few of the talents necessary for command in the field. John of Gaunt certainly had military and chivalric pretensions, but he proved himself a mediocre strategist and failed to rival his elder brother's reputation for feats of arms. The two major campaigns mounted by the duke ended disastrously, and for this his inept strategy was much to blame. Walsingham was not the only one to despise his talents as a general. His failure to take St Malo in 1378 was severely criticized in England, while during his 1386–7 invasion of Castile he lost even the confidence of his own troops. Decimated by starvation, dysentery, and plague they poured scorn on Gaunt's competence, concluding that 'He does not show that he knows how to conduct a war.' Their opinion was endorsed by the enemy. Froissart has a speech supposedly made by the count of Lerna to rally his troops in 1387. The count admitted that the English had gained a great victory at Nájera twenty years before, but at that time they had the flower of the world's chivalry in their midst, each knight resembling an Oliver or a Roland. But the great captains who had fought with the Black Prince were either dead or had turned French, and the duke of Lancaster's army was insignificant by comparison. As a result 'The business is by no means so perilous for us as it was in times past.'[75]

Other leaders scarcely fared better in the eyes of contemporaries. The earl of Arundel, who had been largely responsible for the failure of the siege of St Malo, was in disgrace, and no one mourned the death of his brother, Sir John Arundel, whose viciousness and cruelty in Brittany in 1379 had shocked even his compatriots. As Gower lamented in *Vox Clamantis*, the leaders of England's chivalry, once renowned for their prowess, had been replaced by lesser men who 'have not become worthy of either divine or human praise'.[76]

In these circumstances the few captains of proven worth to serve in Richard's armies were powerless. Sir Hugh Calveley was still widely respected both by the English and the French, but during the infamous Norwich Crusade of 1383 the advice of this experienced campaigner was ignored time and again by Bishop Henry Despenser, the *Pugil Ecclesie*. In Froissart's account of the 'crusade' Calveley advised against the bishop's plan of campaign. It was, he argued, ill-advised to invade Flanders since the Flemmings were good Urbanists like the English, as well as being skilled fighters. Events were to prove him correct. Despenser ignored Calveley's objections and marched against Dunkirk which he took with ease. His victory was short-lived, however, for on the arrival of Charles VI with a large army the English were forced into headlong retreat. At this point, according to Froissart, Calveley could no longer contain his chagrin:

Sirs, by my faith, we have made a most shameful *chevauchée* in this season; none so poor nor so disgraceful ever issued out of England. You have done according to your desire and have believed this Bishop of Norwich who wished to fly before he had wings. Behold now the honourable end which you have won. During the whole of this campaign I was never believed in any thing that I said, so that I say to you: Behold Bourbourg, withdraw therein if you wish. But I shall go on and make directly for Gravelines and Calais, for we are not the men to fight the king of France.

When the French appeared before Bergues, which was being held by the English, a herald informed Calveley that the enemy had 26,000 men in the field. The knight's reactions, as reported by Froissart, are interesting. At first he mocked the herald for his exaggeration; he had been on many campaigns against the French and had never known them to raise an army of more than 6,000. But when the French moved up to invest Bergues Calveley was able to confirm the herald's report for himself. In dismay he counselled the immediate abandonment of the town.[77]

Sir Hugh Calveley was an experienced captain, but he was clearly out of touch with developments. The balance of military power had changed since the days when the Black Prince and his father had raided with impunity through France. The English military were no longer accounted the finest in Europe; in the 1370s and 80s, on the contrary, they were once more heartily despised by their enemies. The Scots boasted to their French allies that the English feared them more than any other nation 'for we may enter England at our ease and ride far into the country without any hindrance from the sea.' The French were equally scornful, and in the 1380s increasingly confident of their ability to take the initiative. In reviewing the successful campaigns of Charles V in 1377 the compiler of the *Chronique des Règnes de Jean II et de Charles V* was cautiously optimistic about the future; but eight years later, when plans were being laid for the (abortive) invasion of England, the final destruction of the enemy was taken for granted: 'England will not be able to endure and hold out against us. The time has come when we will be greatly avenged for the cruel deeds and attacks which they have made in France.'[78]

Inevitably the reversal was keenly felt in England. Where, asks Bishop Brinton, is the might of England's chivalry, 'once powerful and beloved, now however feeble and disgraced'? The answer he finds typically in the decadence and injustice of the knightly estate: 'and for that reason God's hand is against them because "their hand is against God".' The bishop was not alone in making the equation between morals and military success. It was an inevitable and commonplace reaction. If the lords of the realm are no longer successful in their wars, complains one anonymous preacher, it is because they have abandoned love and charity:

... now is envi and wrouthe reynyng, euery man to accuse othur of treson and falsenes. And thus thei be the cause of here own destruccion. And thus this world is transposed vp-so-downe. Synne is cause of this gret myscheff that we haue here in oure lyvyng, and will be cause of oure dampnacion but iff we han grace to amend vs.[79]

Contemporary critics of England's military failure were generally content with such fulminations. Few looked beyond the obvious moral failings of the knights and clergy, and so the real causes of the realm's decline escaped them. In particular, the significance of the new French defensive measures went unnoticed – even, it would seem, by the English commanders in the field, for they clung stubbornly to the well-tried formula of the *chevauchée* with disastrous results.

The author of these innovations was Charles v, the humane hero of Christine de Pisan and Froissart and the 'greatest enemy of the king of England' of Walsingham. His strategy had two objectives: control of the English Channel and the disruption of enemy raids in France by means of a form of passive resistance. With the first of these objectives in mind Charles developed a royal fleet under the command of Jean de Vienne, although the decisive factor in France's favour was the alliance with Castile in 1369. French troops had helped place Enrique on the throne, and in return the formidable fleet of Castilian royal galleys was placed at Charles's disposal. This was used to good effect both in defence and attack. An English fleet was routed by the galleys off La Rochelle in 1372, while between 1377–80 a Franco-Castilian fleet intermittently harried the south coast of England in some of the worst raids of the war.[80]

In France Charles's strategy was dictated by necessity, for since the beginning of the war the French had been defeated almost every time they took the offensive. The king's response to this was both simple and effective. If the enemy could not be defeated in the field, the destructive power of his raids could at least be diminished by a policy of passive resistance. Such a strategy inevitably met with opposition from the conservative and impetuous chivalry of France who considered it 'a great disgrace' not to engage the enemy. But the sound reasoning behind the king's strategy: 'Let them go their way. They will exhaust and ruin themselves – and all without battle', and its manifest success, soon seems to have converted them.[81]

The new defensive measures centred upon a network of heavily fortified castles and towns which could not be taken without a long and expensive siege. The countryside, on the other hand, was abandoned to the enemy after livestock and other victuals had been removed to the safety of the nearest fortified place. Then, as the enemy moved across country, they were followed at a distance by the French army, ready to cut off stragglers and forage parties, whilst avoiding pitched battle. This effectively contained the cavalry raid which had been the mainspring of the English offensive since the 1340s. The new French strategy was employed during Edward III's great *chevauchée* of 1359 and thereafter it provided the basis of the French defence. It was used against raids led by Knolles (1370), Gaunt (1373), and Gloucester (1380), and proved especially effective since the English were reluctant to abandon a formula which had been so successful in the past.[82]

Gloucester's raid may be taken as typical. The duke started from Calais with the intention of raiding through Artois and Picardy en route for Brittany. He soon discovered, however, that most of the towns in his path were too well defended for anything short of a lengthy siege. More seriously, it proved impossible to live off the land for 'although they were in good and fertile country and rich in wines and victuals, they found nothing, because the people had taken everything into the towns and castles and the king of France had abandoned to his men-at-arms all that they found in the open countryside.' Foraging was made even more difficult by the proximity of the French army which forced Gloucester to maintain close formation. By the time the army reached Brittany supplies were so low that only the timely arrival of victuals from

from the Channel Islands and England saved the troops from starvation.[83]

Not surprisingly Charles's subjects came to regard him as a saviour, for he had 'through his great understanding won over to himself and vanquished a great part of his enemies'. He was the particular hero of Christine de Pisan who admired him for his humane attempts to mitigate the miseries and sufferings of war, and of Froissart whose basic humanitarianism was rarely totally obscured by his preoccupation with chivalry. In the pages of the *Chroniques* the significance of Charles's innovations in strategy is fully realized. The king appears as the precursor of the modern general who commands from behind the lines for which, says Froissart, he was greatly to be recommended. Without stirring from his chambers he recovered all that his predecessors had lost in the field 'with helm on head and sword in hand'.[84]

The success of the new strategy did much for French self-esteem. In the *Chroniques* there is a new assertiveness in the speeches which Froissart attributes to the French people. Of these none is more eloquent of changing conditions than the jests current after the failure of the English expedition to Castile in 1387. Gaunt, with the remnant of the English army, was said to be recuperating at Santiago, much to the amusement of his enemies. Froissart records how the French joked with pilgrims on their way to the Spanish shrine:

You go to Santiago and there you will find the duke of Lancaster who lives the good life and keeps in the shade and in closed chambers for fear of the sun. Recommend us to him and ask him by your faith if we French know how to wage war, if we have made him fair war, and if he is content with us. The English used to say that we could dance better than we could make war. Now times have changed. They rest and dance and we guard our marches and borders in such a manner that we lose nothing nor have any injury (XII, 344).

French successes after 1369 were not unqualified, however. Charles VI might consolidate his father's gains in Aquitaine, but his ambitious plans for a full-scale invasion of England in 1386 had proved a costly failure. The two kingdoms had reached an impasse, the absurdity of which is summed up in the French ambassadors' arguments for peace during the negotiations of

1390: 'The French declared they were well aware that they were insufficient for the conquest of England and that the English were by no means so powerful that they might subjugate France, and that through such unprofitable expeditions each kingdom was impoverished in various ways.'[85] Peace had become a matter of overriding concern to the governments of both kingdoms. From the late 1380s to the end of the century diplomatic activity was intensified in an attempt to formulate a settlement acceptable to both sides. In 1389 a truce was agreed upon which was extended three times until in 1396 a twenty-eight year truce was sealed in Paris. A permanent settlement had proved impossible, but in the last decades of the fourteenth century a *de facto* peace had become a necessity.[86]

The Popular Response

In fourteenth-century England those who were close to the court or involved in government were likely to be well informed about contemporary events; so were the members of large and influential religious houses like St Albans. Outside these circles, however, reliable news was hard to come by. Recent studies have shown how Edward III used the administrative machinery of local government and the Church to disseminate propaganda in support of the war with France.[1] Despite its obvious limitations this provided an important source of news for the majority of Englishmen. But information gleaned from royal letters broadcast via the sheriffs or from prayers offered for the success of English armies was inevitably meagre, and in a culture which was still predominantly oral, informed opinion gave way to rumour and hearsay the further one moved from the centres of power.

The paucity of reliable information available to Englishmen at large, and the distortion of what little there was, may be illustrated from the chronicles. The period 1337-9, for example, was one of confusion and bewilderment. It was generally known that war with France had been declared but beyond that fact, certain knowledge was replaced by surmise. A comet appeared in 1337 'probably foreboding a dreadful war about to take place between the kingdoms'; the *tyrannus Francorum* was said to have outlawed, killed, or imprisoned all Englishmen in French territory, confiscating their goods; parliament made grants to Edward 'as a subsidy for the impending war'.[2] An atmosphere of fear and suspicion prevailed. The Lanercost chronicler hints darkly at a highly placed fifth columnist at work in the northern marches. According to him it had been rumoured 'commonly, but in secret, for a long time' that a certain nobleman aided the Scottish raiders in 1337: 'which, if it is true, may God reveal such cunning traitors to the king and the kingdom.' The rumour was persistent. Knighton reports that the northern authorities were thought by many to be in league with the Scots in 1346 'to the great disrepute of the northern magnates'.[3]

French coastal raids of 1338–9 added to the confusion. Froissart says that news of the sack of Southampton spread throughout England: 'whence the English were well aware that the war was open between France and England.' The chroniclers describe the raids in some detail, and at least one, the author of the *Chroniques de London*, feared that they were the prelude to a full-scale invasion in which Philip planned 'to have seized and slaughtered the entire realm of England'. Apart from fear the raids caused anger and a desire for revenge. Laurence Minot declared that

> ... it mun be ful dere boght
> That thir galay men* haue wroght.   *these galley-men

Minot patriotically minimizes the success of the French attack on Southampton. He admits there was a great deal of slaughter and burning 'bot noght so mekill als sum men wend [supposed]'. Baker adopts the same attitude to the raids in general, though he does say that the attack on Southampton had been serious. Clearly the raids produced widespread alarm.[4]

Perhaps the most important source of news – and rumour – was provided by soldiers who had served in France. There is obviously little direct evidence for this in surviving literary and historical documents, though occasionally the chronicles contain information or reflect attitudes which can scarcely have been derived from any other source. Almost all the chroniclers who report the campaigns of the 1340s and 50s, for example, comment on the great fortunes to be made from the war, and much of their information must have been gleaned from the impressions of returning soldiers and from the rumours which spread abroad after the completion of a successful campaign. As one would expect if this were so, they report only the sensational aspects of the 'advantages of war'. They are either unaware of or, more likely, take for granted such established practices as the payment of regular wages to troops and the customary procedure governing the division of spoils.[5]

·   ·   ·   ·   ·

This emphasis in the chronicles goes far in explaining the re-markable popularity of the war in its early stages. The disputed inheritance might be used as a rallying point for patriotic senti-ment and as a justification in royal propaganda, but the reasons for the widespread support of Edward's cause in the 1340s and 50s should be sought elsewhere: in a deep-seated fear and hatred of the French, and later in a growing confidence and pride in England's military capability, but above all in the opportunities which the war offered for personal advancement and enrichment.

Edward III was well aware of the importance of material incentives as a means of gaining support for his campaigns. Recent studies have revealed how he extended his grandfather's practice of encouraging recruitment by offering regular and, in theory, prompt payment of wages of war. This was accompanied by repeated offers of pardons to criminals in return for war service.[6] At the other end of the social scale, faithful military service on the part of the nobility was rewarded with grants of land and positions of authority.[7] But it was the expectation of gain from the spoils of war which was the real attraction of the early campaigns. This is made clear in an exhortation which the Black Prince is said to have delivered before the battle of Poitiers. Addressing himself to the archers he declared that more than his speech, their sense of honour, their love of their native land, and the chance of great booty will encourage them to follow the example of their fathers. In a similar vein Edward III encouraged the troops before Sluys with the promise that 'each may keep whatever he can seize.' Froissart says that when news of Edward's great expedition of 1359 became known, knights, squires, and men-at-arms flocked to Calais to await his arrival. Some came 'to advance their honour' but others 'to loot and pillage the fair land and plenteous realm of France'. Of the Gascons he says that they preferred the English to the French because of the opportunities which their war offered for plunder.[8]

Froissart plausibly accounts for the success of the early *chevauchées* in France by reference to the inhabitants' lack of preparedness for war. He believed that Edward was persuaded to invade Normandy in 1346 by the exiled Godfrey de Harcourt who impressed upon him the almost legendary wealth of the region: 'In Normandy you will find populous towns which are completely undefended where your men will have such great plunder that they will be better off for twenty years to come.' According to Godfrey, the duchy's wealth was only paralleled by the ease with which it could be overrun: 'We will enter the richest country in the world and the most plenteous, and we will have our way, for they are simple people who do not know what war is.' The ensuing expedition proved him right, for the English army met with little or no resistance outside a few strongly defended positions. In the countryside and in many of the towns 'they did for the most part whatever they pleased, for they found no one to resist them'.[9]

Such were the spoils taken during this expedition that even Froissart professes to be at a loss to describe them. When the English took the great drapery town of St-Lô 'there is no man living who could credit or imagine the great riches that were seized and plundered there, nor the great abundance of cloth that they found'. During the sack of Caen they loaded their barges with 'cloth, jewels, vessels of gold and silver, and many other treasures of which they had great plenty'; while after the battle of Crécy the English were 'at one time dancing and at another rejoicing' so great were the spoils.[10]

Henry of Grosmont's *chevauchée* in Guienne (1345–6) and the war in Brittany provided further opportunities for plunder,[11] though in this respect the Crécy campaign was paralleled only by the Black Prince's expedition to Guienne in 1355–6. Froissart describes in detail the prince's profitable raid through Languedoc in 1355, but it was the raid on Poitou in the following year which proved most lucrative. The sack of the French camp after the battle of Poitiers revealed such wealth that all who had fought there 'became rich in honour and possessions, as much from the ransoms of captives as from the gain of gold and silver which was found there in the form of vessels, and gold and silver belts, and precious jewels, and chests crammed with costly and weighty girdles and fine cloaks'.[12]

Spoils gained in this way were on such a scale that pillagers could pick and choose. At the sack of Barfleur (1346) even the *garçons* spurned furred robes; Castelnaudary (1355) contained such a wealth of silver vessels and coins that the English took no count of fine clothes and furs; and at Poitiers the rich armour and harness of the French were left lying on the field. Sometimes the spoils were resold to the inhabitants at a fraction of their value as happened after the sack of Louviers (1346) when the English 'let go for a hundred florins stuff which was worth a thousand'. Booty which was not disposed of in this way was often sold at an equally low price in Calais or Bordeaux. English raids from Calais in 1351 produced such a glut of livestock in the city that 'a fat cow was hardly worth 16 silver pennies.'[13]

The chroniclers insist that soldiers of all ranks made their fortunes from these expeditions. Murimuth reports that after Crécy 'the English were indeed transformed from rags to riches'; the followers of Henry of Grosmont in 1345 made such gains 'that the poorest were made rich'; and it was said of members of Sir Robert Knolles's company which raided in Normandy in 1358 that 'they seemed more like lords of the realm than hired soldiers'. Knighton adds that 'many who went there as grooms or servants became very powerful knights and came back extremely rich'. Several of Edward's most prominent captains began their careers in this way, including Knolles. Walsingham says that he established his reputation and his fortune during the raids of 1358, by means of which 'from a poor and nondescript esquire he soon became a commander of knights, and at that time his wealth increased to royal proportions'.[14] Sir John Hawkwood rose to prominence by similar paths. The tradition that he was originally a poor apprentice to a London hosier is apocryphal, based probably on an Italian corruption of his name. It is indicative of the times, however, that such a story was easily credible.[15]

Many of the fortunes so gained were no doubt lost as soon as made. On their return from Poitiers the English troops 'squandered foolishly and lavishly the gold and silver they had won and whatever their ransoms were worth'.[16] But much of this wealth must have found its way to England where it created a false appearance of prosperity and helped confirm the populace in their support for the war. Walsingham says that in 1348 'throughout England it seemed to the English as if a new sun had risen on account of the sufficiency of peace, the abundance of supplies, and the glory of victories.' He goes on to list the spoils which found their way into English homes:

For the woman was of no account who did not possess something from the spoils of Caen and Calais, and other cities overseas in the form of clothing, furs, quilts, and utensils. Scattered throughout England in every house were to be seen table-cloths and jewels, bowls of murra and silver, linen and linen cloths.[17]

It is tempting to see some relation between the influx of these material gains into the country and the frequent confirmation (and failure) of the Sumptuary Laws, though the chroniclers never make the connection themselves.[18] But civilians must certainly have shared in the prosperity which resulted from the spoils and the more adventurous could profit from such side effects of the war as the government plans for the redevelopment of Calais. The town was partially resettled with English families after 1347, and Froissart says that their number increased daily 'for the king provided and confirmed such great privileges and franchises that everyone came there willingly'.[19]

Ransoms often provided an equal if not greater source of profit than the spoils of war, especially for those who were fortunate enough to capture some prominent commander. Once the enemy was routed confusion prevailed as all ranks scrambled after prisoners. At Poitiers, according to the Chandos Herald, one might see archers, knights, and squires 'running in every direction, to take prisoners on all sides'. Froissart says that so many prisoners were taken that they outnumbered their English captors by two to one, and even the meanest archer had as many as six French captives. After the fall of Castelnaudary there was such a surfeit of prisoners that 'when they took a man, a bourgeois or a peasant, they kept him prisoner and ransomed him, or did him bodily harm if he did not wish to ransom himself.' At Poitiers King John was almost killed in the crush of English men-at-arms who milled around him shouting, 'I have taken him, I have taken him.' So great was his ransom that, according to one chronicler, when only half of it had been paid England was flooded with gold specie, so that money-changers and the trading community willingly exchanged a gold coin for silver at 4d below the customary rate. Generally, however, the chroniclers devote little attention to the profit made from ransom. The process of payment was complex, frequently involving years of litigation before the claimant was satisfied – if indeed he ever was. The profit from spoils, on the other hand, was immediate and tangible and, apart from exceptional ransoms such as that of King John, far more likely to arouse public excitement and comment from chroniclers whose interest in military affairs tended to be peripheral.[20]

During these years Edward III was clearly able to draw on wide-spread support for his cause. But although there was no opposition to the war in principle, there was criticism in some quarters of the government's conduct of the war. This is notably true of the early campaigns in Scotland and Flanders where the issue was one of finance. The cost of mounting these expeditions was immense and the returns negligible. As a result, amongst other expediencies, Edward was obliged to extort heavy taxes from parliament and to extend the already unpopular practice of purveyance – measures which led to widespread discontent. Knighton recalls how government attempts to levy aids for the expedition of 1338 in the form of a quarter of corn, oats, and bacon caused 'a great outcry' amongst the people, 'and greater evil would have grown out of it had not the king taken wiser counsel'. The war taxes of 1340 were if anything more unpopular. The author of the *Brut* says that Edward asked for a seventh of movable goods, a tax on wool, and the ninth sheaf of corn, 'and al he had and helde at his owene liste and wil. wherefor, yf y shal knowliche the verrey treuthe, the ynnere loue of the peple was turned into hate, & the commune prayrs into cursinge, for cause that the commune peple were strongliche ygreued.' Knighton notes that the king had to appease the people and ease their burden by granting pardons for a variety of crimes.[21]

Discontent was increased by the fact that few people were in a position to know whether or not these taxes were wisely spent by the government. The majority depended on rumour for their information, and this was inevitably inaccurate and often exaggerated. As an example of this the Lanercost chronicler reports that the army raised in 1337 cost 'an almost countless sum of money' for its maintenance. But he has no means of ascertaining the exact amount and can only repeat the conflicting estimates of hearsay: 'It was said indeed that it used up 1,000 marks a day, and according to some 2,000 pounds.'[22]

The dishonesty of government officials gave further cause for dissatisfaction since it was believed that the king's financial difficulties and the failure of the early campaigns in Flanders were the direct result of their maladministration. The author of the *Brut* complains that Edward was forced to make a truce with the French in 1340 because he failed to gain sufficient financial support from England. The reason for this was that 'his procuratours & messagers cursidly & ful slowly serued him at his nede, & him deceyved'.[23] Government purveyors were especially hated, and opposition to them grew as Edward extended the practice of the pre-emption of goods to supply the needs of his armies.[24] Discontent was caused not only by the corruption of individual purveyors but by the inherent injustice of a system in which prices were arbitrarily set below market value and were accompanied by frequent delays in payment. Incidents like the one described by Murimuth in 1344 increased bad feeling amongst those whose goods were pre-empted for the war in this way. Corn and other provisions had been collected for a projected expedition to France, but after the inevitable delays it was cancelled and plans were made for Edward to winter in England. Despite this, no attempt was made to restore the pre-empted victuals although Murimuth says that their seizure in the first place had been 'to the great harm of the common weal'.[25]

Discontent with the practice was nothing new. As early as *c.* 1330 an unknown but probably highly placed cleric wrote the *Speculum Regis Edwardi*, an address to the king on the injustice of purveyance.[26] To him it was inexcusable that victuals should be taken against the will of the owner, or for less than he was prepared to sell. The *Speculum* is a stern warning to Edward. Unless he mends his ways he will never earn the love of God nor of the people of England. The subjects of a good king rejoice at his coming, 'but, as is commonly said, the English people are grieved at your arrival, on account of the exactions which your servants make.'[27]

The *Speculum* was written as a protest against the use of purveyance to provision the royal household. Its extension in the 1340s and 50s to include the provisioning of the king's armies added greatly to the long-standing opposition to pre-emption. At times this reached such proportions that the government was forced to appease public resentment by the punishment of purveyors who abused their positions. This happened in 1346 when Edward took action 'on hearing the great outcry and the complaints common amongst his subjects.' In 1362 a statute was enacted which implemented some of the reforms suggested by the author of the *Speculum* thirty years previously. Purveyors were henceforward to be known as 'buyers of victuals', and no goods were to be taken unless paid for in advance; while those buyers who were found guilty of deceit were to be punished in accordance with the law. John of Reading says that these measures allayed public disquiet and there are certainly fewer complaints in the chronicles after this date, though the malpractices of individual purveyors had to be condemned by statute again in 1369.[28]

The other serious cause of public concern directly related to the war was the increase in crimes of violence. Here again the war was instrumental in aggravating a perennial problem rather than in creating a new one. Disbanded soldiers, grown accustomed to the conditions of the *chevauchée*, at times preferred to adopt a life of brigandage on their return home, and the royal policy of pardoning criminals in return for war service did little to mitigate this tendency. The problem was particularly acute during the years between the Treaty of Bretigny and the renewal of the war in 1369. John of Reading observes that the prevalence of crimes of violence in 1367 was such that 'the regular clergy could hardly secure their church ornaments from robbers, or travellers their goods and persons by day or night.' Even foreign potentates travelling under royal protection were not free from danger. In 1363 King Peter of Cyprus was attacked and robbed of all his possessions by thieves while on his way from London to the coast.[29] Highwaymen of this kind were not infrequently members of the gentry, like the Folvilles who divided their time between fighting in the king's wars in Scotland and France and defying his laws in their native Leicestershire. They provide an extreme example of the riotousness and disrespect for law and order which seem to have been widespread amongst the military at this time. Just how widespread it is impossible to tell from contemporary historical and fictional literature, and a thorough study of the problem using parliamentary and judicial records has yet to be made.[30]

It cannot be over-emphasized, however, that such criticism was directed against the government's inept war policy and not against the war itself. The *Melsa* chronicler, writing with hindsight, might lament the 'continuous and sorrowful war' in his account of its inception in 1339 and Minot might conclude his poem on Halidon Hill with a prayer for peace; but such sentiments were exceptional, and neither the historian nor the poet doubted the justice of Edward's cause nor his right to involve the country in a dynastic war.[31] The lament of the peace-loving Richard de Bury in his 'Complaint of the books against war' in the *Philobiblon* is entirely untypical of the age. Here he regrets the infinite losses which books have suffered from wars and tumults and prays that the 'Ruler of Olympus and the Most High Governor of all the world may establish peace and put away wars and make the times peaceful under his protection'. [32] As we shall see, such sentiments were to fall on deaf ears until the turn of England's fortunes in the last decades of the century.

In England itself the war must always have seemed somewhat remote and unreal. Increased taxation and the practice of purveyance no doubt added to the hardships of everyday life, but for many, the harsher realities of warfare could only have been experienced vicariously through the tales of returning soldiers. There were, however, two exceptions to this: for Englishmen living in the northern marches and along the south coast experienced at first hand the miseries which their fellows inflicted year after year on the French.

In the north there was an almost continuous state of war and although Scots raids were inevitably on a small scale they were also frequent and over the years caused real depredations to the inhabitants of Cumberland and Northumberland.[33] The Commons' petitions for the 1370s and 80s tell their own story. In 1376 the county of Cumberland petitioned that the citizens of Carlisle were so poor they could not afford to repair the defences; in 1377 Cumberland, Northumberland, and Westmorland petitioned that the defences of Carlisle, New Castle, Roxburgh, and Berwick were in such a state of disrepair that they could not be held against the enemy; the following year Cumberland again complained that Carlisle was without defences, and that the land between the city and the border had been laid waste. In 1378–9 the people of the three border counties claimed to be in a state of chaos because of pestilence and 'from the continual destruction by the enemies of Scotland'. The same year the members for Northumberland petitioned that the people were so impoverished by Scots raids that they were unable to pay taxes.[34] Such claims must be treated with caution as it was customary to exaggerate the extent of damage from enemy raids in order to gain relief from taxation. But the cumulative effect of the petitions for these years indicates a serious state of affairs in the north.

Behind the complaints lay widespread dissatisfaction with the government's defence of the border, a dissatisfaction which reached a climax in the 1380s. Between 1383 and 1387 the Commons petitioned no less than five times that those who received revenues from the marcher castles should see to it that these were sufficiently fortified, armed, and victualled.[35] The complaint was a long-standing one. In 1376 the county of Cumberland petitioned that it was without a governor or guardian of the marches so that there was no one to prevent internal disorder or 'to resist the malice of the enemies of Scotland'; because of these defaulting marcher lords the border had been 'entirely laid waste'. There are even hints that the continued lack of good governance might lead to rebellion and disaffection. A petition of 1382 requests that the guardians of the march 'be charged to treat your subjects of Tevedale with such reasonable justice that they may have no cause to rebel, nor to adhere to your enemies of Scotland'.[36]

But by the 1380s the men of the north had clearly little expectation that the king and the marcher lords would provide effective defence, and still less that they would pursue the war into enemy territory. In such circumstances the way of peace seemed to offer most hope. In 1382 the Commons reported rumours that the Scots were preparing for war: 'and that would be the strongest and the most evil war that could befall us'. They petitioned that the marcher lords should reside in their castles, and that the king should proceed to York to ensure a truce or at least to learn the purpose of the enemy. In the second session of this parliament the Commons returned to the same issue with greater insistence, petitioning Richard to sue for 'truce or peace' with the Scots so that his subjects might live in peace and security equal to that enjoyed by the king's enemies. Clearly the situation in the north was out of hand and the Scots were enjoying an ascendancy which they had not known since the days of Robert Bruce.[37]

There had, however, been a long history of trouble on the Scottish marches and the inhabitants of the northern counties were consequently inured to the sudden violence of enemy raids. But this was not the case with the prosperous fishing and trading communities along the south coast whose inhabitants had come to expect a state of comparative peace. French naval raids consequently caused great dismay in this region. Government measures existed for the defence of the shoreline,[38] but many towns and villages were inadequately fortified and it proved difficult to contain the raids of a seaborne enemy whose mobility and elusiveness almost always ensured the advantage of surprise. Franco-Castilian expeditions may have been infrequent and restricted to hit-and-run raids along the coast, but within these limits they were capable of inflicting serious local damage. Certainly after the raids of 1338–9 no town from Cornwall to Kent could feel assured of its safety.[39]

The inhabitants of the south coast did not always respond well to finding themselves in the front line of the war. In 1385–6, for example, there was widespread panic in the London area as news reached England of Charles VI's massive build-up of ships and men at Sluys in Flanders.[40] Rumour was rife. Knighton reports an oath said to have been sworn by the leaders of the expedition to the effect that they would conquer and depopulate England or die in the attempt. The size of the expeditionary force was exaggerated out of all proportion. It was believed that a fleet of six hundred ships was ready to carry an innumerable army which would overflow the land 'like a swarm of locusts'. The St Albans chronicler, Thomas Walsingham, was well placed to observe the effects of these rumours on the populace in the south-east and the picture he draws is one of despondency and defeatism not only amongst the common people but, more disturbingly, amongst the military:

... but there, as if there were no hope of deliverance, not only did the common people begin to panic, but the military as well who were once disciplined but now effeminate; once undaunted but now full of fear; once prudent but now witless and unnerved. And they did not think in terms of resistance but of flight and surrender.[41]

A short truce was arranged and, as Walsingham puts it, England was able to breathe 'because it was not at once brought under the sword of the enemy'. But with the expiration of the truce in 1386 the fears of the previous year returned, and in London there was something like mass hysteria. This is described with contempt by

Walsingham who is admittedly hostile to the Londoners at this time. The citizens were, he claims, as timid as hares and, despairing of resistance, sought out lurking places for themselves. Others, as if drunk with wine, ran to the walls and pulled down the houses which bordered them. Such was the custom in times of emergency, but no Frenchman had set foot in a boat, let alone put to sea – yet the Londoners acted as if the enemy were at the very gates of the city. 'Thus, thus, the men who, bold in time of quiet, warlike in peace, present a fair spectacle for one another; they do not offer an example to be followed of how to behave if they sensed battle approaching, danger imminent.'[42]

The government responded to the emergency by raising an army for the defence of the realm which was stationed near London, but what ensued was little short of a fiasco. No doubt with 1381 in mind, the movements of the troops were severely restricted. They were to be quartered within thirty leagues of the city, but were not to approach within more than ten leagues of the walls. This applied equally to the retainers of lords and magnates. When, however, the enemy failed to materialize the militia was disbanded. It was at this point that government organization broke down. Each soldier was expected to make his own way home, but many of them had not been paid with the result that those from the remoter parts were forced to live off the land. Knighton records how the Welsh and the men of Cheshire and Lancashire plundered Warwickshire as they made their way north and west. As an example of their violence and extortion he quotes an incident in which some villagers were forced to buy them off for £10 under threat of death to themselves and the destruction of their village by fire. 'And so,' he adds, 'through such men evils without number were committed in various parts of the kingdom.' Walsingham says that they did everything in their own land which is done between enemies, 'with the single exception that they refrained from arson'.[43] This was by no means the first time that an army had run riot in recent years. In 1380 an English force stationed in Northumberland had made such a nuisance of itself that the inhabitants swore they preferred the arrival of the Scots to their compatriots, since at least they could legitimately offer resistance to the enemy.[44]

Not everyone responded to times of crisis with the Londoners' hysteria. In 1378 the men of Winchelsea and Rye organized a raid on the Normandy coast in revenge for recent attacks by the French. Such raids were not always successful. The same year a group of raiders from Northumberland was cut to pieces in Scotland, and Walsingham, perhaps reflecting current north-south antipathy, saw the cause of its defeat in the northerners' imprudence and arrogance. Generally, however, he approved of such private enterprise and contrasted it favourably with the inept expeditions mounted by the authorities. In 1385 an English fleet led by Sir Thomas Percy and the Master of the Hospital of St John failed to engage the enemy, 'either impeded by private disagreement or driven back by folly'. This he compares with a spirited raid on the French coast by the men of Portsmouth and Dartmouth: 'But not so the men of Portsmouth and Dartmouth, not so did they grow less from idleness. Whom none had led none had paid to inflict injury on the enemy, but their own valour had prompted them, their inborn worth had fired them.'[45]

Directly or indirectly, then, the Hundred Years War influenced the lives of all Englishmen from its inception in 1337 to the end of the century. This was true even during periods of extended truce or peace, for these were little more than interludes in an unresolved conflict. As a result , the French and the Scots came to be regarded as *the* enemies of England, and it is hardly surprising that hatred for their antagonists became a habit of mind for the English. From the beginning this was expressed in terms of crude generalizations about the character of the French and Scots. Such stereotypes satisfied popular and learned curiosity alike, and over the years were to harden into unchallenged truths.

A word of caution is necessary at this point. In fourteenth-century England any prominent group of aliens was liable to attract hostile criticism. At one time it might be Lombard bankers and merchants who came under attack; at another, the merchants of Flanders, the German allies of Edward III, or Queen Anne's Bohemian retainers.[46] Hatred and distrust of foreigners was in fact endemic, and contemporary hostility to the French and Scots should be considered as differing in degree rather than kind from hostility to other racial groups.

During the early years of the war hatred of the French was based upon fear, for the kings of France with their vast resources were long thought to have plotted the destruction of England. Murimuth noted that Philip VI was the son of Charles of Valois 'who never loved the English', and it seemed to some that he had inherited his father's prejudice. Minot feared that Philip and his counsellors planned 'To stroy Ingland and bring to noght', and an actual invasion plan drawn up in 1339 and discovered by the English at Caen in 1346 confirmed such suspicions. Not surprisingly, the discovery was made much of by Edward and his council, and details of the plan found their way into some of the chronicles. Knighton, probably confusing the plan of 1339 with the year in which it was discovered, reveals the would-be conquerors' intention of partitioning England amongst themselves.[47]

Inevitably there were rumours about the cruelty and spite of the French. The author of the *Brut* reports a terrible storm at sea as Edward was returning from France in 1341, 'the whiche was seyd that it was done & areysed thorugh evel spirites made by sorcery and Nigromancye of hem of Fraunce'.[48] Knighton tells of a treacherous plan of Philip's to arrest Edward in 1329 because of his superior claim to the crown of France; while Minot believed that ten years later the French king ordered his men to sail

> Till Ingland, and for no thing spare
> Bot brin* and sla† both man and wife   *burn †slay
> And childe, that none suld pas with life.

He completes his grim picture with the assurance that

> The galay men held vp thaire handes
> And thanked God of thir tithandes.*[49]   *these tidings

Philip's pride and treachery were early established in the minds of Englishmen. Baker reports how the *tyrannus* stirred up the French against the English, 'swollen with the spirit of madness and pride', and he is echoed by the Lanercost chronicler who calls Philip 'proud and passionate' for his refusal to accept a peaceful settlement of the dispute over Guienne.[50] But in the 1340s it was cowardice rather than pride which characterized the French king for the chroniclers and poets. His refusal to accept pitched battle in 1339 was interpreted as conclusive evidence of his wretched nature. The patriotic author of the *Chroniques de London* declares that for all his 'lofty arrogance' Philip did not dare approach the

young King Edward, and even more damning, at the siege of
Tourney he sent a woman to sue for terms 'like a coward and
craven knight'. To describe Philip's behaviour during the Crécy
campaign, Laurence Minot summons up his reserves of contempt
and sarcasm. In mock pity he describes the French king's sorrow
at the sack of Caen:

> The teres he let ful rathly* ren†   *quickly †run
> Out of his eghen,* I vnderstand   *eyes

while at Crécy itself the poet upbraids the Valois as a vile coward
who 'fled and durst noght take his dole [share]'.[51]

This view of Philip's character confirmed the English in their
opinion that he was a usurper. As the author of the *Chroniques de
London* observed, through his cowardice he had forfeited the right
to be called king. Baker, indeed, makes the dying Philip confess to
the injustice of his cause, and Erghome maliciously 'prophesies'
his descent into Hell.[52] The mocking tone adopted by these
writers indicates the relief felt by Englishmen on discovering that
the French were not so formidable as their reputation had
suggested. It became apparent that England had little to fear from
Philip and he was consequently demoted from proud and
avaricious tyrant to despised and wretched coward.

A new confidence amongst the English is also suggested by this
readiness to ridicule the French, for one is less inclined to mock
an enemy one fears. Typical is the joke preserved by the *Melsa*
chronicler which circulated in England in 1340. After the battle
of Sluys the fish were said to have been so glutted with corpses
that if God had granted them the power of speech they would have
spoken fluent French. Even the Bridlington prophecies contain a
joke which reveals a surprising vein of ribald humour in the
venerable 'prophet'. Interpreting the words 'four fundaments'
in the prophecy, Erghome explains that the canon referred to
King John and his sons in this improper manner in response to
the French taunt that the English had tails.[53]

One anonymous poet writing in the 1340s used such altercations
as the basis for a more vicious attack on the French.[54] It takes the
form of a fliting (a poetical invective) between a Frenchman and
an Englishman, in which each in turn is reviled for the supposed
defects of his national character. The poem is of particular interest
because it suggests that some of the traits traditionally associated

with the two nations were already well established by the fourteenth century. The Frenchman begins by reviling his enemy as
'the dregs of mankind, the shame of the world, and the uttermost
of beings', and continues with an attack on the gluttony of the
English which reduces them to the level of beasts: 'their belly is
their god, and they are zealous in sacrificing to it.' In reply, however, the Englishman effectively silences his opponent by accusing
the French of effeminacy and the worst excesses of sexual per-
version.[55]

The poem is found in a single manuscript together with *An
Invective against France*, *The Battle of Neville's Cross*, and *On the
Truce of 1347* and it is likely that they are the work of one man.
They certainly share a virulent hatred of the French which it is
hard to parallel elsewhere. There is nothing in Latin or the
vernacular, for example, to compare with the vituperation of the
opening lines of *An Invective*:

> France! effeminate, Pharisaical, shadow of vigour,
> Lynx, viper, foxy, wolvish, Medea,
> Sly, siren, heartless, repulsive, proud . . .[56]

Poets like Minot, however, did share with the anonymous cleric a
willingness to interpret men and events in simplistic terms of
right and wrong – typified by his prayer to the Virgin to avenge
'gude king Edward on wikked syr Iohn' – and with the decline in
England's fortunes after 1360 this tendency became more pro-
nounced.[57]

Adversity often proves more favourable than prosperity for
jingoism and xenophobia, and this was so in fourteenth-century
England. The reversals of the 1370s and 80s had a profound
effect on those who have left a record of their reactions. The
French were no longer a source of ribald or cruel humour. They
provided, or so it seemed at the time, too serious a threat to
England's sovereignty, and Englishmen reacted with an excess of
hatred and fear.

Extensive French raids brought the realities of war to Englishmen living along the south coast, while their compatriots inland
were fed with rumours of atrocities. Knighton says that an
attack on Winchelsea was driven off, but only after the enemy had
captured nine women 'whom they violated so shamefully that it is
horrible to recite'. Walsingham gives a more circumstantial

account of the same raid. He too emphasizes the excesses of the enemy against English women, adding the detail that some women who sought refuge in the church were mercilessly raped to death.[58]

The St Albans chronicler makes a point of collecting such stories. He notes the ruthlessness with which Charles VI dealt with the contumacious citizens of Paris in 1382; the many cruel excesses committed by the French at Oudenarde the following year; and their horrible mutilation of Ghentish prisoners of war.[59] There were also the familiar rumours of French deceit and treachery, some of which are highly implausible. The fact that men were willing to believe them, however, suggests a hardening of attitudes towards the enemy. Knighton believed that during his captivity in England King John organized large-scale arms smuggling. He is said to have employed spies who bought up bows and arrows 'and put up to a thousand bows in sacks of wool and he collected a large supply of arms for shipment to France'. In proof of this, Knighton makes the dying John confess his duplicity to Edward who benevolently forgave him – at the same time taking steps to arrest the smugglers. Other, more credible, stories derived from the same conviction that the French could not be trusted. Charles was thought to have renewed the war from malice while Edward only desired to live peaceably and 'to keep faithfully the covenants and ordinances made previously'; truces were being used to stockpile arms; the English were being duped because the French 'were treacherously contemplating war not peace'.[60]

During these years hostility to the French clearly became a habit of mind for many Englishmen; but it is hardly surprising that they reacted most intensely to the Scots. The war in the north had a long history and, for England, had been accompanied by a number of set-backs. In the early years of the century the depredations of the Scots had been even worse than in the 1370s and 80s, and Knighton's comment on Robert Bruce that 'there had never been in former times any other king in Scotland who so grievously harassed the English as this one in his day'[61] was hardly an exaggeration. Moreover it was fought by the English on the assumption that the Scots were contumacious vassals, and something of the bitterness of civil war may be seen in the atrocities committed by both sides.[62] Scottish incursions over the border were frequent, and at times Englishmen as far south as Yorkshire and Lancashire experienced the devastation and misery of an enemy *chevauchée*. At their worst, such raids affected a greater proportion of the population than the French and Castilian attacks along the south coast, and the English consequently reserved their most bitter invective for their northern neighbours.

Not without justification the Scots had a reputation as a rude and uncivilized people. Higden writes learnedly of their unstable nature. They are, he observes, 'very savage and wild' and only improved somewhat by contact with the English. The men prefer to die in the field than in bed, and are so conservative in their customs that they despise those of others. Even their French allies found them intolerably uncivilized. A party of French knights sent to Scotland in 1384 were so ill-treated that they considered it a better plan to join forces with the English and destroy their allies utterly: 'for they never saw such evil people as the Scots in any country, nor found any so false, nor so treacherous, nor of such little worth.' The highlanders who took part in the *chevauchée* of 1346 were even worse, according to Froissart. He refers to them as 'the savage Scots' who obey none but their clan chiefs, one of whom led a contingent of 3,000 'of the most outrageous men of his country'.[63]

One may doubt whether such men were worse than the common soldiers employed by Edward in France, but they were certainly brutal in the extreme and greatly feared in the north. Froissart describes in detail the ruthless sack of Durham by the Scots in 1342 which he condemns as 'a great pity and a cruel act of madness'; and Knighton gives an equally circumstantial account of the ravages committed by a raiding party in 1388:

... both killing and burning, they committed many atrocities against infants suckling at the breast, women pregnant and in labour, and in the neighbourhood of Gilsland in the lordship of the lord of Dacre they confined, as it was said, two hundred or more weak and decrepit old men in their dwellings and with the doors shut, they unpardonably and without mercy burned them to death.[64]

The English reacted to such atrocities with bitter hatred, the more so because the conquest or even the pacification of Scotland was beyond their power. After the battle of Halidon Hill in 1333 many hoped that the war in the north was over, but, says Murimuth, they were sadly mistaken. In his poem on the battle Minot says that although the Scots were defeated

neuer the les ay er thai boune*   *ready
To wait Ingland with sorow and schame.

In 1336 Edward once again thought he had chastised their malice and pride, but, observes the canon of Bridlington, the Scots are like dogs forever returning to their vomit. Experience taught the English to be less optimistic. With great bitterness the author of a poem celebrating Neville's Cross urged Christ to destroy the hearts of the proud Scots for they are like the many-headed Hydra – 'when one [head] is cut off, three grow in its place without any harm to the body.'[65]

Like their French allies, it was widely held that the Scots could never be trusted to keep a truce or peace and they became a byword for deceit and bad faith. One Wyclifite preacher used the Scots as the type of treachery in illustration of his attack on 'anticristis prelatis', and in a long list of Arthur's conquests the author of the *Morte Arthure* singles out only 'noxious Scotland' for unfavourable comment.[66]

English writers vied with one another in producing terms of opprobrium to express their hatred of the Scots, who are variously described as thieves, turncoats, traitors, deceivers, wretches, sots, cursed caitiffs, 'berebags', sons of iniquity, Satan's satellites, and degenerates.[67] But in a society which thought habitually in terms of personal loyalties and conflicts, it was natural that David Bruce should be the main target of their abuse. In fact no rumour was too gross to find credence amongst the English. There was a scurrilous anecdote current in the north which claimed that as a child David defecated on the altar – hence the epithet *cacator* which the Lanercost chronicler delights in applying to him. Later in life he was said to have indulged in sexual excess, spurning his wife in favour of other women. According to Erghome this was encouraged by David's counsellors 'because they wished to disparage the queen in despite of the king of England whose sister she was'.[68]

Such malice on the part of the English was the result of hatred mingled with fear. For a few years after the death of Robert Bruce, England had been in the ascendancy; yet, despite repeated efforts by Edward III to crush Scottish resistance once and for all, it proved beyond England's military and economic capacity to gain a lasting victory in the north. Even Neville's Cross and the capture of King David proved no more than a temporary triumph, despite the jubilation of the chroniclers and poets; until the end of the century Scotland was to remain a potent threat to England's security in the north.[69]

Throughout the period there was a firm conviction at all levels of society that England faced a third, and in some ways more insidious enemy: the papacy. There had been a tradition of hostility to the papacy some time before the outbreak of the Hundred Years War. Amongst laymen especially there was resentment at the levying of papal provisions and antagonism towards the servants of the Church whose duty it was to collect them.[70] Throughout the century they were to remain a popular target of reformist satire and complaint,[71] and once again, the war should be regarded as aggravating an already existing grievance, rather than as creating a new one.

There can be no doubt, however, that the war gave a new impetus, and to some extent a new direction to anti-papal feeling in England. The fact that the curia was situated at Avignon on the borders of France, and that an unbroken succession of popes from Benedict XII to Gregory XI were French by birth, made this inevitable. It is to the credit of the papacy that it used its authority in a genuine attempt to mediate between England and France,[72] but it is hardly surprising that in England its efforts were consistently misinterpreted and distorted. From the outset it was widely held among Englishmen that the papacy favoured France. It was an opinion they were loathe to abandon.

This suspicion led inevitably to renewed opposition to the collection of papal provisions after 1337.[73] It was not only feared that England was being drained of its wealth but that gold collected by the servants of the pope was being used to finance the war effort of England's enemies.[74] There was a growing conviction that the English were being duped, typified by Murimuth's report that 'amongst the courtiers of the papal see it has become a proverb that the English are good asses, bearing all the intolerable burdens imposed upon them.'[75]

The origin of this fear lay in the conviction that the popes openly or covertly did everything in their power to advance the cause of the French. Clement VI (1342–52) in particular was thought to be an ally of France. In 1343 Edward III prohibited the collection of papal provisions and sent an embassy to Avignon to remonstrate with the pope. Knighton clearly believed that Clement's partiality was amongst the king's grievances, for he observes that although the pope was disturbed by Edward's prohibition 'nevertheless in as much as he could, but secretly, he favoured the king of France and aided him.' Erghome believed that Clement 'was always favourable to the French against the English', and in proof of this he tells how a troop of French soldiers were saved from drowning during the Crécy campaign 'through the masses and prayers of Pope Clement'. When in 1344 Clement created Luis de la Cerda 'Prince of the Fortunate Isles' and equipped a fleet for their conquest, it was suspicioned that this was intended for an attack on England 'alleging it to be one of the Fortunate Islands and rebel to the papal see'. Equally fantastical tales were told of other popes, and the fact that they could be entertained at all by a restrained and reasonable historian like Murimuth suggests the extent of anti-papal feeling in England.[76]

In fact Clement VI genuinely desired to further peace between England and France,[77] but in such an atmosphere of suspicion and mistrust, any attempt at intercession by the papacy was bound to fail. This was especially true during the 1340s and 50s when England seemed on the verge of a military victory. If papal nuncios negotiated a truce, it was to save France from collapse; if hostilities were renewed, then it must be the result of connivance between the king of France and his papal ally.[78]

Cardinal Talleyrand's attempt to avert the battle of Poitiers may be taken as typical in this respect. He succeeded in negotiating a truce for Sunday, 18 September, but was unable to bring King John and the Black Prince to terms and battle was engaged the next day.[79] After the French débâcle all kinds of rumours were spread concerning the cardinal's motives. It was said amongst the English that Talleyrand negotiated the truce to gain time for the arrival of French reinforcements and that the prince refused to extend it for that reason. Others believed that, after the breakdown of negotiations, many of the cardinal's men fought with the French army, and in confirmation of this the body of Talleyrand's nephew, Robert de Duras, was found amongst the slain. Froissart says that the Black Prince had the corpse sent to the cardinal with the message, 'I greet him with these tokens.'[80] Not everyone believed in Talleyrand's duplicity. The Chandos Herald is careful to stress his innocence and so is Sir Thomas Gray. But the Herald adds that both the English and the French believed that they had been betrayed by the cardinal, and Gray certainly thought that the French used the truce to bring up reinforcements. Nevertheless, he insists that 'the cardinal did everything with good intent.'[81]

The author of the *Anonimalle* also accepted Talleyrand's good intentions, calling him 'the particular friend of the king of England and of the prince', but he believed that the cardinal was exceptional and that the aftermath of Poitiers revealed the curia's true sympathies. He claims that a false report of a French victory reached Avignon to the delight of the pope who at once ordered victory celebrations. Later, however, the true outcome of the battle was announced in a message to Talleyrand who promptly held celebrations of his own amongst the English clerks at Avignon. The story is apocryphal, for Talleyrand was at Poitiers and not Avignon after the battle, but it reveals the extent of English suspicions concerning the good faith of the papacy.[82]

Even after the decline in England's fortunes in the 1370s and the consequent desire for peace, papal intervention was regarded unfavourably. The English viewpoint is clearly expressed in *Mirour de l'Omme*, composed about 1376–8. In a bitter attack on the corruption of the papacy Gower makes an officer of the curia confess that war is more advantageous to the pope than peace. The pope has often been requested to secure 'peace and unity' between England and France, but because of the 'little charity' of the curia such pleas are in vain. Papal intervention would in any case have little hope of success:

> ... We are not disinterested
> But are predisposed to one side,
> So that our arbitrament
> Cannot be made impartially.

Why, the officer argues cynically, should the papacy further peace when war is more profitable? Each king is eager to pay for an alliance with the pope although the Holy Father is careful to lean towards the one who pays best, for in this way his treasury is always on the increase:

> Wherefor we never want a settlement
> As long as we get such a good toll.[83]

One of the few men to defend the rectitude of the papacy during the war was Bishop Brinton. In a sermon on peace preached in about 1373, he chides clerics who seek advancement by reporting vacant benefices to the curia. Nowadays, he complains, it is impossible for English prelates to advance deserving friends as they once did. Even worse, if such men fail in their ambitions they spread rumours that the pope favours the French and 'does nothing for the English'. Brinton was no more afraid than Gower to upbraid the curia for its corruption, but he believed that such accusations represented a wilful distortion of the truth: 'And notwithstanding I truly believe that our lord the pope did more for the English than the French as regards favours granted.'[84] The bishop's position is exceptional, however. The tradition of hostility to papal provisions and attempts generally to exploit the revenues of the English Church (a hostility shared by Brinton) predisposed Englishmen against papal mediation. The impartiality of the papacy was prejudged and discredited, and the popes were established with David Bruce and Philip VI as implacable enemies of England.

Over a long period of time this complex of hatred, fear, and suspicion had a profound effect on English social mentality. Surrounded by enemies bent on the kingdom's destruction, Englishmen were forced into an awareness of common identity and purpose which in times of crisis overruled regional and class differences. As we shall see, there emerged from this a crude form of patriotism which was a distinctive feature of English social and political life in the second half of the fourteenth century.

3
Aristocracy, Knighthood and Chivalry

With few exceptions the armies put into the field by Edward III and Richard II were commanded by princes of the blood or by prominent aristocrats. Their lieutenants were knights who made a profession of war, although few of them were 'professionals' in the modern sense of the word. The social differences between these men were often very great, but they shared many basic assumptions about the nature of warfare and were conscious of forming a military élite within society. At the centre of their élitism was the ideal of chivalry.

It is, however, extremely difficult to evaluate the nature and significance of chivalry in late medieval society. Various statements and codifications of the ideal are readily available to the historian through such works as Ramón Lull's *Libro del Orden de Caballería*;[1] what is not clear is how far the ideal was ever taken seriously as a basis for social and political behaviour by the aristocrats and knights themselves. The evidence for this has to be gleaned piecemeal from chronicles and from the (rare) contemporary biographies of men like the Black Prince and Bertrand du Guesclin. For reasons to be discussed later, such evidence is hard to evaluate and conclusions drawn from it are of necessity qualitative.

There is a further complicating factor. To most moderns chivalry is an alien and fantastical concept, and it scarcely seems credible that the men of the Middle Ages could have taken it seriously. This conviction is shared by many historians and it has resulted in the neglect or misunderstanding of the function of chivalry in late medieval society. It has been neglected largely by social historians whose study of manorial and judicial records has revealed no evidence for the influence of chivalric ideas on the land-owning aristocracy and gentry. This neglect has encouraged their conviction that such ideas had no real influence at all. It has been misunderstood especially by literary historians who tend to be most familiar with the ideal formulations of clerics and romancers. When these are compared with the harsher aspects of medieval warfare, glaring discrepancies are revealed. On the basis of this historians infer the decline of chivalry as a social influence of any importance in the later Middle Ages. The ideal, it is asserted, had reached a decadent phase.

The charge of decadence rests upon the belief that the ideals of conduct essential to chivalry became divorced from the realities of life during the fourteenth century, to be replaced by mere externals of lavish spectacle and empty ritual. According to R. L. Kilgour, one of the main exponents of this theory:

> Chivalry had thus become a sort of game, whose participants, in order to forget reality, turned to the illusion of a brilliant, heroic existence. ... It became more and more a code of public display, divorced from the duties of everyday life, in which less elevated conceptions would be far more convenient.[2]

The corollary, of course, is that the realities of fourteenth-century life lay elsewhere. So Dr Hewitt observes:

> At a time when idealized knightly conduct coloured the pages of literature, when war and romance might appear to go hand in hand, when new orders of chivalry were being founded, the stark realities of war were known to all men and not disguised by the founders of the Orders of the Garter and the Star. Whether operations are conducted in Scotland, northern England, Brittany or France, the chroniclers (English and French) use the same terms. And the two kings, judged by their official letters, see war in the same light: it consists in destruction and is accompanied by other evils.[3]

The acts of chivalry reported by Froissart and other chroniclers are, therefore, mere romantic excesses. They are foolish and wasteful, and irrelevant both to the high standards of the chivalric ideal of former times and to the real business of war.[4]

As these quotations imply, many historians refuse to take the ideal seriously in its later manifestations. Moreover they make the assumption that their attitude was shared by the knightly estate itself. This is evident from the language they use in discussing chivalry. According to Hewitt, when men did act by the code of knightly conduct it was with 'theatrical' bravery and 'ostentatious' daring, all of which was the merest 'posturing'. Huizinga writes of chivalry as a 'continual illusion' and a 'fiction'. Chivalry, as Kilgour never tires of reminding his reader, was a 'game' to be abandoned 'whenever the grim horror of war came too near'.[5]

This approach is founded on the assumption that the chivalric code of the knightly estate may be equated more or less exactly with one or other of the two major formulations of the ideal: that of the Church and that of romance. A wealth of evidence survives in the form of chivalric manuals, exhortatory sermons and romances which encourages the assumption, but it is misleading in the extreme. The formulations of learned clerks and romancers were far too complex and theoretical ever to be taken seriously in their entirety by those who made a profession of arms. The chivalric code acknowledged by such men was at once simpler and more eclectic. As we shall see, it was influenced in some important respects by the clerical and romance ideals, but it was essentially the code of a military caste based on inherited values and ideas independent of either. Some of these values (honour, pride, fealty) were held to be immutable. Others (techniques of warfare, standards of civility) were open to change as contemporary practice or fashion dictated.

It is difficult to assess the influence of the clerical ideal in the fourteenth century. Its origins lay in the Church's desire to bring the second estate within its sphere of influence and to direct its energies towards approved goals – notably through the crusades.[6] But amongst the knights themselves the pious desire to recover the Holy City was always inextricably involved with the pursuit of land and plunder.[7] Few men were able or willing to live according to the exacting precepts of Christian chivalry as conceived by idealists like Lull.[8] There is, however, a sense in which they recognized its validity as an absolute standard of knightly perfection, and the individual who did embody the ideal in his life was admired to excess. Such men were rare, yet each generation saw at least one outstanding figure whose life took on a symbolic meaning for contemporaries often far in excess of his importance as an individual. Earlier examples are Godfrey of Bouillon and St Louis; fourteenth-century England produced one of the most remarkable Christian knights of all, Henry of Grosmont, first duke of Lancaster (1310–61).

The duke is of particular interest in the present context. At the height of his career he was possibly the most powerful man in England after the king, and in the 1340s and 50s he played a major role in the conduct of the war with France. But Henry was also an ascetic, deeply attracted by the rigorous idealism of Christian chivalry, and there was a resultant dualism in his life which is curiously reflected in the opposition between modern and medieval estimates of the duke's importance and achievement. The modern historian is understandably concerned most with Henry's position as a great magnate and landowner and with his career as a general and diplomat;[9] but while the duke's abilities in these areas were recognized by contemporaries, his reputation during his lifetime and for many generations after his death was centred elsewhere. To Englishmen of the fourteenth century Henry of Grosmont was pre-eminently the very type of religious chivalry.

In the surviving notices of his life the duke is consistently described in terms of the perfect knight. Even the hostile author of *Les Voeux du Héron* found little with which to discredit him, while the Scots chronicler, Andrew of Wyntoun, who had no cause to praise an Englishman, wrote that he was:

> . . . ay worthi, wycht* and wysse,†   *brave †wise
> And mast ranownyt of bownte,*   *bounty
> Off gentrice* and of honeste,   *gentility
> That in til Inglande liffande was.[10]

In the pages of Wyntoun's chronicle Henry emerges very much as the secular knight who engaged in the wars with Scotland for personal glory – he had, we are told, 'gret yarnynge to wyn prysse [praise]'.[11] There is a degree of accuracy in Wyntoun's assessment of the duke's chivalry, but his account is very partial. Henry of Grosmont was no mere knight-errant in pursuit of renown. He was in fact one of Edward's most trusted and accomplished lieutenants whose generalship won the field on more than one occasion. He alone is praised by Erghome for his conduct at the siege of Calais in 1347 where he is described as the good duke 'from whom England received many honours and great glory through the warlike deeds and great exertions which he sustained'. Henry was also a stern conqueror who, as Capgrave records in his encomium, 'conquered many provinces, oppressed many towns, subdued villages and castles by force, and brought rebels to their destruction'. On more than one occasion he put the inhabitants of a city which had resisted him to the sword – men, women and children – but such acts were justified by contemporary laws of war and were in no way thought to detract from Henry's chivalry.[12]

Prominent amongst the qualities of a good commander was largesse, a quality which, according to Thomas of Walsingham, the duke possessed to a high degree. We are told that whenever a city was taken by storm Henry reserved to himself only a portion of the spoils and at times took none at all, placing everything at the disposal of the troops. As Christine de Pisan knew, such was the practice of 'valyunt conquerours that be past' by which means they gained the respect and obedience of their men. Such, Walsingham assures us, was the case with Henry of Grosmont: 'Indeed he was so liberal, so lavish with gifts, that everyone thought it agreeable to serve under him.' Capgrave, who accounts for the duke's popularity by reference to his noble disposition and reputation for prowess, says he was known as 'the father of knights'. So great was his fame that 'other young men of the world, the sons of dukes and lords of France and Germany, were wont to serve in his divisions and under his standard.'[13]

During his lifetime Henry's renown was international. When he visited Avignon in 1354 at the head of an embassy to the pope, so many people turned out to see him that it was only with difficulty that he entered the city. Knighton says that on the same occasion he bore himself so graciously to one and all that it was said his equal was not to be found in all the world. In Bordeaux such was his popularity that on his arrival there in 1345 the citizens showed him 'great reverence and every honour, and put at his disposal supplies and provisions'.[14]

So far there is nothing in this image of the duke to suggest the pious devotee to the ideal of Christian chivalry. Indeed, a man who dedicated much of his active life to a secular war of dubious legality fought between two Christian kingdoms might seem, to modern eyes, a long way from that ideal. But the duke's reputation was for piety as much as for prowess, the two being closely associated in his person in the minds of contemporaries without any apparent awareness of inconsistency. We are seemingly faced with an area where medieval moral sensibility differed radically from our own. As we shall see, this difference is fundamental to an understanding of certain aspects of chivalry in late medieval society.

Henry of Grosmont was in fact one of the last prominent men of the age to take the crusading ideal seriously, fighting for the faith in Lithuania, Rhodes, Cyprus, and the Near East. Capgrave claims that the young nobles of France and Germany were eager to serve under him for his renown as a crusader rather than his success in the Hundred Years War. As one would expect in such a man, he was also assiduous in individual acts of piety both in the form of endowments to the Church and in alms-giving. Capgrave praises him for his 'many pious deeds' which included the founding of monasteries and the building of churches and hospitals. He especially notes the duke's charity towards the poor and defenceless: 'His eye could not behold a poor man and pass him by empty handed. He personally heard the causes of the poor and of widows, and dealt with them according to God and good conscience.' As an example, he made provision for the care of a hundred paupers at the hospital founded by his father at Leicester, as well as enlarging the original foundation to include a college with a dean and canons.[15] Henry's charity was coupled in the minds of contemporaries with his justice. Capgrave says that he was just in all things and 'sought nothing contrary to justice'; while Thomas Hoccleve, although he recognized that the 'good duke' possessed all the chivalric virtues in his 'excellent man-hode', gives greatest weight to his justice which is 'writen and auctorised'.[16]

Normally there would be little further evidence than that provided by chroniclers and poets for the assessment of such a magnate's character and ideals. But the first duke of Lancaster was a literate if not a learned man and he wrote a book, *Le Livre de Seyntz Medicines*. This remarkable work is in the form of a devotional treatise and was intended as a confession of his own sins and as a warning and a guide to others.[17] To this end he classified his transgressions under the seven deadly sins, and for the historian this catalogue provides a rare insight into the style of life and the chivalric idealism of an aristocrat in the middle decades of the fourteenth century.

In his notice of the duke's death Sir Thomas Gray of Heaton

allows him the conventional epithets associated with the good knight: he was 'wise, glorious, and valiant'. He adds that in his youth he was 'renowned in honour and arms and before his decease he was an exceedingly good Christian'.[18] The *Livre* was written in 1354, towards the end of Henry's life, and one of its main themes is the tension between his duty as a Christian and the delight in the noble life which so often led him into sin. The work is inevitably austere in tone. In the search for salvation the 'exceedingly good Christian' could not recall without anguish even the most trifling pleasure of his youth which may have turned him momentarily from God. There is no sense, however, of a man who in later life attained a state of perfect piety. In his youth he frequently fell below his own standards of behaviour and, as he freely confessed, often succumbed to temptation in middle age. As a result, the acts of charity and justice for which he was admired by contemporaries hardly atoned in his eyes for a life spent in the pursuit of worldly pleasure and power. But it must be remembered that Henry's view of the Christian life was more than usually austere for a man of his class, and many of the faults which his puritan conscience dwells upon seem insignificant now and his self-condemnation excessive. Nevertheless they highlight the differences between the worldly chivalry actually lived by a young aristocrat and the ideal of religious chivalry towards which Henry strove in later life.

In Part 1 of the *Livre* he discusses the various ways in which the five senses have led him astray. One of the most prominent aspects of the duke's youth which this reveals is his awareness of and pleasure in simple physical sensation. He delighted, for example, in all kinds of sounds: 'a delightful song made by a man or woman, or by a nightingale or some other bird or instrument, or the barking of a dog'; as well as in the smell of flowers, leaves, herbs, and fruit, and the scent of women 'or anything belonging to them'. He goes on to describe how he had 'great delight' in costly things 'such as in fine cloths which I have coveted more for their scent than anything else'. He listened eagerly to the details of a feast being discussed: 'the good viands and the delicacies and the drinks – strong wines, or verdelés, or clarés, or vernage* – and all those other delights which one has heard spoken of or heard

* *Verdelé*, a tart, slightly acid wine; *claré*, wine mixed with honey and spices; *vernage*, a strong sweet white wine from Italy.

planned with too great a concern'. His taste for good things led him to eat to excess and at forbidden times, a habit which had its inevitable consequences: in later life the duke was subject to bad attacks of gout after an evening's heavy banqueting.[19]

Worse still in the duke's opinion was his addiction to lechery since this had caused him to lead others into sin. He clearly regarded this as his greatest fault, for he returns to the subject repeatedly: 'from that sin my hands have been greatly sullied, through myself and others, with all the filth and vileness which any man could think of or devise.' To gain the affections of a lady whom he lusts after he adopts the pose of a courtly lover, to which end he boasts of his prowess and tells many lies. He sings 'many an amorous song', stretches out his stirrups at tournaments, and dances 'with nimble foot'. If the lady is *daungerouse* [disdainful] he employs a go-between whose aid he piteously beseeches: 'I am but dead if you do not help me.' But he well knows that the friend who pleads his case 'shows me little friendship and will destroy himself and me also'. Despite this he cannot contain his lust and confesses that he always prefers the kisses of a low woman 'immodest of her body' to those of a good woman of rank 'were she never so fair'.[20]

Henry's ascetic idealism had more to contend with than his natural instincts alone. It also had to combat the values and assumptions which the duke inherited from his aristocratic background. Some of these were indeed so habitual with him that in the *Livre* he is able to reiterate them without any apparent awareness that they conflict with his declared Christian duty. His concept of nobility, for example, is rooted in the aristocratic belief that *gentilesse* depends upon lineage. He acknowledges the importance of nobility of character, but to establish whether or not a man is truly *gentil* he considered it important to know whether his parents were *gentil* as well. Such a belief was widely held amongst the upper ranks of society in the fourteenth century, but its validity was denied by the Church and frequently condemned by the moralists.[21]

For the most part, however, Henry is well aware of the ways in which the pursuit of the noble life can lead a man into sin. In this respect he has surprisingly little to say on the subject of chivalry and war. But the numerous illustrations which he adduces from personal experience reveal, in a fragmentary form, his youthful preoccupations and aspirations, and many of these reflect the values of an aristocratic military élite.

In his youth, he tells us, he was a proud man. He thought he surpassed all others 'in strength, in bravery, in sense, in power'. He was proud of his strength and the beauty of his hands which he adorned with rings, going to great lengths 'that they should be praised by people'. Vainglory led him to boast and to lie about himself in order to be the more honoured, a practice he continues even now in later life.[22] Envy caused him to advance his own reputation at the expense of others 'to be held the best in this world'. Such implacable concern for personal honour at the expense of others is a common feature of any aristocratic and militaristic society and is frequently admired in its literature, but, as Henry well knew, the pursuit of such worldly vanities led him further from 'the kingdom of paradise'.[23]

Something of the duke's austere qualities as a general is suggested by his confessions concerning the sin of anger. Often, he laments, it has led him to command the death of a fellow man, or to have him beaten or mutilated. At times he is beside himself with rage: 'out of charity, out of sense, and of all reason'. Then his hands are eager 'to accomplish the evil promptings of sin, such as to strike out and beat, be it with fist, dagger, sword or staff, and from great anger to pull, to tear, and to rend my own or another's hair and clothes'.[24]

Occasionally he uses imagery which illuminates aspects of his military experience. He adopts, for example, the allegory of the body as a castle defending the soul against the hosts of the devil. This is a commonplace figure in sermons and devotional literature[25] but in the *Livre* it is enriched by Henry's knowledge of the techniques of siege warfare. A castle or town, he observes, is as often taken by storm at the walls as at the gate, since the former are usually less carefully defended. The castle is his body which guards the soul; the enemies are the seven deadly sins; and the walls are his hands and feet. The sins are like miners who undermine the walls, but even though the castle were taken all would not be lost. The *donjon* (the heart) still remains and if it is strong and well defended 'may yet guard the treasure well, and rescue the whole castle from that tower, and defeat all the enemies who have entered the suburbs, killing them or casting them into everlasting imprisonment'. But in his case the situation is desperate: even the *donjon* is lost, for he failed to defend it against the devil, keeping it instead against his own Lord.[26]

Henry was well aware of and apparently given to the temptations confronting a great landowner. He confesses to taking the goods of others without mercy to the poor; to acquiring lands, castles, and manors for the profit alone; and to obtaining them by means of cursing and harassment when persuasion failed. To this end he resorted to maintenance, forcing judgements in his favour in his courts. Three things, he reflects, encouraged him in this sin: the desire to be rich, the fear of being poor, and 'consent without conscience'. Through them he was always willing to receive but never to give.[27]

The *Livre* reveals aspects of the duke's life and character which admiring contemporaries chose to ignore or of which they were unaware. From his confessions it would be possible to portray him as an acquisitive, unjust, brutal man who was no better if no worse than other members of his class. But this would be only a half-truth. The chroniclers and eulogists were not entirely wrong, for by medieval standards his devotion to the crusading ideal, his alms-giving, and other acts of charity justified his reputation. Only Henry, who was, to judge by the *Livre*, his sternest critic, knew that he gave to the poor reluctantly, urged on by shame for his wickedness and fear of death and damnation. The *Livre* is a record of the duke's failure to achieve the exacting ideal of religious chivalry, but it is also the testimony of a man who came closer to realizing it than any of his contemporaries.[28]

It is important to note, however, that Henry's ascetic idealism may already have appeared somewhat old-fashioned by the mid-century. His commitment to the crusading ideal, for example, was certainly considered praiseworthy, but chivalry was no longer intimately linked with the cult of the soldier of Christ. The duke's younger contemporary, the Black Prince, was equally admired as an exemplar of chivalry although he paid the merest lip-service to the idea of the Holy War and never went crusading himself. As we shall see, the secularized ideal of the prince was more in keeping with the needs and capabilities of the second estate. For the majority of knights chivalry was a less elevated code of honour which prescribed their behaviour in relation to society generally and their peers in particular.

.   .   .   .   .

There is even less evidence for the influence of the romance ideal on the knightly estate at this period. There were certainly men who modelled themselves on the pattern of the knight errant or courtly lover, as the pages of Froissart testify.[29] Yet even in the *Chroniques* they are exceptional, and Froissart was careful to record their extravagant exploits whenever they came to his notice. Romance was mainly influential in civilizing the relationship between men and women in court society through its emphasis on *courtoisie*, the refinement of speech and manners. In this context, it also helped to refine the pastimes of the aristocracy. During the thirteenth century the brutal and often fatal *mêlée* was replaced by elaborate tournaments and jousts based upon precedents in romance which if no less dangerous were at least aesthetically more pleasing.[30] Romance was always essentially an entertainment. Embodying an ideal which challenged some of the basic assumptions of feudal society through its insistence on the primacy of the love relationship between a knight and his lady, it could scarcely be anything more. Marriage was based on more mundane principles: the enlargement of estates, the ratification of alliances, or the need for an heir.[31] This may help to explain the insistence in some romances on an extra-marital relationship, but romance rarely reflects the actual practice of the day. A love match such as that between the Black Prince and Joan of Kent was always the exception.

The fashion for chivalric orders based on the extravagant example of romance did lead to one significant development in England: the founding of the Order of the Garter. Edward III took pains to associate himself with King Arthur. At the great 'round table' or jousts of 1344 he planned to inaugurate a fellowship of three hundred knights after the pattern set by the British king, which was to meet each year at the feast of Pentecost. To accommodate such a gathering he gave orders for the construction of a 'most noble hall' at Windsor, although this was never completed. The choice of Windsor was not fortuitous. According to tradition it was Arthur himself who founded the great castle, 'and there where the Round Table was first begun, whence so many good and valiant knights issued forth and laboured in arms and in prowess throughout the world'. In the end Edward's grandiose scheme was abandoned in favour of the less ambitious Order of the Garter.[32] It has been the fashion for historians to minimize the

military importance of Edward's Arthurian pretensions in general
and the Order of the Garter in particular. But as Professor
McKisack has argued, by his adoption of the role of a second
Arthur and the creation of an exclusive fellowship, Edward
'harnessed the idealism of chivalry to his cause and bound to
himself under an obligation of honour nearly all the greatest
names in the land'.[33] Throughout his reign Edward's captains
worked together with a remarkable harmony, and nothing is
heard of the rivalries which marred the efficiency of Richard ii's
campaigns. In this, the king's fostering of current fashions in
romantic chivalry was a contributory factor which should not be
ignored.

Before turning to the knights themselves, one further formulation
of the chivalric ideal deserves attention: that of the fourteenth-
century legists in their tracts on the nature of war and the laws by
which it should be governed. These are in effect manuals of
chivalry though they differ greatly from those produced by clerks
like Lull. They are of significance to an understanding of fourteenth-century chivalry since they are the particular products of
the age, combining civil and canon law, the theory of late Roman
strategists, a rationale of contemporary practice, and on occasion
the testimony of knights themselves. Tracts of this kind were
popularized in French versions in the late fourteenth and early
fifteenth centuries by Honoré Bonet and Christine de Pisan.
Bonet's *L'Arbre des Batailles* (1387) and Christine's *Le Livre des
Faits d'Armes et de Chevalerie* (1408–9) were immediately popular
and in many respects provide a more accurate reflection of
chivalry as understood by the knights themselves than the courtly
fantasies of romance or the complex moral structures of the
Church.[34] To begin with, their concept of chivalry was far more
eclectic. Bonet and Christine discussed the legal and theological
bases of the just war, the theory of strategy and tactics, the
qualities essential to knighthood, and the niceties of points of
honour. They also examined more mundane problems arising
from such contemporary practice as the taking of ransom, the
granting of safe-conducts, and questions of feudal allegiance and
obligation.[35]

Many of the aspects of war they discuss are taken by historians

D

to indicate the decline of chivalry in the later Middle Ages. The mercenary interests of knights in the Hundred Years War are particularly cited in this respect since it is assumed that the pursuit of gain in battle is incompatible with chivalry. Religious chivalry certainly condemned the practice,[36] but there is little evidence to relate this to the actual code of honour acknowledged by the knights themselves. Neither Bonet nor Christine considers ransom contrary to chivalry, and there is reason to believe that they reflect the established code of contemporary knights as well as their practice. Bonet presents a number of current arguments against the practice but he concludes by reasoning in its favour:

Now something must be said on the other side; for according to written law all that a man can win from his enemy in lawful war he may of good right retain. So, seeing that he holds the man's person, and by releasing that can have his goods, why should he be blamed? Also, if a man had all his possessions with him in battle, by written law they would be spoil for the conqueror. Why then should the conqueror not have them sent for before he allows his prisoner to go? Again, by written law, good custom and usage are approved, and among Christians great and small there exists the custom of commonly taking ransom one from another.

There are limitations, however, which a captor should observe. He may only demand a 'reasonable and knightly ransom' which the prisoner can pay without impoverishing himself and his family, and 'if he do otherwise he is not a gentleman but a tyrant, and no knight.' Bonet indeed goes on to condemn the knights of his own day: 'for they take from their prisoners, or cause them to pay, great and excessive payments and ransoms without pity or mercy.' But this does not controvert the basic principle that ransom, when demanded in moderation, is compatible with chivalry.[37]

Through their studies in military history Bonet and Christine are aware of the principle of change in human society. As Christine points out to her reader, 'there nys in the ordres of humayn dedes/ But that it is by long proces of tyme chaunged and tourned.' They apply this principle in their accounts of the techniques of warfare associated with chivalry. Christine draws attention to the differences between the ordering of an army as prescribed by Vegetius and as practised in her own day; commenting in particular on the fact that the ancients commonly fought on horseback while contemporary knights sometimes fight on foot. Similarly Vegetius's instructions on the assault of castles are supplemented by the remarks of knights of her acquaintance because 'it semeth me goode to adde in thys oure sayde werke more partyculerly thoo thinges that be goode and propyce to assaylle Cytees Castelles and Townes after the manere and waye of the tyme present for to gyue thereof a more Intellygyble exsample.'[38]

The consideration of so many practical aspects of war, and the recognition that the knight's role was liable to change in some respects are not thought to detract from the pursuit of chivalry. In both *L'Arbre des Batailles* and *Le Livre des Faits d'Armes et de Chevalerie* analyses of the techniques of warfare and of the moral values appropriate to knighthood are given equal consideration. Christine's account of the ideal commander is an amalgam of the practical and worldly qualities to be looked for in a professional soldier and the conventional attributes of the Christian knight. She has no sense of an uneasy alliance between the two. Chivalry appears in the pages of her book as a flexible institution capable of absorbing change and, perhaps inevitably, involving contradictions in its structure.[39]

In some ways, however, the treatises of the legists do contain elements which are anti-chivalric in sentiment, heralding the changes in outlook which eventually were to outdate chivalry. Typical is Christine's argument that the king should never lead his knights into battle except in time of civil war because of the dangers to which he exposed himself; and her approval of the humane but unchivalric reply of Charles v to his critics who upbraided him for recovering his castles with money when he had the power to seize them by force of arms: 'It semith me . . . that that whiche may be bought ought not to be bought with mannys blode.'[40]

This concept of chivalry corresponds more closely to that of the second estate than the elevated theories so far discussed. It is nevertheless like them in being essentially a theoretical code. It is the product ultimately of lawyers, not soldiers, and this is reflected in its complex structure; in the importance attached to exact legal definition; and in the presentation of detailed arguments for and against each topic. It is significant in that it draws upon the experience and opinions of individual knights, and attempts to provide a rationale of contemporary practice. But its very inclusiveness and complexity diminishes its value as a reflection of the code of honour used by fourteenth-century knights as a guide to their actions and thought of by them as chivalry. In their sense, chivalry was a simpler and at times confusing and contradictory code which cannot be confined within a single coherent pattern.[41]

Essential to that code was the belief that war, governed by chivalry, was a positive, ennobling experience. This is not an attractive proposition to modern man, and it is hardly surprising that historians have seen medieval warfare in very different terms. H. J. Hewitt has revealed many of the baser realities of fourteenth-century warfare: the pillage, slaughter, and unending brutality characteristic of numerous campaigns during the Hundred Years War. In such circumstances chivalry may well seem a mere posture which had 'little relation to the daily work of seizing food, looting and devastation'. Huizinga, referring to chroniclers like Froissart, saw chivalry as 'a sort of magic key' which they used to make intelligible 'the motives of politics and history'. He continues:

The confused image of contemporaneous history being much too complicated for their comprehension, they simplified it, as it were, by the fiction of chivalry as a moving force (not consciously, of course). A very fantastic and rather shallow point of view, no doubt. How much vaster is ours, embracing all sorts of economic and social forces and causes. Still, this vision of a world ruled by chivalry, however superficial and mistaken it might be, was the best they had in the matter of general political ideas. It served them as a formula to understand, in their poor way, the appalling complexity of the world's way.[42]

Hewitt and Huizinga are of course substantially correct, but not entirely so. In a real sense chivalry comprised a system of values effective only in terms of a military élite. Those outside the élite were generally thought to be beyond its terms of reference. A knight was not necessarily under an obligation to extend mercy and courtesy to a social inferior who was in turn deemed unworthy (and even incapable) of aspiring towards chivalry himself. As we shall see, Froissart was under no illusions about the ruthlessness and brutality of the great, but with some justification he made a distinction between the actions of knights and the common soldiery in the Hundred Years War. There is no doubt that Edward III and his captains deliberately embarked upon a policy of wholesale destruction and slaughter in France, but there is equally little doubt that this was made worse by the general disposition of the troops themselves.

Discipline was a notorious problem in medieval armies, and despite strict injunctions to the contrary it often proved impossible for captains to limit the extent of the pillage and slaughter committed by their men, especially during the confusion which followed the storming of a city. This was the case at Caen in 1346. When the city fell, the usual pattern of pillage and massacre prevailed, but this was not surprising to Froissart: 'for in such a host as the king of England leads it cannot be but that it contains base knaves and evil-doers enough and men of little conscience.' He makes it clear that the massacre was the work of the archers and men-at-arms and is careful to distinguish their behaviour from that of the knights. After an account of the slaughter he describes how Sir Thomas Holland rescued the comte d'Eu and the comte de Tancarville who were in fear of their lives from some English archers. In the second redaction of the *Chroniques* Froissart adds that Holland and 'many noble knights of England' rode about the streets 'and prevented much cruelty and many horrible deeds which would have been perpetrated that day had they not opposed them, by which they acted with charity and nobility'. Significantly they saved from rape 'many a fair *bourgeoise* and many a nun'.[43]

To the modern mind, Holland's motives as described by Froissart may not appear entirely disinterested. On learning the identity of his prisoners Sir Thomas was 'overjoyed, for two reasons'. One was that he had saved the lives of such noble men; the other was that he confidently estimated their ransom at 100,000 *moutons*. Such incidents may seem to support the thesis that chivalry no longer exerted any real influence on the behaviour of the second estate. In fact they reveal an area where medieval moral sensibility differed radically from our own. The aristocratic élite of the late Middle Ages simply did not dissociate honour and profit as we tend to do. This may indicate an area of moral insensibility on their part, but it is an insensibility shared by such earlier exemplars of chivalry as William Marshal and is indeed a conspicuous feature of many heroic or militaristic societies.[44]

It is clear that those who concerned themselves with chivalry distinguished between war as waged by the common soldier and war as waged by knights. The destructive potential of the soldiery was used time and again by Edward III and his commanders; it was an established feature of any major campaign. But although the military élite were committed to a general strategy involving rapine and slaughter on the part of the men-at-arms under their command, they comprehended their own role in very different terms. Caste solidarity still united the English and French aristocracy and those knights who espoused the chivalric ideal. This often proved stronger than the ties of nationality and common purpose which one might suppose to have existed between them and the men they commanded. It was accepted that knights fought, or should fight, with their peers according to a well-established code based upon pride and mutual self-interest. When a knight demanded the surrender of the famous Gascon captain Jean de Grailly, he is said to have replied: 'Are you a man of gentle birth? For I would sooner die than surrender to one who was not.'[45] The soldiery were essential to the war effort, but in a sense they fought a different war based on different assumptions. The chivalric code of the military élite meant nothing to such men, while they themselves had little significance within the terms of that code. English knights cut down by a peasant force at Longeuil were mourned by their compatriots on the grounds that 'it was too much that so many of their good fighters had been killed by mere peasants'.[46]

This dual concept made it possible for the aristocracy and knights to think of war as an ennobling and manly occupation. Their military code, together with a strong sense of *esprit de corps* successfully isolated them from the brutality and suffering which characterizes the war for most modern historians. In their terms it was quite legitimate to assess the failure or success of a battle simply by referring the behaviour of the great lords and knights present to the code of chivalry. Froissart does this when he compares Crécy and Poitiers. He considered Poitiers superior on four counts. Crécy was fought in the evening 'without array and without order', while Poitiers took place in the morning and was well conducted; there were more and better feats of arms at Poitiers *with the result that fewer great men were killed*; those who fought at Poitiers acquitted themselves loyally so that it was no dishonour to have fought there; and finally, unlike his father at

Crécy, King John did not flee the field but fought alongside his knights to the end.[47]

A sense of the fineness of war depended very much on one's susceptibility to the flamboyant trappings associated with four-teenth-century armies: the gaudy pennons and devices, the calls of trumpets, the roll of drums, and the flashing of sunlight on lances and armour. The Chandos Herald expresses the feeling of exhilaration which such a sight can arouse in his description of the marshalling of the Dauphin's host before Poitiers: 'Then you might see banners and pennons unfurled to the wind, whereon fine gold and azure shone, purple, gules, and ermine. Trumpets, tabours, horns and clarions – you might hear sounding through the camp; the Dauphin's great battle made the earth ring.' Froissart captures the same atmosphere on numerous occasions in the *Chroniques*. Edward III's army at Calais (1359) was so nobly and richly arrayed that it was 'a pleasure and a delight' to look upon it. He repeatedly writes of the 'beauty' of an army assembled for battle. As Philip VI marched to the relief of Calais it was 'a great beauty to see and to gaze upon their powerful array'; and of the French army before Bergues in Flanders (1383) he observes that it was: 'a great beauty to see the banners, pennons, and basinets glittering against the sun, and such a great multitude of men-at-arms that the eye of man could not take them in, and it seemed that they bore a veritable forest of lances.'[48]

In this the chroniclers and poets undoubtedly reflect the senti-ments of the knights themselves. Froissart has an interesting passage in which he describes how Sir John Chandos went to view the French host during a truce before the battle of Poitiers. Chandos, who was 'a valiant knight, generous and noble of heart, and discriminating of judgement', had great pleasure in contem-plating the ranks of newly armed knights, a pleasure enhanced by the prospect of the honour to be won in the ensuing battle.[49]

Such delight gave way to awe mingled with dread once battle was joined. At Poitiers:

It was a marvellous and terrifying thing to hear the thundering of the horses' hooves, the cries of the wounded, the sound of the trumpets and clarions, and the shouting of the warcries. The tumult and the noise were heard at a distance of more than three leagues. And it was a great grief to see and behold the flower of all the nobility and chivalry of the world go thus to destruction, to death, and to martydom on both sides.

The anonymous chronicler emphasizes the terror and pity which the sight of such destruction aroused, yet in keeping with most historians of the age he finds such scenes neither sordid nor degrading. Froissart, writing of the defeat of the Spaniards at Nájera, describes how the river ran with the blood of horses and men – 'so great and horrible was that defeat' – but he evinces fascination rather than disapproval.[50]

A sense of the fineness of war does not, however, necessarily imply a blindly romantic view of war itself or of the knight's part in it. This becomes clear when one examines the testimony of the knights themselves. Of particular interest is a chivalric treatise written by Geoffroi de Charny in 1352.[51] Not without justification Charny was admired during his lifetime as an exemplar of knighthood. In his youth he had haunted tournaments and jousts; he took the cross in 1345; was active in most of the major campaigns against the English in the early years of the war; and became a knight of the Order of the Star in 1352. He was killed in the battle of Poitiers where he was King John's standard-bearer.[52]

Charny held a high view of knighthood: in his opinion it was a noble occupation worthy to be ranked with clergy. But he also writes of it as a kind of martyrdom, and his book reveals many of the difficulties and dangers, the frustrations and hardships of the chivalric life. His advice to the aspiring young knight is at times far from encouraging: 'You will have to put up with great labour before you achieve honour from this employ: heat, cold, fasting, hard work, little sleep and long watches, and always exhaustion.' Things are even worse when battle is joined:

You will needs be afraid often when you see your enemies bearing down on you with lances lowered to strike you and swords ready to attack you. Shafts and quarrels come at you and you do not know best how to protect your body. Now you see men slaughtering one another, fleeing, dying, and being taken prisoner, and your friends dead whose corpses lie before you. But your horses are not killed, you could well get away. Through them you could save your skin; you could ride off without honour. If you stay, you will have honour ever after: if you flee you dishonour yourself. Is not this a great martyrdom?[53]

Charny is clearly aware of the real dangers of war, but he regards them only from the viewpoint of the military élite, and as the above quotation demonstrates, that viewpoint is inextricably bound up with the concept of honour. Julian Pitt-Rivers has well defined honour as 'the value of a person in his own eyes, but also in the eyes of his society. It is his estimation of his own worth, his *claim* to pride, but it is also the acknowledgement of that claim, his excellence recognised by society, his *right* to pride'.[54] Honour in this sense is an aggressive concept. The honourable man must demonstrate his honour continually before his peers, and this in turn often involves challenging the honour of others. As Pitt-Rivers observes: 'The ultimate vindication of honour lies in physical violence.'[55] This is of fundamental importance to an understanding of medieval chivalry.

Honour is at the centre of the chivalric code of the aristocracy and military élite and it frequently involved violence. Such violence was often of an extreme kind which may seem revolting or quixotic to the modern mind and certainly 'unchivalric'. The fact that medieval knights did not regard violence in this way suggests that we are dealing with a fundamental cultural difference between medieval man and his modern western descendant. Some illustrations from the life of the Black Prince may make this clearer.

For most of his adult life the prince was active in the wars with France and Spain and it was his conduct at Crécy, Poitiers, and Nájera which earned him an international reputation as a commander who waged war according to chivalric principles. But contemporary notices of Edward's life reveal clearly the way in which his chivalry was intimately bound up with a rigid sense of honour and its concomitant violence. In many ways the prince was a stern and gloomy man and he waged war with a ruthlessness which terrified his enemies as much as it gladdened his allies. This is typified by John Gower in a vigorous piece of description in *Vox Clamantis*. The poet begins conventionally enough by comparing Edward to a lion breaking through the ranks of the enemy, and to a ravening wolf running amok in the sheepfold. Those who were bold enough to oppose him in battle he cut down with his sword as a wild boar tears to pieces the pursuing hounds with his jaws. He then continues with an elaborately rhetorical description of Edward's ferocity in the face of the enemy:

He was always sober in his actions but his sword was often drunk with the blood of the enemy. Harshly assaulting his foes, he fought and overcame them. His sword point refused to go back into the sheath dry. His hostile blade was sated with enemy gore; a torrent of blood slaked the thirst of his weapons. His broadsword was unwilling to drowse within the scabbard, it disgorged itself out of its mouth.[56]

Other writers give a similar impression of Edward, and although few do so with the same elaborate rhetoric and obvious relish, no Englishman condemns him for these traits.[57] Knighton, who calls him 'the flower of earthly chivalry', says that under him 'to serve as a knight was to be a lord'. Walsingham calls him another Alexander the Great of whom it was said: 'he did not assail any nation which he did not conquer; he did not besiege any city that he did not take.' Froissart, describing the prince at Poitiers, says he was 'like a lion fell and cruel, and . . . had great pleasure that day to fight and press closely upon his enemies.'[58]

The passage from *Vox Clamantis* was intended as a guide to the young Richard II who is admonished by Gower to follow his father's example when taking arms against the enemy.[59] The portrait stresses justice untempered by mercy, and accords with Edward's own outlook as represented in most of the chronicles. When the people of Carcassone tried to buy him off in 1355 he replied that 'he did not come hither for gold but in pursuit of justice, and to capture the citizens rather than put them up for sale.' Edward could be prodigal with the lives of others. When he heard that the Gascon nobles had appealed to the courts of the king of France against his alleged injustices he is said to have commented that they must all appeal to the courts of his father, 'and before it be otherwise it will cost a hundred thousand lives.'[60] That such threats were not idle is revealed by the sack of Limoges, an event which has been largely misunderstood by later historians who regard it as a stain on the prince's character.[61]

In the confused fighting in Gascony after the renewal of the war in 1369 Limoges held a key position as capital of the Limousin. It was held for the English by its bishop, Jean de Cros, who had been a trusted friend and adviser of the Black Prince. In 1370 de Cros betrayed Edward and turned the city over to the French. The prince, said to have been in a mad rage, vowed to avenge himself on the bishop in particular and the citizens in general. He besieged the city with the aid of his brother, John of Gaunt, and when at last the walls were breached by his miners, he commanded a general slaughter of the inhabitants.[62] It has already been suggested that the massacre of its citizens was the common fate of a city taken by storm, but the ruthlessness of the sack of Limoges shocked contemporaries like Froissart who writes of it in the bitterest terms:

There were pitiful scenes. Men, women and children flung themselves on their knees before the Prince, crying: 'Have mercy on us, gentle sir!' But he was so inflamed with anger that he would not listen. Neither man nor woman was heeded, but all who could be found were put to the sword, including many who were in no way to blame. I do not understand how they could have failed to take pity on people who were too unimportant to have committed treason. Yet they paid for it, and paid more dearly than the leaders who had committed it. There is no man so hard-hearted that, if he had been in Limoges on that day, and had remembered God, he would not have wept bitterly at the fearful slaughter which took place. More than three thousand persons, men, women and children, were dragged out to have their throats cut. May God receive their souls, for they were true martyrs.[63]

This is one of the most famous quotations from the *Chroniques*. It expresses sentiments to which the modern reader readily responds, and it is hardly surprising that most historians have taken Froissart's narrative as the basis for their own account of the siege. But although the sack was certainly vicious it was not outstandingly so by contemporary standards[64] and one may suspect Froissart of partisanship here. By 1370 the *Chroniques* are already showing signs of the pro-French sympathy which dominates his narrative of the later years of the war.

It is instructive to turn to English accounts of the sack which are understandably less sympathetic to the fate of the citizens. Walsingham makes an implied criticism of Edward's part in events prior to the siege when he says that Limoges turned French because of the insupportable taxes imposed on the citizens by the prince's misgovernment.[65] But he clearly considered Edward within his rights when he put the inhabitants to the sword. If Walsingham's version of events is correct, then Edward acted entirely in accordance with the law of arms governing siege warfare.[66] According to Walsingham he sent messengers to Limoges demanding that the citizens place themselves at his mercy. This they refused to do and the prince consequently informed them that he would raze the city to the ground and put those within to the sword if they continued in their revolt. But 'the undisciplined populace wished to hear nothing of them, but looked down on the messengers with a proud eye and fortified the city completely on all sides.' The prince therefore quite legitimately carried out his threat. The Chandos Herald makes the same point. The sack was the successful conclusion to a punitive expedition against traitors. All the inhabitants were killed or captured by 'the noble prince' which caused his friends to rejoice and his enemies to regret that the war had ever been renewed.[67]

At the time of the siege the prince was racked with pain from the lingering disease which was to kill him six years later. Some historians have used this fact to explain his apparently uncharacteristic savagery at Limoges. His illness, it is argued, temporarily unbalanced his mind and caused him to act contrary to chivalry.[68] This explanation may sound attractive, but it is instructive to compare it with that of the seventeenth-century historian Sir Richard Baker, who in many ways comes closer to a true estimation of Edward's motives:

At this time, the Dukes of *Anjou* and *Berry*, with two great Armies enter upon the Territories of the Prince of *Wales*; whereof the Prince advertised, assembles Forces to oppose them: but when the newes was brought him of the taking of Limouges, he was so much troubled at it, by reason of the Bishop of that place was his Gossip, and one in whom he specially had affiance; that he resolved to recover it at any price, and not to spare a man that had any hand in the rendring it up: and thereupon taking it by force, he commanded to sacke and pillage it, and would not be staied by the cries of the people, casting themselves downe at his feete; till passing through the Towne, he perceived three *French* Captaines, who themselves alone had withstood the assault of his victorious Army, and moved with the consideration of their valour, he then abated his anger; and for their sakes, granted mercy to all the Inhabitants. So much is vertue even in an enemy, respected by generous minds.[69]

Baker (who in many of his attitudes is closer to the Middle Ages than we are) is in no doubt about the prince's motives. His honour had been affronted by the treachery of de Cros. The army assembled to oppose the invading French force was therefore diverted to Limoges, not primarily on strategic grounds (though Limoges was strategically important) but to vindicate Edward's honour. The citizens suffered as much as the commanders, at the Prince's express command, because honour is collective as well as personal.

The treachery of de Cros was also their treachery.[70] Pitt-Rivers's axiom that 'the ultimate vindication of honour lies in physical violence' would have been quite understandable to Sir Richard Baker, and was certainly so to the Black Prince and his peers.

It has already been suggested that social historians tend to dismiss chivalric excess of the kind described by Froissart as theatrical posturing and therefore, in a sense, hypocritical. To do so is to misunderstand seriously the aristocratic mind. Much of the behaviour of medieval aristocrats and knights which now seems quixotic or merely foolish should be re-examined in the light of the concept of honour outlined above. Again the life of the Black Prince may furnish us with examples.

Bertrand du Guesclin, the constable of France, had been captured by the English at Nájera in 1367. Du Guesclin was one of France's foremost military commanders and his capture was a great coup. Yet in 1368 the Black Prince ordered his release in return for a large ransom. There are two main accounts of the incident, by Froissart and Cuvelier. According to Froissart the prince had been advised not to ransom the constable by his counsellors, who feared that if released he would renew the war in Spain. But when du Guesclin taunted Edward that he dared not release him from fear, the prince impetuously offered to free him on the payment of a ransom of 100,000 francs, supposing this an impossibly high figure. The constable, however, agreed to the terms, and with the aid of the king of France succeeded in raising the ransom. Edward was urged by members of his council to revoke his offer but the prince refused, justifying his decision by reference to his reputation for honour: 'Since we have agreed to it we will keep [our promise] and will not go back on it. It would be a rebuke and a shame to us if we were reproached that we would not put him to ransom when he is content to pay such a great sum as 100,000 francs.' Cuvelier's account is essentially similar except he says that the taunt that Edward dared not release du Guesclin came from a member of his own council, the Lord d'Albret, and not from the constable himself.[71]

Militarily, as Edward's advisers foresaw, the decision was disastrous. The same year du Guesclin was instrumental in replacing the French candidate, Enrique, on the throne of Castile, and

on the renewal of the war between England and France in 1369
he was recalled from Spain by Charles v to command the French
defence. Edward's action was clearly based on a mixture of
motives. From Froissart's version it may well be that his initial
offer to ransom du Guesclin may have been little more than a pose
on his part. But, once the constable took him at his word, the
prince had no alternative but to stand by his offer if he wished to
maintain his reputation for chivalry. Politically and militarily it
was an act of the greatest folly. In chivalric terms it was the only
logical course open to the prince since honour and reputation are
more important than temporary military advantage. Froissart
admiringly observes of the incident that Edward was 'always a wise
and loyal knight', while Cuvelier claims that after he had agreed
to the ransom his barons declared: 'Well have you spoken'.[72]

An overriding concern for honour also explains many of the
more quixotic examples of courtesy that one finds in Froissart and
the verse biographies of aristocrats like du Guesclin and the Black
Prince. Nowhere is this seen more clearly than in the prince's
treatment of King John after his capture at Poitiers. It is reported
fully by Froissart and with less detail by the Chandos Herald. In
Froissart's version, Edward held a feast after the battle which
was attended by John and the French lords captured that day.
The king was served by the prince in person 'as humbly as he
could', and no matter how often the king begged him to sit at his
table he refused on the grounds that: 'he was by no means yet of
sufficient rank to sit at the table of so great a prince and so valiant a
man as he was and as he had shown himself in that battle.' Edward
courteously consoled John with the thought that he would be
honourably treated by his father the king, and that a reconciliation
and a new peace might be negotiated. Moreover, he protested,
John through his valour had won the prize for chivalry that day.
This was not said to flatter the captured king, for everyone who
saw the feats of arms performed that day was in agreement, 'and
awards you the prize and the chaplet if it please you to wear it'.[73]

It is easy to be magnanimous in victory, and it may be argued
cynically that the Black Prince had a vested interest in the king's well-
being, considering the vast ransom he might reasonably be expected
to pay. The capture of John was in fact one of the biggest financial
coups of the entire war. Ultimately only half of the ransom was paid
by the French, but even this amounted to 1,291,200 crowns.[74]

Without doubt Edward was motivated by such considerations in his treatment of the king, but it would be an over-simplification to conclude from this that his behaviour was hypocritical or that it merely provides yet another example of chivalry as 'a splendid pageant, an elaborate game to mask the coarser aspects of existence'.[75] In the fourteenth century symbolic action was the accepted means of expression for a wide range of human experience, and nowhere was this more so than amongst the English and French aristocracy. For them, ritualistic courtesy of the kind performed by the Black Prince at Poitiers was an essential element in the ideal of the noble life which they professed to follow.[76] The elaborate forms of address and behaviour associated with courtesy were used to give public recognition of an individual's status within the aristocratic hierarchy, and of the obligations and rights which this entailed. Acknowledgement of one's inferior position in relation to a fellow nobleman was most readily expressed by the idea of service, and Edward's serving at King John's table acknowledged in symbolic form what was self-evident to all those present: the French king's superior status even in captivity. In this context the action was not hypocritical, nor was it mere public display, but a meaningful ritual. The same is true of the prince's action in assigning a chaplet to John in recognition of his prowess that day. Edward was aware that his intentions could be misconstrued: 'I say this by no means . . . to flatter you.' But again he acted with the utmost propriety according to contemporary practice. The international chivalric milieu in which he lived was largely unaffected by the chauvinistic tendencies of the age and admired feats of arms for their own sake. It was not uncommon to acknowledge the prowess of an enemy in this way, and the prince's action won the approbation of the assembled company, English and French. Froissart reports that they whispered amongst themselves that the prince had spoken 'nobly and to the point' and concluded that 'in him one had and will have in the future a noble lord if he might survive and live long in such a fortunate manner.'[77]

In Sir Richard Baker's account of the sack of Limoges it will be noticed that the Black Prince's desire for revenge was slaked only when he witnessed the gallant last stand of the French garrison commanders. Baker's account is based on Froissart who reports that at last the exhausted French knights gave up their swords with the words 'Sirs, we are yours and you have conquered us. Deal with us according to the law of arms.' John of Gaunt is said to have replied: 'By God, Sir Jean ... we would not think of doing otherwise, and we retain you as our prisoners.'[78] The passage reveals an essential element in the chivalric idealism of the noblemen and knights who were closely involved in the Hundred Years War. It is based almost entirely on caste solidarity and mutual self-interest. Chivalry in this sense is not necessarily devoid of noble principles, but such principles generally operate only in the knight's relations with his equals or superiors. Mercy may be extended to social inferiors, but it is not obligatory. The cries of the men and women of Limoges were ineffectual, but Jean de Villemur's appeal for mercy according to the law of arms was granted without hesitation by the duke of Lancaster; and the sight of the French knights' defence was sufficient to assuage the anger of the Black Prince against the city.

The response of many Englishmen to the war was characterized by a growing chauvinism, but as the actions of these French and English knights suggest, this was not the case with the aristocracy. The main reason for this was the intense caste solidarity which they possessed. Aristocrats like Henry of Grosmont and knights like Sir John Chandos considered themselves members of a chivalric élite which transcended national boundaries and which was governed by an internationally recognized code of honour.

This sense of community was often strengthened by ties of kinship which lifelong enmity could not entirely efface. This was especially true at the higher reaches of the aristocracy, and as an example one may take the relationship between the Valois and Plantagenets. When John the Good died in 1364 he was mourned by his Plantagenet cousin, Edward III; and when Charles V learned of the death of the Black Prince he caused an impressive mass for the dead to be celebrated at Paris, which was attended by the king's brothers and numerous prelates and barons of the realm. The author of the *Quatre Premiers Valois* feels it necessary to explain why Charles behaved in this way to a lifelong enemy. It was, he says, 'for reasons of lineage'. Froissart, more in touch with court society, finds the king's action quite understandable.[79]

Not only kinsmen were mourned. The heroic death of the aged

and blind king of Bohemia at Crécy was admired and lamented by many. King Edward and his eldest son 'grieved excessively' when they heard the news, and dressed in black 'for love of him'.[80] Even lesser men were sometimes honoured in this way. The respect and importance which a knight like Chandos could attain within chivalric society may be measured by the general grief of the English and French aristocracy at his untimely death during a skirmish in 1370. Charles v and the lords of France are said to have wept at the news, greatly regretting the loss of one who was so wise. He alone, it was felt, could have brought about a peaceful reconciliation between the two kings.[81] The tendency to honour in this way kinsmen and great knights who were at the same time one's enemies suggests the extent to which the English and French royal houses regarded themselves as members – if exceptionally elevated ones – of an élite which transcended boundaries of allegiance and nationality.

Both Edward iii and John ii undoubtedly fostered chivalry with the aim of enhancing their reputations within this circle. One of the statutes of the Order of the Garter proclaimed that any spotless knight could be elected whether or not he was a subject of the sovereign, providing he did not defend or favour the king's enemies.[82] In effect this excluded the French, though Edward iii, eager to give the great round table of 1344 an international air, sent heralds to proclaim the tournament in Scotland, Germany, Flanders, Hainault, Brabant, Aquitaine, and France. The latter were offered safe-conducts for the duration of the tournament, but as Edward took the opportunity of sending his defiance to Philip vi at the same time, it is hardly surprising that no French knights took advantage of his offer. But many knights from Flanders, Hainault, and the Empire did attend, and amongst the founder members of the Order of the Garter were the Gascon, Sir Jean de Grailly, Sir Henry Eam, a Brabanter in the service of the Black Prince, and Sir Eustache d'Aubrécicourt from Hainault. Later, a fellow-countryman of his, Sir Walter Manny, was also admitted to the Order.[83] It would be unwise to make too much of their inclusion since all four were heavily committed to Edward's cause, but their acceptance into the Order does indicate the king's desire to give it an international air when circumstances permitted.

The numerous tournaments and round tables held during his

reign are further indications of Edward's desire to earn a reputation as a patron of chivalry. The chronicles contain many notices,
not always favourable, which hint at their splendour and wide
appeal. A 'most beautiful' tournament was held at Smithfield in
1362, attended by the king and queen, numerous lords and
knights of England and knights of France and other regions.
Jousts were held at Windsor on St George's Day 1358 which were
attended by the chivalry of England and Scotland as well as
captive French knights then in England. In keeping with his
custom, Edward sent invitations to foreign knights to attend under
guarantee of safe-conduct and Knighton adds the detail that the
duke of Brabant as well as many Gascon knights attended.
According to the *Eulogium Historiarum*, such jousts were 'unseen
since the time of King Arthur'.[84]

Edward III saw his role on these occasions in a romantic light.
At Dunstable in 1342 he jousted disguised 'in the manner of an
ordinary knight'; while at a tournament held at London in 1359
the king, his sons Edward, Lionel, John, and Edmund together
with nineteen nobles fought in disguise against all-comers 'and held
the field with honour'.[85]

Not all the chroniclers approved of Edward's indulgence in
tournaments. This is especially true of some of the monastic
historians who did not share the king's concern for the trappings
of chivalry. They make the usual complaints that such places are
the haunts of vice and corruption. The compiler of *Melsa* notes
that the pestilence of 1348 was preceded by the profligacy of the
upper classes, especially at tournaments. Knighton, also under the
year 1348, rants against the opportunities which they afforded for
lasciviousness, and complains that the military 'expended and laid
waste their wealth' on lewd dress and costly destriers (war horses).
The great expense of tournaments is a perennial complaint. In
1340 Edward held tournaments at York and other places 'spending
money as if it were water', while the round table of 1343 was held
'at outrageous expense and great cost'. Only the Lanercost
chronicler reflects the court attitude that such immense expenditure
was 'befitting the royal dignity'.[86]

Through such activities Edward eventually rivalled John of
France as an arbiter of chivalry. A notable acknowledgement
of this took place in 1350 when Thomas de la Marche, Bastard
of France, and John Visconti presented themselves at Edward's

court and demanded to settle their quarrel before the king in trial by battle. Thomas won (wrongly, as many thought) but when he returned to France he had to contend with the wrath of his half-brother, King John. According to Baker the king was incensed that Thomas should have taken his quarrel for judgement before the English king. In reply the Bastard praised Edward's nobility, justice, and renown, which had spread throughout the world. As an example of his open-mindedness Thomas pointed out that Edward had judged in his favour even though he was the close kinsman of his greatest enemy. This account comes from Geoffrey Baker which contains several inaccuracies, and there is every reason to believe that he invented the dialogue between Thomas and King John. But it suggests that some at least of Edward's contemporaries took his chivalric pretensions seriously and that the duel was considered a signal triumph for the king.[87]

The ability to judge feats of arms impartially was highly regarded in chivalric society. True knighthood was admired for its own sake irrespective of the allegiance of the knight concerned. Charles v, looking back on the career of his arch-enemy, the Black Prince, could avow that he had indeed ruled 'mightily and bravely'; the great Castilian nobleman, Pedro Lopez de Ayala, said of his enemies, who had captured him at Nájera, that they were 'at that time the flower of chivalry of Christendom'; while amongst historians of chivalry the Chandos Herald, no blind partisan in such things, found cause to praise the French generals at Poitiers and especially the Marshal d'Audrehem who was 'ever at all times right greatly to be esteemed, for he was a very goodly knight'.[88]

Where complexities of allegiance allowed, it was perfectly honourable for such men to fight side by side. During the peace between England and France after the Treaty of Bretigny, English, French, Bretons, Normans, Picards, and Gascons fought in Castile under the banner of Enrique the Bastard. Amongst them was Sir Hugh Calveley who willingly served under his old enemy Bertrand du Guesclin. The brotherhood of arms co-existed with feudal loyalties, and nowhere is this illustrated more clearly than in an incident which occurred during Enrique's Castilian campaign of 1365-6. There was a plot amongst some members of the English contingent in the army to assassinate du Guesclin. This was revealed to Calveley in the hope of gaining his support, but instead he immediately informed the constable: 'For the said Sir

Hugh Calveley did not wish to be culpable for, nor consenting to, the death of so noble and valiant a knight as Sir Bertrand du Guesclin.' Yet when the news reached Enrique's camp that Edward III had declared in favour of Pedro the Cruel and that the Black Prince was preparing an army in Gascony for the invasion of Castile, Calveley formally took leave of du Guesclin on the grounds that 'he could not and should not be against his lord the prince'. Shortly afterwards Calveley was prominent amongst the captains of the English army which defeated Enrique and captured du Guesclin at Nájera.[89]

The most notable expression of this international spirit throughout the Middle Ages was the crusade, although it is a commonplace that by the fourteenth century it had lost much of its impetus. The political structure in the Near East which had ensured the success of the early expeditions no longer prevailed, and the whole concept of the Holy War had been debased by its use as an instrument of papal politics in Europe.[90] Despite this, the idea of the crusade still had some hold on the imagination of the military élite. Dedicated crusaders like Henry of Grosmont were rare, but when great lords and professional captains were out of office or temporarily disgraced, or when no war offered employment nearer at hand, the possibility of a crusade was often considered and sometimes acted upon.[91] Fear and hatred of 'the innumerable throng of Satan's satellites' was in itself sufficient justification for crusades against the Turk and Saracen, even though such enterprises consistently ended in disaster. The Christian chroniclers rarely had the satisfaction of recording that the enemies of God 'hasten to Hell in their hundreds', despatched by the swords of Christian knights.[92]

Nevertheless the idea proved tenacious that it was right and proper for a knight to advance himself by fighting against the heathen. In 1366 the Black Prince ordered the Lord d'Albret to bring only two hundred lances on the expedition to Castile instead of the 1,000 originally agreed upon. D'Albret was said to have been extremely angry at this and wrote to the prince to point out that he had held back his men in readiness at a time when they were naturally eager to advance themselves: 'for some of them were all set and ready to go abroad to Prussia, to Constantinople, or to Jerusalem as every knight and squire who wishes to advance himself does.'[93]

Typically d'Albret also makes the association between honour and profit, and the expectation of spoils from the rich cities of the East may still have provided an added incentive to those who took the cross. When King Peter of Cyprus temporarily captured part of Alexandria in 1365 some of the booty in the form of cloth-of-gold, silks, and jewels found their way to Gascony and England.[94] But such victories were rare in the fourteenth century, and those who engaged in war for profit alone tended to look nearer to home.

For some who found themselves with conflicting loyalties during the Hundred Years War, the crusade provided an honourable solution. During the fighting in Aquitaine after the renewal of the war in 1369 Sir Aymenion de Pommiers found himself in this predicament. He resolved it by declaring that while the war lasted he would take arms for neither party. Instead he went as a pilgrim-crusader to Cyprus, the Holy Sepulchre 'and on many other fair voyages'.[95]

The crusade was taken more seriously in France than in England. There is little reason to doubt the sincerity of Philip VI when he took the cross at the pope's instigation in 1329 or of John in 1362 although the latter's motives reveal a nice calculation of piety and personal advantage. John, we are told, committed himself to a crusade in order to fulfil his father's vow; to save his own soul; and to remove from the realm the companies of disbanded mercenaries who were causing so much trouble. Edward III was not backward in proposing a crusade when it suited his purpose, but neither he nor the Black Prince ever seriously projected an expedition. It was always an instrument of policy directly related to his continental ambitions. In the 1330s when Edward felt insecure in his relations with France, he dangled the bait of a joint crusade before his Valois cousin in the hope of strengthening his precarious hold on Gascony. But when a breach between the two kingdoms seemed inevitable he quickly appropriated the money collected for the crusade for the war with France. The pope revoked the tenth levied on the clergy for the crusade but 'in England nothing was returned because it had been granted to the king by the clergy.' Edward's attitude was undoubtedly influenced by suspicion of the French king's designs. Knighton believed that Philip's proposal of a joint crusade in 1335 was a feint to draw attention away from his real purpose: the destruction of the realm of England. According to him Edward replied bluntly

that he was quite willing to take the cross, but not while his
enemies were being aided and abetted by Philip 'who by right of
consanguinity ought the more to adhere to him with his aid than
to support his capital enemies so strongly against him'.[96]

The fact that acknowledged arbiters of chivalry like Edward III
and the Black Prince did not feel obliged to take the cross,
together with the increasing use of the crusade as a move in international politics, are important factors in its decline. They also
suggest the way in which chivalry itself, and the international
spirit which it fostered, were undergoing modifications in the
fourteenth century. The great lords and knights who served in
the Hundred Years War still retained a sense of caste solidarity
which to some extent governed their attitudes to their equals in
France and Spain; but there was a growing tendency for the practice of arms to become associated with royal policy, a tendency
hastened by Edward III himself who took pains to appropriate
chivalry to his cause. At the same time, however, the king undoubtedly gained more general support for the war by fostering
the latent patriotism of his subjects. In itself this may have had no
immediate influence on the chivalric pretensions of the aristocracy
and the *milites strenui*, but the successful yoking together of chivalry
and patriotism in the name of royal ambition inevitably created
a more restricted framework within which men became accustomed to view chivalry. As we shall see, this in turn enabled the
patriots of the late fourteenth century, who had little interest in
the knightly ideal *per se*, to seize upon chivalry and its practition-
ers as outstanding examples of the spirit of patriotism in action.

So far evidence has been drawn mainly from the lives of great
aristocrats like du Guesclin and the Black Prince. One reason for
this is simply the greater abundance of documentary evidence for
a study of their thoughts and actions. Another is that chivalry
was undoubtedly more important to the lives of the higher
nobility than to lesser men of the knightly estate. M. H. Keen has
drawn attention to the dictum of Taine that while the lower and
middle classes are motivated by self-interest the aristocracy is
motivated by pride. He comments:

As regards the greater nobility, at least, of the later middle ages,
there is much truth in this statement. Princes, such as Philip the Good

or Henry v, were jealous of their good fame, and punctilious in discharging obligations in which their honour was involved. It is true, no doubt, that it was chiefly the very great who were as careful as they, and that this was partly because they had to play to a wide audience – they knew that every action they took would be observed, and judged by severe critics.[97]

It is extremely difficult to judge the influence of chivalry on the behaviour of lesser knights and captains who made a profession out of the Hundred Years War; but in varying degrees there can be little doubt that it played a significant part in their lives. Keen shows how many men were more concerned with obeying the letter rather than the spirit of chivalry, but he goes on to demonstrate that an appeal to knighthood was often more successful than the threat of legal reprisals in ensuring that an agreement was honoured – even when the most hardened *écorcheurs* were concerned.[98]

Detailed biographies of the lives of many such men would reveal interesting evidence about the nature and function of chivalry at this level of society; but such a study is beyond the scope of the present work. Something of the complexity of the problem may be suggested, however, by contrasting the careers of two knights: Sir John Chandos, an intimate of the Black Prince and one of the most renowned knights of his day; and Sir Thomas Gray of Heaton, who spent a lifetime working unobtrusively in the king's service on the northern marches and in France.

Chandos was the particular hero of Jean Froissart and from the pages of the *Chroniques* it is possible to build up a fairly comprehensive picture of the chivalry for which he was internationally famed. We are told that the knight combined in his person the four cardinal virtues of chivalry: prowess, loyalty, courtesy, and *mesure* (moderation). There was no knight living who was so *courtois* and *gentil* and he was not beyond the kind of knight-errantry which led to the rescue of young ladies from the hands of ruthless archers. But in general *mesure* and a strong sense of duty restrained him from romantic escapades.[99]

Froissart goes out of his way to establish Chandos as a loyal and wise servant of the Black Prince. At Poitiers he counselled and protected Edward, refusing to leave his side when others scattered in search of booty and prisoners. He proved equally mindful of his duty to John of Gaunt at Nájera for which he was highly praised: ' . . . and with good reason, for a valiant man and a good knight who thus carries out his duty towards his lord should be greatly recommended'.[100] Such a disciplined and loyal captain was all the more to be valued when one compares him to headstrong knights like Sir Hugh Calveley and Sir William Felton. Such men made discipline extremely difficult in medieval armies. Calveley almost lost the battle of Auray for the English by refusing to take command of the rearguard on the grounds that it was dishonourable and an insult. Chandos was in charge of the host and no matter how often he urged him to obey Calveley remained intractable: '. . . and held and confirmed that it was a great shame, and he prayed for God's sake and with hands joined, to put some other [in that command] for, in short, he desired to fight with the foremost'. Chandos, almost crying with anger and frustration, at last put it to him that one or the other of them would have to command the rearguard: 'Now consider which would be better.'[101] At last Calveley, humbled by Chandos's pleadings, accepted the command.

The ability to control the respect and obedience of such a self-willed man was no mean feat. The turbulent individualism of an earlier age was far from dead in the fourteenth century. The overreacher who risked all in an act of individual daring was still widely admired in chivalric circles. Chandos's own herald, a man of judgement in matters of chivalry, could praise Sir William Felton for what now seems the foolhardy enterprise in which he lost his life in Castile in 1367. A small detachment of the English army was surprised by a superior Spanish force. The English rallied on a small hill and their leaders 'who cared not two cherries for death' prepared their defence. Felton, however

. . . very boldly and bravely charged among the enemy like a man devoid of sense and discretion, on horseback, lancè couched. Striking a Spaniard upon his flower-emblazoned shield, he made him feel through the heart his sharp blade of steel. Down to the ground he hurled him in the sight of all the people. Like a man full of great hardihood he rushed upon them, with drawn sword, and the Castilians by their might followed him on all sides, and threw spears and darts at him. They slew his horse under him, but Sir William Felton defended himself stoutly on foot, like a lion-hearted man; albeit his defence availed him little, for he was slain. God have mercy on him.

Militarily Felton's death was meaningless: in terms of a chivalric code based on an unbending sense of personal honour, there could be no finer way to die.[102]

It was not without reason that Froissart praised Chandos for his *mesure* or that he was highly regarded by Edward III and his sons. There is no reason to doubt their grief at the news of his death in 1370. He had spent a lifetime in the service of the crown during which time he had proved himself on many occasions as an able administrator and diplomat as well as one of the foremost knights of the day.[103] He was buried at Mortemer where his epitaph is indicative of the twin poles around which his life revolved: the pursuit of arms and the service of the king.[104] But the terse and clumsy verse reveals nothing of the chivalry and courtly accomplishments which Geoffroi de Charny recommends in his book and for which Chandos was so much admired during his lifetime. Once again it is Froissart who provides a glimpse of this side of the knight's life: '. . . he was a gentle knight, courteous and amiable, generous, bold, wise, and loyal in every circumstance.' During his lifetime, he laments, it was impossible to find a better knight.[105]

The life of Sir Thomas Gray of Heaton forms a distinct contrast with that of Chandos. He was a member of a Northumberland family whose father had taken an active part in the defence of the Scottish marches in the early decades of the century. On his death (probably in 1344) this role was assumed by the son who inherited the lordship of Heaton Manor and the wardenship of Norham Castle, an important border fortress on the eastern marches. These factors determined Gray's career, for from 1344 his life was spent mainly in arms in the king's service. He fought at Neville's Cross in 1346 and was summoned to a council at Westminster in January of the following year. At the conclusion of the truce with Scotland on 30 October 1353 he was called to the defence of the border. In 1355 he was captured with his son, Thomas, during a sally from Norham Castle and imprisoned in Edinburgh. He wrote to Edward III requesting help towards the payment of his ransom and was released a year later in August 1357 when he was appointed guardian of one of King David's hostages. He probably accompanied the Black Prince to France in the autumn of 1359 and was made warden of the east marches in 1367. He is said to have died in 1369.[106]

Such is the bare outline of Gray's career. It is not particularly remarkable and could be paralleled in the lives of many other north country knights. But Sir Thomas was also a *miles literatus* and during his period of captivity in Edinburgh he employed his learning in the composition of a chronicle. It is this which makes him so interesting to the historian of chivalry. Earlier in the century historical works had been commissioned by knights (the *Chronicon* of Geoffrey Baker was written at the instigation of Sir Thomas de la More) but the *Scalacronica* of Sir Thomas Gray is unique. So far as I am aware it is the only chronicle actually composed by an English knight to have survived from the period.

In the prologue Gray explains how he came to write the *Scalacronica*. During his captivity he developed an interest in history from reading a number of verse and prose chronicles written in Latin, French, and English. He became so engrossed in the subject that he greatly regretted not having come to it earlier. It then occurred to him that his enforced idleness might be put to good use by translating and condensing those chronicles which dealt with Great Britain and the deeds of the English. Gray explains his method and excuses his plagiarism by way of an allegorical dream. While he was pondering this scheme a sibyl appeared to him in his sleep and revealed how he was to make use of the work of certain historians for each period of his history. The result was a world history from the creation to Gray's own times. It is divided into five sections the first four of which are entirely derivative; it is the final section which is of particular interest, for here Gray deals with the period from the reign of Edward I to 1362–3. It contains much original material relating to the border wars based on Gray's personal experience and the reminiscences of his father. This section of the *Scalacronica* has been used extensively by historians of Anglo-Scottish affairs, but it has not received the attention it deserves from historians of chivalry, despite its great significance as a first-hand narrative by a knight intimately concerned in the campaigns he describes. It provides a unique insight into the mentality and conduct of a well-placed but by no means prominent knight of the mid-fourteenth century.[107]

The most remarkable feature of the *Scalacronica* is its objectivity. Gray seems to have been uninfluenced by the chauvinism which as we have seen characterized the response of many Englishmen to the war. As warden of Norham Castle and later of the east marches he was deeply involved in the Anglo-Scots war, yet his account of the conflict reveals nothing of the hysteria and hatred of the Scots current amongst those who, like the Lanercost chronicler, lived on or near the border.

Gray's attitude to the French is similar. Most of the writers who have left their impression of the enemy raids along the south coast responded with alarm, anger or despondency. Above all, the raids fed their hatred and suspicion of the French. Gray, on the other hand, viewed them with the impartiality of a professional soldier. Unlike many of his non-military contemporaries, he sought an explanation for the raids in terms of a coherent strategy. In his opinion, the assembled force of French, Normans, and Picards 'made an attack on England in the semblance of an invasion in order to force the said king of England to retreat from France to rescue his country'. He then proceeds to give an account of the movements of the raiders which has all the objectivity of a campaign report.[108] Gray belonged to a class of professional soldier-administrators whose importance increased during the later Middle Ages. In the course of duty such men habitually made decisions based on a consideration of fact which would have been obscured by patriotic fervour. His objectivity and circumspection as an historian owe much to the habits of mind developed in this way.

The same is true of his attitude to chivalry. In common with most men of the age he did not make a distinction between chivalric exploits and the 'business of war'. Like Froissart he considered it the historian's duty to record feats of arms for posterity, and when he discovered some notable feats which took place in Gascony and which he had overlooked, he interpolated them after his account of the battle of Poitiers. He makes a point of describing individual feats of arms such as the challenge to single combat at Fregeuil by a French knight calling himself the 'White Knight'. But there is a judicious limit to his interest in such romantic escapades. The deeds of arms engaged in by the English during the war were so numerous that he decided to record only the most notable: 'for it would be too prolix a subject to narrate them all'.[109]

More significant is Gray's account of an incident which occurred during the Scots wars of Edward II's reign. William Marmion, a Lincolnshire knight, was given a helmet of gold by his mistress and commanded to make it known wherever glory was most difficult to attain. This was put to the knights present who agreed that Norham Castle was at that time the most perilous place in the country. Soon after Marmion's arrival, Alexander Mowbray appeared before the castle with 160 men-at-arms. Gray's father, the warden of Norham, was about to mount an attack when Marmion approached him, splendidly armed and wearing the golden helmet. He was greeted by the elder Sir Thomas with these words:

Sir knight, you have come here as a knight-errant to make that helm known and it is more fitting that chivalry be accomplished on horseback than on foot *where that is practicable*. Mount your horse; behold there your enemies; spur on your horse and go and do battle in the midst of them. May I renounce God if I do not rescue your body alive or dead, or die in the attempt.

Marmion accordingly charged into the Scots host and fought until surrounded and on the point of death. Only then did Sir Thomas rescue and remount him with the aid of the garrison forces.[110]

Gray's account of this incident is interesting for two reasons. His father's advice to Marmion reveals a cautious, practical approach to chivalry which was in itself a distinguishing feature of English knighthood at this time. According to this view it was right and proper for a knight to fight on horseback rather than on foot – *but* only where this was practicable. It was the willingness of English knights to abandon their traditional role as offensive cavalry and to fight on foot in a defensive position which gave them their superiority time and again over the French in the Hundred Years War.

Equally significant is the fact that this encounter took place in the time of Gray's father. Sir Thomas records many feats of arms which occurred during the Hundred Years War, but there are few as flamboyant as this, and one has the impression that for the son war was a more sober affair. Gray was one amongst many professional *milites strenui* who lacked the wealth, and perhaps the inclination, to sustain chivalry on the grand scale associated with aristocrats like the Black Prince or with wealthy knights like Chandos who were intimately involved in the chivalric ethos of the royal courts. Nevertheless the *Scalacronica* makes it clear that chivalry did influence their ideas about warfare and how it should be conducted even if their general outlook was less idealistic and more practical. In the anecdote concerning Marmion one feels that the elder Sir Thomas would never have acted with such self-conscious panache; but it is equally clear that neither he nor his son condemned such acts of individual self-assertion or thought them foolish and 'theatrical'.

Referring to the concept of honour Julian Pitt-Rivers has written:

A system of values is never a homogeneous code of abstract principles obeyed by all the participants in a given culture and able to be extracted from an informant with the aid of a set of hypothetical questions, but a collection of concepts which are related to one another and applied differentially by the different status groups defined by age, sex, class, occupations, etc. in the different social (not merely linguistic) contexts in which they find their meanings.[111]

In this chapter an attempt has been made to apply this principle to the study of chivalry in the fourteenth century. Chivalry was a complex and often contradictory code and one of the ironies of the ideal is that its noblest virtues contain *in potentia* the very vices it strove to overcome. This is especially true of the social virtues: courtesy may often come close to hypocrisy, and at times it is very hard to distinguish princely largesse from bribery. But it is also true of more specifically military qualities: prowess is often indistinguishable from foolhardiness and overweening pride. Indeed, as we have seen, in some circles such aggressive self-assertion was highly respected. Added to this, the knightly estate as a whole did not make certain moral distinctions which we consider self-evident. The relationship between honour and financial gain in war is the most obvious example. Modern historians tend to make a rigid distinction between the two, and so did many fourteenth-century moralists. But the latter reflected the Church ideal of chivalry and there is plenty of evidence to suggest that those most closely connected with the practice of chivalry did not make this distinction, justifying their behaviour in the light of what seemed to them a perfectly honourable code. They were aided in this, of course, by the fact that chivalry was the prerogative of a particular social group whose interests were reflected in the ideal. The association of chivalry with material gain may indicate an area of moral insensibility on the part of the second estate, but this should be seen as one of the limitations of chivalry itself rather than as a new factor indicating the decline of chivalric idealism in the fourteenth century.

Such a complex of motivation, and the ease with which the ideal may be subverted to ignoble ends, preclude any simple analysis of the importance and function of chivalry during the period. Not everyone approached chivalry with the same degree of seriousness, or even agreed as to the exact nature of the ideal to be followed. Besides, the habitual frailty or baseness of human nature put the ideal beyond the reach of most men. But imprecisely defined and self-contradictory as it often was, chivalry provided a substructure of ideas and values which influenced the characteristic outlook and not infrequently the actions of the aristocrats and knights who were closely concerned in the war with France. To such men the style of life attained by the Black Prince must have seemed a near-perfect embodiment of the ideal they professed to follow. As the Chandos Herald admiringly said of him:

Those who dwelt about him esteemed him and loved him greatly, for largesse sustained him and nobleness governed him, and discretion, temperance and uprightness, reason, justice and moderation: one might rightly say that such a Prince would not be found, were the whole world to be search throughout its whole extent.[112]

4
Patriots and Patriotism

Nationalism may be defined as a people's awareness and articulation of its collective identity, based on common racial, linguistic, and geographic factors.[1] In this fully developed sense it is vain to look for nationalism as a major force in fourteenth-century social and political life. The reign of Edward III did see the beginnings of a crude form of patriotism, however, which grew in importance during the reign of Richard II; but nationalism in its fullest sense was the product of the fifteenth century.[2]

One of the greatest obstacles to its growth during our period was the failure of Englishmen to develop a terminology with which to express the patriotic sentiments they dimly felt. The language of feudalism still dominated their thinking, and it was easier and more natural for poets and chroniclers to express their patriotism in feudal terms than it was for them to seek new forms of expression. So the nascent nationalism of the day was channelled into asseverations of loyalty to the king and enthusiastic support for his personal cause against the 'usurper' of France. Only towards the end of the century were there signs that the vocabulary of feudalism was felt to be inadequate. In the 1370s and 80s chroniclers and poets were clearly experimenting with language in an attempt to define their patriotism more exactly – although, as we shall see, they were only partially successful.

In *From Script to Print* H. J. Chaytor remarks that: 'Medieval and modern times are in striking contrast in their attitude towards language, regarded as a mark of nationality.' Language, he asserts, 'had little or no political significance in the middle ages'.[3] Dr Chaytor is more concerned with the early medieval period, but with some qualifications his observations hold true for the fourteenth century as well. The internationalism of the aristocracy and military élite has already been remarked upon and in fourteenth-century England a knowledge of French rather than English was the indispensable language for anyone with social, professional, or cultural ambitions. It was the language of the court during Edward III's reign and remained influential at that of his grandson. Richard II probably had English as his mother tongue, and he certainly patronized poets writing in English; but as Froissart reminds us, the king 'spoke and read French extremely well', and he was an acknowledged francophile.[4] Amongst the aristocracy French remained a fashionable if acquired language – the traditional medium for a *miles literatus* like Sir Thomas Gray who was also conversant with English and Latin, and for a devout nobleman like Henry of Grosmont. In the law courts, too, French maintained its hold, despite the much publicized act of 1362 which substituted English for French in pleading 'at the request indeed of the commons'.[5] Towards the end of the century there was even a short-lived revival of literary French in which writers like Gower attempted to emulate the more sophisticated French of Paris. But Gower's French was very much that of 'a fairly well-taught and fluent foreigner', and the poet himself felt obliged to excuse it on the grounds that he was an Englishman.[6]

This may simply have been a rhetorical humility topos on Gower's part, but Henry of Grosmont's plea in the *Livre de Seyntz Medicines* that 'if the French is not good I should be excused because I am English and not well versed in French' is probably sincere.[7] It is quite clear that many of the nobility and gentry spoke French only with difficulty and some, perhaps, not at all. Froissart claims that in about 1337 Edward III ordered the gentry and bourgeoisie of England to teach their children French 'so that they would become more able and better qualified for their wars'.[8] If such an attempt was made, it met with little success, for by the end of the century even the royal court was sufficiently anglicized for the king to patronize poets writing in English – a practice probably already well established amongst the more provincial nobility and gentry.

Humphrey de Bohun, earl of Hereford, for example, commissioned a translation of *William of Palerne* from the French original, as the anonymous translator informs us. He also claims that he is writing 'for hem that knowe no frensche ne neuer vnderston' which, as Dieter Mehl points out, must in the context refer to the earl's household. Another romance, *The Gest Hystoriale of the Destruction of Troy*, was translated at the request of an anonymous north-country knight, and Trevisa informs us that his translation of Higden's *Polychronicon* was commissioned by Thomas Lord Berkeley. It is worth remembering that a romance as sophisticated as *Sir Gawain and the Green Knight* was not a popular work and must have been written for a provincial aristocratic household. It is interesting that these works have strong provincial associations. Humphrey de Bohun in particular led a retired life, taking little part in contemporary politics and war. If the English translation of *William of Palerne* reflects his literary tastes, it is instructive to compare him with a prince of the blood like Thomas, duke of Gloucester, and Sir Simon Burley, the prominent courtier. Gloucester had a large and varied library comprising eighty-three volumes but only three were in English: two gospels and a bible. Burley possessed nineteen books of which one was English, the no longer extant *Romance of the Forester and the Wild Boar*.[9]

Clearly, English was establishing a superiority over French amongst the country gentry and more provincially minded aristocracy. In this context one may recall Trevisa's well-known account of the revolution in the grammar schools whereby English was substituted for French as the language of instruction for Latin. Writing in 1385 Trevisa claimed that the disadvantage of this was that 'now children of gramer scole conneth na more Frensche than can hir lift heele, and that is harme for hem and they schulle passe the see and trauaille in straunge landes and in many other places.' He adds significantly that 'Also gentil men haueth now moche i-left for to teche here children Frensche.'[10]

But there is evidence that even at the royal court, where it was still a prestigious language, French was in decline by the late fourteenth century. This is suggested by the prominence of Chaucer as a court poet, but it also appears in other less expected ways. During the peace negotiations of 1393, for example, it was agreed that each party should submit its grounds of treating in writing so that they might be considered at leisure. Froissart says that this was insisted upon by the English who feared that the enemy might introduce 'subtle and dissembling words with double meanings', in order to turn the negotiations to their advantage. The English consequently examined each clause of the French proposals demanding clarification of 'any language which was obscure and hard or difficult for them to understand'. To excuse such meticulousness they explained that: 'the French which they had learnt at home during their childhood was not of the same nature and condition as that of France and which legists used in their agreements and conferences.' The leaders of the English embassy were the dukes of Gloucester and Lancaster, and if such eminent princes of the blood found difficulty with their French, one may doubt whether lesser men outside the international milieu of the court fared any better.[11] Moreover, Gloucester's hatred of the French and his suspicions of their trickery and deceit must have been strengthened by the humiliation of being unable to follow the subtleties of the French proposals. For so proud a man it would be galling to find himself in a position where he had to apologize to his peers for speaking an uncouth provincial dialect.

English attempts to speak French had long been the subject of ridicule and satire in France,[12] and even in England the degenerate Anglo-Norman of the late fourteenth century was sometimes considered a joke. Chaucer's mockery of the Prioress who only spoke French 'After the scole of Stratford atte Bowe' is well known, and in *Piers Plowman* unlettered Avarice is made to confess: 'I can no frenche in feith but of the ferthest ende of norfolke.'[13]

In view of the francophobia which the war generated and the decline in the standard of Anglo-Norman, one might expect to find a new assertiveness and confidence amongst writers of English, but with some exceptions, this was not generally so. French maintained its reputation, at least, as a literary and professional language, while English was still considered by many a purely utilitarian tongue for the instruction or entertainment of the unlearned.[14] Even those who, like Chaucer, considered it a suitable medium for court poetry, were distressed by the diversity of dialects and the instability of orthography which might lead to the misinterpretation of their works. As Chaucer observed in the envoy to his greatest poem, *Troilus and Criseyde*:

> And for ther is so gret diversite
> In Englissh and in writyng of oure tonge,
> So prey I God that non myswrite the,
> Ne the mysmetre for defaute of tonge.

Earlier in the century Higden had complained of the corruption of English due to borrowings from Danish and Norman, to which Trevisa added the comment that 'som vseth straunge wlafferynge, chiterynge, harrynge, and garrynge grisbayting'. Trevisa was a Cornishman by birth, and would clearly have been in agreement with Chaucer's Parson who proudly proclaims that he is 'a Southren man' who 'kan nat geeste "rum, ram, ruf," by lettre' – a slighting reference to the alliterative verse tradition of the west midlands and northern dialects. Such comments serve to remind one that the diversity of Middle English dialects was more often than not a divisive factor in English society at this period.[15]

Perhaps because of this divisiveness there is still less evidence to associate the growing use of English as a literary language with any parallel development in nationalist sentiment. Laurence Minot may have chosen English as the best medium for his patriotic outbursts; and the west midlands poets were perhaps expressing national as well as regional feeling in their choice of a traditional English alliterative verse form, together with their interest in Brutus, the eponymous founder of Britain, and Arthur, its greatest king. It is interesting to note, for example, that Humphrey de Bohun, earl of Hereford (d. 1322), named his youngest son Eneas; and that the earls of Warwick actively culti-vated the legends surrounding Guy of Warwick, the supposed English founder of the family.[16] But there is nothing in the period to compare with the prologue to the late thirteenth-century *Cursor Mundi* which remains isolated and unexplained. In it the anonymous north-country author declares emphatically that he is writing for the love of 'Englis lede [men] of meri ingeland'. He even goes so far as to complain about the prevalence of works in French which are of little use to those who do not know that language, and he concludes aggressively that each nation should keep to its own tongue:

> Of ingland the nacione
> Er englijs men in comune,
> The speche that men may mast wid spede
> Mast to speke thar-wid war nede:
> Seldom was for ani chance
> Englis tong prechid* in france,

*Bodley MS Fairfax 14 substitutes 'praysed' for 'prechid'.

Gif we thaim ilkan* thair language,   *each one
And than do we na vtetrage.[17]

If, however, such sentiments could be harboured in the late thirteenth century, it is most likely that they gained ground in the fourteenth under the impact of the Hundred Years War. The evidence for this is slight, but there is an interesting detail in the report of the parliament held at Westminster in 1344. Edward III urgently required a subsidy for the war and pressure was put on parliament by the council to grant the necessary aid. In a speech before the Commons it was claimed that the king had firm information that Philip was 'fully resolved . . . to destroy *the English language*, and to occupy the land of England'. Some forty-four years later the same fear was roused during the 'Merciless Parliament'.[18] It is significant that in each instance the threat to the English language is isolated as an example of the enemy's ruthlessness should French armies ever land in England. This suggests at least that by the mid-fourteenth century there was a fairly widespread association of 'Englishness' with the English language which the authorities could manipulate to their advantage. The association was certainly fully developed by the early fifteenth century which saw a proliferation of patriotic verse in English.[19]

In conclusion, it may be said that despite the lack of positive evidence, there is likely to have been some relationship between the growth of English and the development of patriotic sentiment – though not so close a one as might be expected. It would be misleading to make comparisons with modern nationalist movements in which a common linguistic heritage plays an important role. As Professor Galbraith has remarked, some of the most ardent patriots during the medieval period were the chroniclers (and, one may add, the poets) writing in Latin: men who as historians were aware of England's past and fostered her legends and traditions.[20]

If Englishmen had yet to develop a sense of nationality based on linguistic unity, there can be no doubt that by the late fourteenth century there was a growing awareness of national identity in other areas:

And thus you have what Scripture says '*Pacem super Israel*', peace over Israel, because Israel is naturally the heritage of God as is England. For I truly think that God would never have honoured this land in the same way as he did Israel through great victories over their enemies, if it were not that he had chosen it as his heritage. May God grant us that peace.[21]

These words were spoken by the chancellor during his opening address to the parliament of 1376–7 in which his purpose was to persuade the members of their duty to acknowledge Richard as Edward III's heir. His choice of a comparison between England and Israel was by no means fortuitous, for in reminding the members that they belonged to a chosen race he was appealing to them as Englishmen and as patriots.

The chancellor had caught the mood of the day. The great victories of Crécy, Neville's Cross, Poitiers, and Nájera had convinced many Englishmen that they enjoyed the favour of divine protection.[22] It was a conviction which the reverses of the 1370s and 80s did little to weaken, for these were explained as a punishment visited by God on the sins of his people. If only society would reform, it was felt, England would be made victorious once more. The conviction is implicit in Walsingham's thanks to God for checking the hand of the French during the raids of 1377: 'But through all, blessed be the Lord who preserved the English through his mercy, calling them to repentance by means of such terrors, so that at all events they should be recalled by fear from the error of their ways – they who did not know how to enjoy his mildness.'[23]

This belief is closely allied to the growth of patriotic feeling, for it encouraged Englishmen to identify with one another on racial grounds. At a simple level this found expression in enthusiastic acclaim for England and the English – typified by Thomas of Erceldoune's supplication to Christ to 'saue jnglysche men whareso thay fare' and Minot's prayer:

> Now Ihesus saue all Ingland
> And blis it with his haly hand.[24]

More significantly, it was instrumental in providing a means whereby various elements in society could identify their interests with those of the second estate.

The outstanding victories of the early years of the war established England temporarily as a military power of some importance in western Europe. One result of this was a renewal of national self-confidence which expressed itself in a fresh pride in the prowess of the English military. The days seemed past when Knighton commented gloomily that two Englishmen were hardly a match for one puny Scot. With pardonable exaggeration the author of the *Acta Bellicosa* claimed that the French took to their heels when they saw Edward landing in Normandy in 1346, 'believing a thousand to have been present for one Englishman'. A more modest boast on the part of a captured English knight – that one Englishman was worth two French – is said to have precipitated the famous Battle of the Thirty. As Sir Richard Baker aptly observed in the seventeenth century:

> Martiall men were never more plentifull then in this Kinges Raigne: whether it were that the Starres have an influence to produce such men at one time more then another: or whether it were *Regis ad exemplum*, the Kings example made his subjects like himselfe: or lastly, that his continuall exercise of Armes put them as it were into a mould of fortitude.[25]

The legend soon developed that the English were invincible in the field. After the sack of Caen in 1346 Philip VI followed Edward at a distance, not daring to attack, 'so great and wonderful' was the might of the English army. When the two hosts did finally engage at Crécy the French panicked and turned on their heels, for 'such was the host of the English that all the world could not resist them.' With unconcealed pride Robert of Avesbury reports the supposed reactions of a French envoy at the sight of the English army in 1350:

> ... he inspected the three battles of the English, nobly arrayed, and [composed] undoubtedly of alert men, and ready for battle, and extraordinarily spirited. And he was astonished that my lord the king of England had at that very moment such might from which my lord the prince of Wales, his first-born son, had so great an army in Gascony.

When the envoy returned to the French camp he reported all that he had seen, whereat John 'greatly perturbed' decided to withdraw. He again refused battle when Edward rode out from Calais in 1355. Like his father nearly ten years before, he contented himself with following the English at a distance lest, sneers the Kirkstall Abbey chronicler, 'by chance he should see his standards [which were] so dreadful to him'.[26]

This should not be dismissed too easily as the braggadocio of patriotic English chroniclers. Some at least of England's enemies

shared their view. When the Black Prince invaded Castile in 1367
Enrique was advised by his French captains and in letters from
Charles v not to seek a pitched battle 'for he made it quite plain to
him that with the prince of Wales came the flower of the chivalry
of the world.' Instead he was advised to block the passes into
Castile and force the prince to retire into France. In Froissart's
version, Arnould d'Audrehem offered similar advice and urged on
the king in even stronger terms the fighting quality of the English
military: '. . . when you assemble for battle with the prince you
will find real men of arms, for there is the flower of all the chivalry
of the world. And you will find them hard, wise, and good fighting
men whom not even death would make retreat a single foot.'
But like their French allies before them, the Spanish were to learn
from bitter experience. Years later the count of Lerna accounted
for the fiasco at Nájera by reference to the tried quality of the
enemy. The prince's army, he estimated, was composed of 10,000
lances and 6,000 archers, and in his opinion, 'of those men there
were at least 3,000 each of whom was worth a Roland or an
Oliver.'[27]

Comparison with the heroes of old was of course axiomatic.
Roland and Oliver never accomplished greater feats of arms than
did the English knights at a skirmish at Inglesmendi; and at
Nájera itself the deeds of the English beggared comparison with
them. Froissart considered the feats of arms in the early years of
the Hundred Years War so fine that they equalled those of Charle-
magne's reign; while Sir Henry Percy's exploits at Neville's Cross
earned him comparison with Gideon, Samson, Joab, Solomon,
and Gawain from one enthusiastic poet.[28]

It was suggested in chapter 3 that the aristocracy and the
milites strenui saw their role in the Hundred Years War in terms of
chivalric internationalism: an élitist concept which isolated them
from the rest of society. But aristocrats like the Black Prince were
also Englishmen, and this enabled their fellow-countrymen to
approve of their exploits without in any way sharing their
chivalric idealism. For those outside the military élite, knighthood
became associated with patriotic rather than chivalric and feudal
ends.

The association was advanced with greatest enthusiasm in the
northern counties where the knight's military activities were most
clearly beneficial to society at large. The battle of Neville's Cross in

particular was celebrated as an example of patriotic endeavour on the part of the northern barons and knights. No doubt the fact that the English army comprised a hastily assembled body of knights, clerics, and peasants fighting side by side encouraged this view: 'and all the remaining knights, chaplains, and clerks from these regions were assembled all with one assent, ready to live and to die for the salvation of the kingdom.' In such circumstances clerics like the Lanercost chronicler could happily interpret the actions of Henry Percy or Gilbert de Umfraville in the light of their own patriotic fervour, although the real motives of these barons were certainly different. Thus Umfraville is praised for his readiness to fight with spirit for his country, while the valour of Sir Thomas de Rokeby 'stood out as a model to all who saw it of how to fight valiantly for the pious cause of the fatherland'. Percy is praised in similar terms by the unknown cleric who composed a poem in celebration of the victory. Armed with the breastplate of faith he fought magnificently in the defeat of 'our enemies'. Such magnates, the poet concludes, 'we ought always to cherish who seek during their lives to defend the people.'[29]

For these north-country clerics, at least, the virtues of chivalry had been assimilated with no sense of incongruity into their own system of patriotic values and assumptions.[30] Almost certainly, however, these values were not shared by the aristocrats and knights who made a profession of arms – although such sentiments are occasionally attributed to them in the chronicles. Knighton, for example, in his account of Henry of Grosmont's duel with Otto of Brunswick, says that Henry refused to leave the lists until his honour and that of his king and country were satisfied: 'so that the English nation should not incur the reproach of shame through him.'[31] Such statements should be regarded with caution, for the sentiments attributed to the duke are out of keeping with what is known of his character. As might be expected of such a man, the challenge seems to have been made solely on the grounds of a slight to his personal honour. What is significant is Knighton's readiness to attribute a patriotic motive to Henry's actions. It provides another example of the way in which the chivalric code of the military élite was reinterpreted by their patriotically minded fellow Englishmen.

But if the military élite did not share such idealism there were others involved in the war who did. As we have seen, it was not only in the north that all sections of society were occasionally mobilized against the enemy. Along the south coast, too, church-men and merchants were forced to fight beside knights when the enemy suddenly appeared before Winchelsea, Rye, or Southampton. Such men were far removed from the international court milieu of Henry of Grosmont and the Black Prince and they fought from very different motives. It was not chivalry or feudal obligation which impelled them, but the basic desire to defend their homes and their native land.

The failure of the military in the later years of Edward III and during the reign of Richard II heightened the achievement of such men. Not only did they frequently defend the coast against the enemy when the government failed to do so, but they mounted successful counter-attacks as well, to the discredit of the barons in charge of the fleet.[32] The motives of such men were undoubtedly mixed. The hope of plunder was probably a dominant motive for raids along the Normandy coast, and the defence of the English seaboard was a practical necessity. Many were no doubt like Chaucer's Dartmouth Shipman who plied the wine trade with Bordeaux but was not averse to a little privateering against enemy (and other) shipping when opportunity availed. As Chaucer laconically put it:

> Of nyce conscience took he no keep.
> If that he faught and hadde the hyer hond,
> By water he sente hem hoom to every lond.

Others seem to have been professional privateers. Díez de Games describes in *El Victorial* how the Franco-Castilian fleet was particularly keen to sack Poole in revenge for the privateering of one Harry Paye who used the port as a base for his operations. Díez de Games gives a detailed account of Paye's activities. He had a large fleet which he used against French and Spanish shipping in the Channel, but he raided as far south as Finisterre, causing a great deal of damage along the Castilian coast. 'And although other armed ships set out from England', he concludes, 'he was the one who kept it up longest.'[33]

It would be rash to speculate too much about Paye's motives. He may have been no more than the professional corsair depicted by de Games, but he may also have had a genuine concern for England's welfare. At a time when government naval operations were, to say the least, inadequate, it is perhaps significant that Paye's activities seem to have been centred on keeping the English Channel free of enemy shipping. According to de Games, he quartered the Channel so effectively 'that no ship sailed to Flanders that was not taken'. Concern for England's security was certainly shown by the Kentish peasants during the Revolt of 1381. At an assembly held at Dartford it was decided that 'no one who lived within twelve leagues of the sea should go with them, but should guard the coasts against enemies.' The peasants were merely maintaining the long-established *garde de la mer*,[34] but there can be little doubt that patriotic sentiment was often involved in the upkeep of what was potentially a burdensome duty. Describing the response to the raids of 1360, John of Reading observed: 'the clergy and laity in England came together in arms to resist the aforesaid enemies and, if it were granted, to fight for their native land.'[35]

To contemporaries, the most outstanding example of the new patriotic spirit in action was John Philipot or Philpot, a prominent London grocer and alderman who was knighted in 1381.[36] Philipot was a man of some wealth and in 1378 he equipped a fleet at his own expense and succeeded in capturing John Mercer, a Scottish pirate who had recently taken a toll on English shipping. This incident, coinciding with Castilian raids along the Cornish coast and Lancaster's failure to take St Malo, made Philipot a national hero at the expense of the military.[37] His popularity made him enemies amongst the nobility who were said to be jealous of the grocer's success in the pursuit of arms. But according to Walsingham, Philipot rebutted his critics in a sharply worded speech which is worth quoting in full:

Learn . . . without doubt, I would not have destined myself, nor my money, nor my men to the dangers of the sea on that account – in order to snatch the good name of knighthood from you or your colleagues and to acquire it for myself. But, pitying the afflictions of the common people and of our native land which now, through your indolence, has fallen from being the most noble kingdom and mistress of nations into such wretchedness that it lies open to plundering by whom it please of the most ruthless people; so long as none of you applies his hand to its defence, I have exposed me and mine for the salvation of my own countrymen and the liberation of my native land.

Philipot was the hero of the hour in a way which would have been unthinkable in the great days of Edward III when the triumphs of the military were on everybody's lips. Such a man could only come into prominence at a time when the military no longer fulfilled its obligation to defend the realm. If Walsingham's report of his speech can be trusted, Philipot clearly saw himself as a public-spirited citizen acting under his own initiative for the benefit of society. But he fought with no desire to usurp the role of the military; he was not interested in war as a profession; and still less was he concerned with chivalry. As a London merchant it was no doubt in his interest to keep the sea lanes clear of enemy privateers like Mercer. It is his self-justification which is significant. Most men like to ascribe to their deeds noble motives: for Philipot, the noblest were concern for the welfare of the people and the *patria*. It was in these terms that he was judged by his fellow-countrymen.[38]

Philipot's patriotism expressed itself in prompt action in defence of the realm. Others, motivated by a similar concern for their native land, attempted to analyse the causes of England's decline and to suggest reforms which could restore the kingdom to its former prosperity. This is properly the subject of the next chapter, but it will not be out of place to mention briefly the foremost of such men, the poet and moralist John Gower.

As he watched the kingdom's progressive decay under what he considered Richard's misgovernment, Gower became obsessed with the welfare of England. It was an obsession typified by his rededication of *Confessio Amantis* to England rather than to King Richard, and it had its roots in an intense love for the land of his birth. But we must look to *Vox Clamantis* rather than the *Confessio* for an elaboration of Gower's patriotic concern. In a remarkable passage in Book VII, the poet dutifully asserts that he loves all the kingdoms of Christendom but, he adds, ' . . . above all I love my own land, in which my family took its origin.' It is the starting point for the most self-conscious and articulate declaration of patriotic sentiment to have survived from fourteenth-century England:

Whatever other lands may do, I am not shaken by it, as long as I stand apart at a distance from them. But if the native land which bore me as a young child, and within whose realms I always remain fixed –

if she suffers anything, my innermost feelings suffer with her, and she shall not be able to suffer her misfortunes apart from me. I am almost overwhelmed by the weight of her adversities. If she stands firm, I stand firm; if she falls, I fall.[39]

Love for his native land is a most important factor in Gower's Latin and English poetry, for his identification with England intensified his anguish at the social and political turmoil of the 1380s and 90s. His condemnation of the immorality of the three estates and his growing disillusionment with Richard II should be seen, at least in part, in its light. Like many of his contemporaries, 'moral' Gower related the decline in England's fortunes to the moral collapse of society. But he also believed that if the people would reform and live in harmony, there would be no nation on earth to compare with the English. It is a conviction which finds expression in an earlier passage in *Vox Clamantis*. In Book I Gower presents an allegorical dream in which he is driven in a rudderless ship to the shores of an island. The poet asks an old and wise man its name and is told that it is 'the Island of Brut'. The old man then gives an account of the inhabitants who are characterized as a lawless, treacherous, violent race given to bloodshed and war. And yet, he concludes, 'I do not think there is a worthier people under the sun, if there were mutual love among them.'[40]

Gower's most significant contribution to the development of a patriotic consciousness should perhaps be sought in the language he employs. More than most, he seems to have been aware of the limitations of feudal terminology as a vehicle for the expression of patriotism. His own eloquence in *Vox Clamantis* is largely the result of his attempt to evolve a more accurate language to convey his ideas and feelings. But this is an aspect of Gower's poetry which leads forward to the fifteenth century, for his contemporaries were for the most part content to express themselves within the limiting terminology already at their disposal. The most outstanding example of this is the widespread identification of national interest with Edward III's feudal and dynastic war with France.

Among contemporaries and for many succeeding generations, Edward III was held in the highest esteem. It was true, as Sir Richard Baker observed, that he 'out-lived the best of himselfe'

and that 'his later years were not answerable to his former'; but
men found it easy to forgive the senility of Edward's old age when
in his prime he had possessed all the qualities appropriate to kingship. 'In short', wrote the seventeenth-century historian Joshua
Barnes in his monumental biography:

He had the most Vertues and fewest Vices of any Prince, that ever I
read of; He was Valiant, Just, Mercifull, Temperate, and Wise; the
best King, the best Captain, the best Lawgiver, the best Friend, the
best Father, and the best Husband in his Days. And after all this his
very Enemies will be found to say much more of him.[41]

Modern historians of the fourteenth century have not endorsed
Barnes's judgement. Beginning with James Mackinnon, who published his *History of Edward III* in 1900, Edward has either been
the subject of somewhat hostile criticism, or he has been ignored
in favour of Richard II whose complex character is seemingly
more amenable to modern psychological probing.[42] Yet in many
ways Edward is the more interesting historical figure, for in his
acceptance of the conventions and ideals of the age he brings us
closer to the mind and outlook of fourteenth-century England.
Moreover, it is his conventionality which explains Edward's
popularity in his own day and later. The age favoured a strong
king who upheld chivalry and at the same time waged a successful
war abroad; who passed his leisure hours in the noble pursuits of
hawking and hunting; and whose manifest piety did not interfere
with the interests of the state. Mackinnon criticized as 'superficial'
the praise lavished on Edward by his contemporaries,[43] but this
was not mere flattery on their part. Rather, it expressed a genuine
admiration for a man who identified himself completely with the
accepted ideals of kingship of the later Middle Ages.

The king's passion for chivalry naturally gained the support of
the aristocracy and the *milites strenui*, and of men like Froissart and
the Chandos Herald who celebrated the noble life in their works.
From the beginning, Edward invested himself and his court with
a romantic aura which the chroniclers and poets were quick to
reflect. The Order of the Garter was the most successful of all late
medieval chivalric orders, and Edward's personal enthusiasm for
chivalry appeared, as we have seen, in the numerous tournaments
held during his reign and his delight in entering the lists personally in some romantic disguise. The comparison with King Arthur

did not escape contemporaries. To the Chandos Herald, the celebrations at the English court after the battle of Poitiers could only be likened to those of Arthur's reign; not since the days of Arthur were so many kings gathered together in London, exclaims the author of the *Eulogium*; there has not been his equal, laments Froissart at his death, since the days of King Arthur.[44]

Outside court circles Edward's chivalric pretensions were often criticized for their expense and immorality, or because they interfered with the progress of the war.[45] But the war itself generally met with approval, and Edward's popularity in his own day and later owes much to his outstanding success as a general. Even from his enemies Edward won grudging admiration as 'the wisest warrior in the world and the most cunning', while at home a cleric like Knighton, who had no time for the trappings of chivalry, implied the same compliment when he called the king 'the most worthy, vigorous, and powerful knight in Christendom'.[46]

It is easy to understand why Edward was popular with the soldiery, for apart from his undoubted talent as a strategist, he possessed other, more personal, qualities which endear a commander to his troops. Froissart notes the courtesy and good humour with which he rallied the army before Crécy: 'so that whoever was completely downcast was fortified on hearing and seeing him.'[47] Moreover, reckless of his personal safety, Edward fought beside the troops in his early campaigns. At Sluys, says Froissart, he pressed 'bravely and boldly amongst his enemies to cause them the more harm, and to give courage to his men'.[48]

Those at home were reminded of Edward's endeavours through the medium of government propaganda, for as we have seen, the king took great pains to ensure his subjects' support for the war and to inform them of its progress. Edward's frequent injunctions to the clergy to offer prayers for the success of his expeditions kept the war before the minds of the people; so did the mixture of propaganda and information diffused via parliament, where news of victory and fear of invasion were used to persuade the Commons to grant subsidies for the war.[49] But more important in the present context are speeches in which the Commons were told of the king's personal involvement in the war. In 1355, for example, Sir William Shareshull informed them of Edward's 'great labour ... for the defence and salvation of his kingdom'; and again in 1376 they were reminded by the chancellor of how the kingdom was 'most nobly benefited, honoured, and enriched' by Edward and his sons – 'and more was never done in the time of any other king'.[50] Edward's travails and victories were kept before his subjects in other, more tangible ways. After the battle of Sluys the image on the gold noble was changed to show 'on the one side of it, a ship, the king armed and eager within, circumscribed with the royal name; and on the other side of it, a cross firmly stamped with this circumscription, *"Jesus autem transiens per medium illorum ibat"'*.[51]

Propaganda of this sort was instrumental in gaining support for the war, but some Englishmen may have responded to it in a way which may not have been calculated by the king and his council. There is little doubt that so conventional a king as Edward III saw the Hundred Years War entirely in feudal and dynastic terms. According to this view, the people of England were implicated in the war in that they were subjects of the king: as such it was their duty to support his cause. Such assumptions are implicit in Edward's appeal to the troops before Crécy to defend his honour and his right; in Shareshull's statement before the Commons that the king wished to end the war with least grievance to his people and greatest profit to himself; and in Edward's request for a subsidy, 'or otherwise he would be shamed and dishonoured and he and his people destroyed for ever.'[52]

But certain aspects of royal propaganda lent themselves to a different interpretation. It was possible, as some of these quotations suggest, to view the war as a conflict waged by the king for the benefit of his subjects rather than his own dynastic ends. In other words, Edward and his policies were capable of a metamorphosis similar to that of chivalry and the aristocracy: the king's motives and actions could likewise be reinterpreted in terms appropriate to the emergent patriotism of the age.

This view is expressed in *An Invective Against France*, a poem which may well have been written, as Wright conjectured, to encourage a continuation of the war after the Crécy campaign. The piece contains several echoes of government propaganda, notably in its attempt to stir up fear and hatred of the French, and in its emphasis on the justice of Edward's cause. But the poet is also concerned to show the king labouring tirelessly on behalf of his subjects ('We sleep securely, while he rarely sleeps') and in so doing he is appealing to the nascent patriotism of his audience who are reminded of Edward's selflessness – 'giving himself for us' – and of the many hardships he has suffered for their sakes. The propagandist aims of the poet emerge, however, when he continues that the king's subjects should in turn give their all for him, their all being specified in some detail: 'Therefore let us give him our goods, money, heart, body, and love.'[53]

There can be little doubt, as such government apologists were quick to observe, that the image of the king labouring unceasingly for the good of his subjects appealed to their growing sense of patriotism. Yet, surprisingly, it rarely finds expression in the literature and even the author of *An Invective* falls back on more conventional motifs in his praise of Edward. There may, however, be a purely literary explanation for this apparent failure of propagandists to exploit patriotic sentiment more fully. The Middle Ages had inherited from classical oratory a scheme governing panegyric which was frequently applied to the praise of contemporary kings and heroes.[54] Most of the poets and chroniclers who wrote in Edward's praise were educated men whose literary medium was Latin. Consequently they would have been familiar with the topics of epideictic oratory from rhetorical handbooks such as Cicero's *De Inventione* and the pseudo-Ciceronian *Rhetorica ad Herennium* or their medieval derivatives.[55] These were popular texts in the schools and educated men naturally drew upon them when writing in praise of famous contemporaries. The extent of their debt varied from the provision of occasional ornament to total dependence, but in varying degrees the rhetorical schema imposed a significant formal and thematic limit on those who wrote in praise of Edward III.

The topics appropriate to panegyric are conveniently summarized in *De Inventione* where Cicero identifies eleven attributes which may be developed for purposes of praise or blame. These are: name, nature, manner of life, fortune, habit, feeling, interests, purposes, achievements, accidents, and speeches. Together they provide a schema which attempts to formalize all significant aspects of a man's life.[56]

Its importance in the present context may be illustrated from Thomas of Walsingham's *Historia Anglicana*, I, 326f., where the chronicler describes in detail the last days of Edward III. For the most part it is a sordid tale of physical and moral decay, redeemed only by a pathetic deathbed repentance. Yet Edward had been a great king, and Walsingham appropriately concludes with a more general assessment of his character and achievements. It is the occasion for a sustained panegyric in the manner prescribed by the rhetoricians.[57]

At first glance, Walsingham's eulogy gives the impression of casual organization. This is rather an example of the art concealing art advocated by the rhetoricians[58] for the precentor of St Albans draws extensively on Cicero's schema, or one like it, in his presentation of Edward's characteristic virtues and accomplishments. Some examples will make this clear. In epideictic oratory it was customary to praise a man for his physical beauty. The topic was popular throughout the Middle Ages,[59] and consequently we find Walsingham praising the proportions of Edward's body in terms which are entirely conventional: 'he was elegant of body, as the height neither exceeded that which was seemly nor yielded overmuch to shortness.' The king's physical beauty was a joy to all who beheld it, for he had the features of an angel 'in which shone forth such extraordinary beauty that if anyone had openly looked upon his countenance or dreamed of it by night, he would without doubt hope for delightful solaces to befall him that day.'

Under 'fortune' the panegyrist considered, amongst other things, his subject's success in life and his fame, for which special topics were reserved. Walsingham duly praises Edward's attainments in the spheres of government and warfare.[60] The king's fame he embellished with what E. R. Curtius has called the topics of 'inexpressibility'.[61] Thus we are told that Edward's renown spread to remote and foreign nations, 'so that they considered themselves fortunate who were either subject to his lordship or were partly allied with him.' They did not believe, Walsingham concludes, that there could be any kingdom on earth which produced so noble, so high-minded, and fortunate a king, or in the future could produce such another after his decease.[62]

Medieval authors naturally adapted the catalogue of virtues inherited from classical rhetoric to meet the needs of a Christian society. Edward is consequently praised for his conformity to the Christian ideal of kingship. Walsingham notices the reverence and honour which he always showed to the servants of the Church, and commends him for his numerous pilgrimages. He was, moreover like a father to orphans, compassionate towards the afflicted, and sympathetic to the wretched, at the same time giving relief to the oppressed and 'seasonable help to all the poor'.

It is important to recognize that this list is wholly conventional,[63] for together with his dependence on rhetoric, it provides a key to Walsingham's purpose. The chronicler was undoubtedly an ardent patriot who enthused over Philipot's selfless defence of his native land, but he was also an educated man, conversant with the rules governing panegyric. Consequently he was careful to establish Edward's reputation amongst the great kings of medieval tradition by relating his character and actions to the values conventionally associated with kingship. The introduction of patriotic sentiment into panegyric of this sort would have been at once indecorous and irrelevant.

This may well explain the absence from the literature of a specifically patriotic response to Edward of the sort clearly hinted at in the parliamentary rolls and developed by fifteenth-century poets writing in the vernacular. It is a response which may well have been popular and widespread in the fourteenth century, but we can never know for certain because our main source of information, the literature, was governed by rhetorical conventions which were too firmly established to admit of innovation. When men wrote of Edward it was inevitable that they should do so by reference to an internationally recognized and wholly conventional ideal of kingship, and the highest praise of all was to claim that a king outshone not only his contemporaries, but also the great kings of the past in the achievement of that ideal. It is a claim frequently made for Edward by admiring and learned eulogists: 'Through such merits, such warfare, such noble conduct, the glorious Edward, that most excellent man, put all who went before him into the shade, outshining them all'.[64]

5
Conservatives and Intellectuals: The Debate on War

In the reign of Richard II serious-minded Englishmen frequently turned their thoughts to the lamentable state of the realm. They discussed the nature of the crisis in society, explored possible causes, and expounded what they considered to be necessary reforms. Inevitably, the cause of England's decline was found in the corruption of society. Everyone, says Gower, cries out 'The times are bad, the times are bad!' but, he concludes, if this is so they have only themselves to blame. Bishop Brinton is eloquent on the subject in the sermons he delivered during these years. He drew a comparison between England's fate and that of Rome. That great city had flourished while its clergy and knights remained true to their vocation, but when the inhabitants fell into sin, then discord and injustice triumphed and the city was destroyed. Such, he fears, will be the fate of England. In the bishop's view sexual excess was rampant and there was no need to look further for the cause of the kingdom's decline. He berates the lords and knights in particular for their lechery. If England is unfortunate in the war with France it is no wonder when 'luxury, adultery, and incest reign everywhere, for few men – and especially the lords – content themselves with their wives'. Elsewhere he quotes the *Book of Ruth* in support of his argument: 'Wherefore, on account of our pride, injustices, and impurity, the hand of the Lord is against us.'[1]

The bishop contented himself with generalized complaint against the three estates. Others were bolder in accusing individual members of the government. It is well known that Walsingham was particularly outspoken against John of Gaunt, duke of Lancaster, and although many of his accusations may be dismissed as sensationalism,[2] there is a substratum of truth in his charge that the reverses of 1377–8 were partly due to Gaunt's inept leadership.

As an example of his irresponsibility in command the chronicler reports a conversation which allegedly took place in 1377. Some of his retainers are said to have urged the duke to look to the defence of his castle of Pevensey in view of the expected French naval raids. But according to Walsingham who seems very sure of his source of information ('I am about to quote him verbatim') he merely replied: 'If they destroy it . . . completely, I have the power to rebuild it again.' While the French raided the south coast, however, the duke was careful to remain in the north, indulging in the chase. Walsingham reports similar dereliction of duty on the part of the earl of Arundel and concludes with an anguished appeal to the reader: 'Let the judicious reader examine carefully the words of this earl and this duke with their deeds and, if he can, interpret them in a good manner.' Walsingham further blamed the duke for the defeat of an English fleet by the Spanish in the following year, and with more justification, for the failure of an attack on St Malo which Gaunt led in person. Everyone, laments the chronicler, despaired of resisting the enemy under such a leader.[3]

Even the aged king was not free from censure. Walsingham notes Edward's declining health, but he has his own ideas as to its cause. It was not, he says, due to the natural diseases of old age but was 'because of an inordinate passion for venery'. The reference is unmistakable. It is to the king's infatuation for his mistress, Alice Perrers, which became a public scandal after the death of Queen Philippa in 1369. At the time it seemed the most regrettable aspect of Edward's last years and an indelible stain on his reputation. Capgrave, looking back on Edward's career, observed that he was gracious and fortunate in peace and war, devout, and without blemish 'save that in his age he was gretly langaged with lecchery'. Edward's dotage was all the more regrettable when his mistress was compared with his queen. Philippa had been widely respected, she was 'a most noble woman, and a most constant lover of the English', whereas Alice was universally condemned as an unscrupulous, grasping whore. The king, declares the St Albans chronicler, should be considered a slave rather than a lord when he allows himself to be commanded by such a shameless woman. He then proceeds to trace a direct causal relationship between the king's sinfulness and the crisis in society. He urges Edward to repent and to reform his way of life, for only by a return to just rule on his part will the crisis be averted.[4]

The association of morals and politics was of course a commonplace of fourteenth-century political thought. It underlies much of the political reporting in the chronicles and is central to the works of men like Gower and Erghome where the king's dotage is specifically related to the failure of the war effort. Gower's attack on Alice in *Mirour de l'Omme* is typically more allusive than Walsingham's, however. His section on the estate of a king contains an exposition of the folly of the prince who succumbs to the wiles of women, but the cautious poet makes no direct reference to Edward and his mistress. He had no need to. The contemporary relevance of the biblical parallels he used would have been instantly recognizable to his readers, while being sufficiently generalized to save him from reprisal. Like Walsingham, Gower considers the realm to be in great danger where the king is ruled by a woman. He dwells at some length on the unmanning effects of such slavery, with obvious reference to the war with France: 'The king is too greatly deceived by women when he loves them more than his God, whence he abandons honour for foolish pleasure. That king will never be feared who thus desires to abandon his shield and seek battle in bed.' He adds weight to his argument by reference to King David's discomfiture through his infatuation with Bathsheba.[5]

The most sustained attack on Edward's government during these years, however, is to be found in John Erghome's pseudo-prophecy which the Yorkshire friar foisted on to his innocent contemporary John, prior of the canons regular of Bridlington.[6] Its popularity is attested by the existence of twenty-three manuscripts which contain the prophecy in one form or another, and by the frequent references to it in chronicles well into the fifteenth century.[7] Like Walsingham and Gower, Erghome considered the king's obsession with Alice Perrers to be the greatest stumbling block to any improvement in England's fortunes; but he deliberately obscured his attack on Edward's mistress by pretending to be uncertain as to whom the 'author' of the prophecy refers. He may, says Erghome in his ponderous commentary, be speaking 'against the queen of England or against some other woman by whose love and counsel the king was impeded from many fair wars at that time', but since he cannot be sure, he declines to be more explicit. Elsewhere he hints that the 'prophet' knew the woman's name but dared not reveal it for fear of her enmity.[8] The hint that the queen may be the woman in question is yet another example of the way in which Erghome deliberately obscured his interpretation in order to protect himself. His later suggestion that Edward should leave this woman and return to the queen may seem to indicate that he was writing in Philippa's lifetime, and the prophecy is ostensibly referring to the siege of Calais in 1347 when such a reference would be in order. As the piece was almost certainly written between 1369–72, however, this may well be another false trail designed to protect the author from possible reprisals.[9] Such evasiveness serves as a reminder of the dangers involved in such direct political comment.

Whoever this woman is, continues Erghome, she has made the king effeminate. He no longer has a taste for war but remains at home indulging in pleasure and luxury. Erghome makes the inevitable parallels with Samson and Delilah and, like Gower, with David and Bathsheba. Edward is being punished for his sinfulness, though not to the full extent of his deserts because of the justness of his cause against the usurper of France. Earlier he notes that the king was victorious as long as he and his knights refrained from sin, but that later many were burdened and weighed down by the sins 'which they carry in their consciences on account of their evil deeds'. As a result, Edward lacks all measure in his actions and is incapable of good government. He no longer observes the laws of the land as he ought to do, but extorts great sums of money from the people, which he wastes without any benefit to himself or the realm. Because of this the people of England and France have turned against Edward, and his present misfortunes are a punishment from God in answer to his subjects' prayers. The 'prophet' foresees the king's repentance, however, which Erghome interprets as meaning a return to his warlike past as well as a return to virtue: 'he will lead a warlike and virtuous life, by renouncing his lewd life.'[10]

The aim of writers like Walsingham and Erghome was largely to expose the abuses and inadequacies of society through criticism of the individuals whom they believed responsible for them. But apart from the obvious danger of openly attacking people in high places, educated men tended to be more concerned with the failings of society as a whole. It was the general rather than the

particular which concerned them, and it led them to debate contemporary problems within a more abstract and theoretical context. But discussion was limited by a scarcity of ideas about social
structure, for in the fourteenth century the ideal of the three estates
of clergy, knights, and peasants was predominant. Despite its
obvious inadequacy in relation to the social structures of the late
Middle Ages, it had the sanction of ancient authority and provided
an ever-popular framework for the analysis of society. Its wide
currency explains the remarkable degree of unity in the conclusions
of those who debated the troubled times.

Contemporary moralists were naturally concerned with the
failure of all three estates to live up to their social obligations, but
in the circumstances it is not surprising that the knightly estate
received a large share of their attention. Not without justification
it was blamed for the political and social instability which characterized England in the 1380s and 90s. It was particularly blamed
for the failure of the war effort – or for the prolongation of the
war from ignoble motives – according to the disposition of the
writer. Complaint of this sort was frequently accompanied by
exhortation to return to the true calling of knighthood, and this
involved the writer in a discussion of the nature of chivalry and
the just war. As one might expect, the concept of chivalry advanced by such men differed significantly from the code of honour
recognized by the knights themselves.

Opinion differed amongst them as to the origins of knighthood
which was variously stated to have been founded by Christ, by
David, and at Rome.[11] But whichever legend was subscribed to,
there was no doubt as to the duties of the knight. One of the
clearest statements on this was made by Bishop Brinton in a
sermon preached in 1374. The name knight, he observes, involves
both honour and labour. It involves honour because of its foundation in ancient Rome when a thousand warriors were specially
selected and given the name *milites*. It involves labour because of
the knight's solemn oath to obey his lord in all things: 'never to
desert the field, to protect the life of princes, and not to refuse
death for the common weal'. Brinton then analyses the duties of
the knight who has received his sword at the altar. He should
respect the clergy, maintain peace and order, shed blood for his
fellow-countrymen in time of need, injure no man's property, and
live off his own.[12] This concept of the knight is endorsed by

Gower in *Vox Clamantis*. Knighthood, he says, was established for three reasons: to protect the rights of the Church; to foster the common good; and to defend the orphan and widow. For these causes a knight may rightfully do battle: 'Indeed, not long ago the knight did conquer his enemies in such fashion, for which reason his fame in the world lives on.'[13]

Not surprisingly, Gower and Brinton discovered a gap between the chivalric ideal as they understood it and the behaviour of the second estate. They were consequently dismayed by what they considered to be the decadence of the knights of their day. The bishop reproves those who, forgetting the honourable estate of knighthood,

> rise up against the Holy Church of God, violating ecclesiastical laws, and by unjust means seizing the inheritance of Christ; despoiling the poor; aggravating their neighbours; maintaining disputes and violence; defaming prelates of the Church; abominably perjuring themselves on Christ's members – now swearing by the head, now by the body, and so on . . .

Such viciousness was all the more regrettable since social order and stability depended on the good offices of the knightly estate. When knighthood fails, argues Gower in *Mirour de l'Omme*, the rest of society follows in its wake: 'Through their error, present-day knights and esquires (some who go to war, some who stay in their halls, the covetous and the proud) are one and all doing harm, for which reason all the rest of society is embroiled in folly.'[14]

Reform of the knightly estate was inevitably bound up with discussion of the nature of the just war. Gower was a man of peace, but not a pacifist, and in common with most of his contemporaries he accepted the concept of the just war. It was, for example, the knight's duty to fight in defence of the common right, although it was not lawful for him to engage in warfare out of pride or covetousness.[15] When he wrote *Mirour de l'Omme* in about 1376–8 Gower seems to have accepted the legitimacy of Edward III's claim to the crown of France and in consequence the justness of the Hundred Years War.[16] But as the conflict dragged on into the 1380s his attitude changed. In his view it was no longer a just war but a damning indictment of the military and the aristocracy who prolonged it to satisfy their avarice, pride, and lust. In the *Mirour* he had attacked great lords who stirred up wars solely for their own profit,[17] but in *Vox Clamantis* and *Confessio Amantis* this becomes one of his most bitter and repeated complaints against the second estate. He upbraids those who engage in war for the sake of some woman's love or for worldly renown, when such things are the merest vanities;[18] but his most incisive attack is reserved for those aristocrats whose greed impels them to prolong the war with France:

> Outwardly, greedy lords deal in the blessings of peace, but inwardly, wars still stand first with them. As long as it can store up more loot through war than through peace, avarice does not know how to love the good things of peace. And envy on your part does not permit you to conduct yourself peaceably towards me, for my tears are laughter in your ear. It is nothing to you if the downtrodden people bewail their sufferings, provided that the general misfortune brings in money to you.[19]

As a result of such unscrupulousness the pursuit of arms has been debased. It has become more of a business than a sign of nobility, for any tailor's boy may now wear a helmet or a gilded spur: 'And for this reason there is not the honour in feats of arms that there used to be. And indeed, since the poor but proud man does not have the wherewithal to conduct himself with pride, he lives everywhere by plundering.'[20]

Even more iniquitous in Gower's eyes are those members of the clergy who engage in battle personally or who stir up wars for the sake of worldly gain. The pope himself was not considered free from blame in this respect. We have seen that it was widely believed in England that he was in league with the French and was using his vast resources to further their war effort, instead of trying to promote peace in accordance with his Christian duty. This belief lies behind Gower's attack on the papacy in *Vox Clamantis*. The poet makes the traditional distinction between the kingdom of God and the kingdom of Caesar. It is the duty of the knight to wage war in the world and *not* the priest who should devote himself to the care of souls. Yet nowadays even the pope wages war:

> Peter preached, of course, but today's Pope fights. The one seeks souls, the other greedily seeks riches. The first was killed for God's law, the second kills, and yet God maintains no such law as that. The one arouses faith through his innocence, not by force; the other rouses armies on parade.

The wars of laymen, he insists, are regrettable enough, but the wars of the clergy are inexcusable, for it is the duty of the Holy Church to promote peace amongst men, not war 'For worldes good, which may noght laste'.[21]

One of the scandals of the age was the Norwich Crusade of 1383 in which Christian fought Christian under the pretence of waging a holy war. Gower never alludes directly to this event, and his attack on clerics who live like knights is characteristically generalized, but there can be no doubt that he had the *Pugil Ecclesie* in mind. Others, notably Wyclif and his followers, were more outspoken. A Wyclifite tract of the early 1380s attacks those priests who withheld the sacrament from their parishioners for refusing to subsidize the 'crusade'. Such priests do not consider the consequences of their actions when they incite their flock to 'vnpacience & enuye & hate for a litel muk that thei chalengen to hem self'. Elsewhere in the Wyclifite tracts martial prelates are attacked with even greater vigour. They are in 'mahoundis obedience' for they practise 'the deuelis lawe of cruelte': '& so thes worldly prelatis ben chef capteyns & arraiouris of sathanas batailis to exile good lif & charite, but certis no tonge in this lif may telle hou many soulis gon to helle bi thes cursede capteyns & anticristus iurdiccion & censures.'[22]

.The popularity of the crusading ideal had long been on the wane, and the cynical exploitation of the holy war as an instrument of papal policy in Europe was an important factor in its decline. By the end of the fourteenth century few people regarded it with any degree of seriousness despite the tireless efforts of idealists like Philippe de Mézières.[23] In his desire to see the wars between Christian nations ended Gower sometimes revived the arguments of Urban II that the crusade against the infidel provided an honourable outlet for the aggressive spirit of the second estate.[24] But such suggestions seem to have been at best half-hearted and elsewhere the poet condemns the practice. In *Confessio Amantis*, when the Lover asks whether or not crusades are lawful, the Confessor replies that it is lawful to preach and to suffer for the faith, 'Bot forto slee, that hiere I noght'. After Christ's death the apostles preached the gospel and submitted themselves to martyrdom, but they did not use the sword to spread the faith. Had they done so, Christianity would 'yit stonde in balance'. This, continues the Confessor, is proved by the example of the present war, for since Holy Church 'hath weyved/ To preche, and hath the swerd received' many regions have been lost to the true faith.[25]

Gower was never a pacifist in the modern sense, but two generations of war between Christian kings had changed his attitude to the just war. When even the noblest cause could be debased by the viciousness of its protagonists, it became increasingly difficult to label any war 'just'. It is hardly surprising, therefore, that to men of conscience in the late fourteenth century peace should seem the one hope left to Christian society. But as Gower saw so clearly, there was little hope of peace while powerful vested interests favoured war.

Sixty years of intermittent war had left its mark on English society. The military triumphs of Edward III's reign had made a deep impression on the populace, and the king, 'of fair memory', together with the Black Prince had passed into the realms of national legend. One may doubt Froissart's assertion that 'all society' favoured war,[26] but there were certainly many who stood to lose if a permanent peace was established with France. Some were simply adventurers who regarded the war as a potential gateway to wealth and social advancement,[27] but for many more it provided a necessary and even agreeable way of life. Such men were naturally strongly opposed to any attempt to negotiate a settlement with the enemy.

In his account of the Anglo-French negotiations of the early 1380s Froissart has something to say about these professional soldiers, for he considered them the greatest obstacle to peace. His opinion must be regarded with caution in view of the anglophobia of his later years, but the chronicler had visited England in 1395 when he spent some time at the royal court. He was therefore in a good position to observe reactions to the peace talks on the part of the nobles, knights, and officials whom he met there. Moreover, his impression is confirmed in general terms by Gower and Brinton in their complaints against over-mighty lords prolonging the war for their own mercenary ends. It was certainly a firmly held belief amongst other continental writers. The anonymous author of the *Complainte sur la Bataille de Poitiers* believed that King John had been betrayed by his own barons in 1356 who were secretly in league with their English peers to prolong the war out of greed; while Díez de Games believed that the English killed Richard II because he wanted to establish 'peace perpetual' with France.[28]

Froissart insists that the common people were as much in favour of war as the aristocracy, for those who served as archers found that it offered better prospects than their peacetime occupations.[29] There were others who wished to try their luck if opportunity arose, and there was a popular saying that while the English held Calais they carried the keys to the kingdom of France in their belt.[30] But he is quite clear that those who stood to lose most from peace were young men of gentry status, poor knights, and squires, 'who did not know where to employ themselves, and who had got into the habit of being leisured and of keeping a good establishment from the existence of the war.'[31]

These professional captains and men-at-arms were supported by powerful interests amongst the aristocracy. Thomas, duke of Gloucester, especially, led an influential anti-French faction at court which opposed any attempt to negotiate a settlement.[32] In the *Chroniques* Froissart reproduces at length a conversation which he alleges took place between the duke and his close adviser, Sir John Lackingay. As with many other private speeches narrated in the *Chroniques* the duke's speech no doubt represents what Froissart believed he said rather than his actual words. But there is evidence to suggest that the chronicler based the conversation on a first-hand knowledge of Gloucester's opinions concerning the war. G. Brereton has pointed out that Froissart claims to have met the duke at Pleshy where he heard his opinion of the Anglo-French negotiations of 1393. The speech which the chronicler attributes to the duke is therefore based on personal knowledge of Gloucester's views and language. As Brereton observes: 'Froissart's version is about as near as we are likely to get to a genuine speaking voice of the fourteenth century.'[33]

Gloucester begins by ranting against the French. They are full of pride and boasting but they never bring any enterprise to a successful conclusion – as witness their recent expedition against the Turks and their defeats at the hands of his father the late king, and his brother, Edward. The present truce should be abandoned and the war renewed with vigour, for apart from anything else: 'the people of this country want war for without it they are unable, and do not know how, to live, and the cease-fire is no good to them.'[34]

The duke next turns his attention to his nephew, Richard. If England had a good warlike king he would find 100,000 archers and 6,000 men-at-arms ready to follow him. The people are eager to risk themselves in battle 'for the fair and rich spoils which they hope to gain'. But Richard is no true knight: 'No! He is too heavy in the arse, he only asks for drinking and eating, sleeping, dancing and leaping about. That's no life for men-at-arms who ought to win honour through deeds of arms and put their bodies to work.' The present king of France, Gloucester observes, is eager for battle, unlike his predecessors – and this is just what the English want, since it was through pitched battle that they became rich under Edward III. Meanwhile the kingdom is going from bad to worse and in the duke's eyes the people are so overburdened by taxation that they are on the point of open rebellion.[35]

The character of Gloucester which emerges is in accordance with what is known of him from other sources. Whether or not the speech represents the duke's actual words, it is eloquent of the frustrations experienced by men who make a profession of war during a period of enforced inactivity. Gloucester's response to the economic, social, and political crises of the day is characteristically forthright. England's prosperity in the past depended on the war with France. A renewal of the war will therefore avert the present crises and set the kingdom in order once more.

Behind this simple formula lies the duke's deep-seated conviction that warfare alone is a fitting occupation for the nobility. Brought up at his father's court where chivalric virtues were accorded the highest honours, Gloucester could feel nothing but contempt for the sophisticated court of his nephew with its love of literature and art, and the latest French fashions.[36]

Many professional captains and men-at-arms clearly shared the duke's views, as did powerful aristocrats like the earls of Arundel and Warwick. Nevertheless, there can be little doubt that an increasing number of the king's subjects favoured peace even if they frowned on the excesses of Richard's francophilia and disapproved of his government at home. By 1390, at least, few thinking men who have left a record of their views would have concurred with the duke's formula for ending the crises in society. Rather, they turned their thoughts more and more to peace, and it is significant that the usurper Henry IV was most widely praised for the blessing of peace which it was hoped he would bestow upon the realm.

The war itself came to be looked on as something that had outlived its usefulness – if, indeed, as many doubted, it ever had any:

> The harm ne may nat rekened be, ne told;
> This werre wexith al to hoor and old.[37]

The words are those of Thomas Hoccleve who was born in about 1370 and who had therefore witnessed the desultory course of the war during his boyhood and youth in the last decades of the century. Moreover, as he wrote these lines in 1412 France itself was embroiled in a bitter civil war, and despite protestations that he was an Englishman and so an enemy of France, the poet was in fact very much a francophile. Civil war in the kingdom he admired therefore caused him great distress, but he was even more disturbed by the failure of England and France to reach a permanent settlement, and here he wrote as a conscientious Christian. He saw the long-drawn-out war as a disaster for Christendom and clearly felt it his duty to foster peace in any way he could. In *The Regement of Princes* he addressed himself directly to the two warring kings, for if only the 'cristen princes' would agree to peace, the benefits 'Vnto al peple . . . of christen blood' would be incalculable. As heads of state they share a great responsibility, for they act as 'mirours' for the people, who merely follow their example. Consequently, they should provide their subjects with a precedent by ending a war which has caused so much suffering and destruction:

> Allas! what peple hath your werre slayn!
> What cornes wast, and doune trode & schent!*   *ruined
> How many a wif and maide hath be by layn!
> Castels doun bette, and tymbred houses brent,
> And drawen downe, and al to-torne and rent!

Like Gower, Brinton and Langland before him, Hoccleve sought the cause of the war in the avarice of the great lords. He pays the merest lip-service to the claim of English kings to the crown of France by right of inheritance. This may have been used with great success by Edward III to justify the war, but by 1412 it had a hollow ring to it and Hoccleve openly accused the two kings of prolonging the conflict through greed:

To wynne worldly tresour and richesse,
Is of your strif the longe continuaunce.

The poet concludes his anguished appeal by reminding the princes that the pursuit of worldly riches is a vanity. They should therefore content themselves with what they already possess and 'With pees and reste, arme yow and clothe!'[38]

Hoccleve reflects the opinion of educated men in the late fourteenth and early fifteenth centuries. By 1380 there is not a single moralist or chronicler who wholeheartedly supports the war. Even an enthusiastic partisan of the English cause like Thomas Walsingham began to have misgivings, and came to support the peace negotiations of the 1380s. He had praised the attempts of Urban v to establish peace in 1370: 'but alas! before so pious a deed was begun he was prevented by death [and] was taken from this unstable life.' Later, in 1384, he objected to the grants made by parliament 'for the maintenance of this useless royal war'. Elsewhere he gave cautious approval to the Anglo-French negotiations of the early 1390s.[39]

Richard's peace policy undoubtedly attracted growing support. Malvern notes the opposition of the king's council to Gaunt's aggressive policies in 1385.[40] This was at the height of the invasion scares of 1385–6 and to many it seemed more advisable to await the enemy at home 'than to cross over unadvised to foreign parts without adding anything glorious to his reputation'. The truce effected by Gaunt in the previous year was more in keeping with the mood of the day: 'From which peace is most ardently desired by the inhabitants of each kingdom, and especially by the commons'.[41]

Peace became a matter of overriding concern to men of conscience. In about 1378 Wyclif had condemned the war as 'the sin of the kingdom' and he was echoed by his disciples in the following decade. To the Wyclifites the most abhorrent aspect of the war was the threat it posed to the unity of Christendom, and their tracts are eloquent in their condemnation of priests who encourage the people in their violence against fellow-Christians:

... & hereto thei wolen crie *ora pro nobis* abouten the grete stretis that god distroie here cristene bretheren & geue hem schort lif, euyl sped & wicked ende . . . it were betre to crie faste that the peple amendid here lif, & that god helpe vs & oure enemys agenst the fend & make us frendis in crist.[42]

Gower, who was hardly a Wyclifite, had arrived at the same conclusion. As early as about 1376 he had denounced the war as 'the false war' in which 'Christian cruelty' was the cause of 'common slaughter, like beasts in the market-place, made by men without pity'. By the time he came to write *Confessio Amantis* he was even more confirmed in his opinion. In the prologue he declares that the world has reached the age of steel and clay prophesied in Nebuchadnezzar's dream, and that consequently the end is near. Christendom itself is being destroyed by 'dedly werre', the result of division and lack of charity in the world; and 'al this wo is cause of man'.[43]

Gower adduces powerful arguments against war. God condemns it in both the Old and the New Law. Moreover it is against the law of charity and against Nature who commends peace which alone brings prosperity. War leads only to destruction, poverty, and wretchedness as a result of which 'The law is lore [lost] and god unserved'.[44] Gower did not abandon the concept of the just war altogether,[45] but even in a just war he believed that mercy was the virtue most appropriate to 'the worthi knihtes'. Moreover, the course of the war with France made him realize how easily the concept could be misused by unscrupulous men bent on justifying their own rapacity:

> Thou miht a gret ensample take,
> How thei her tirannie excusen
> Of that thei wrongfull werres usen,
> And how thei stonde of on acord,
> The Souldeour forth with the lord,
> The pouere man forth with the riche,
> As of corage* thei ben liche,†　　*disposition †the same
> To make werres and to pile*　　　　　　　　　　　*plunder
> For lucre and for no other skyle* . . .　　　　　　*reason

Consequently Gower believed that the war with France 'In which non wot who hath the werre [worse]', should be ended. But the poet had little faith left in man's ability to reform himself and he concludes with an appeal to God to

Afferme pes betwen the londes
And take her cause into hise hondes,
So that the world may stonde appesed
And his godhede also be plesed.[46]

It is almost certain that Chaucer came to the same conclusions although he is rarely as explicit as his friend, Gower. This is hardly surprising in one whose career as a minor government official was contingent on the patronage of some of the greatest names in the land. It was at best a precarious position, for as his younger French contemporary, Alain Chartier, reminded his brother with respect to life at court:

There knoweth noman in certayn yf hys astate be sure or not/ But who someuer it be, alway he is in doubte of hys fortune/ And whan thou wenest to be most in grace/ Thenne remember the wordes of the poete that sayth/ that it is no grete preysynge/ for to haue ben in the grace of a grete prynce.[47]

During the fourteenth century any involvement in politics was dangerous, but for someone in Chaucer's position it was especially so. As it was, his association with Burley's 'court party' may have lost him two controllerships of customs during the baronial purge of 1386.[48] Moreover, Chaucer's position as a prominent court poet made him at once more privileged and more vulnerable than most. Many of his poems were either commissioned by members of the court, addressed to prominent courtiers, or composed for specific court festivities.[49] A near-contemporary manuscript of *Troilus and Criseyde* contains a frontispiece which shows Chaucer reading before an assembly of lords and ladies,[50] and no doubt his poetry served his career in the sense that it kept him before the ear and eye of the court. It also meant that he had to be circumspect in what he wrote, and his poetry contains few references to contemporary politics and personalities.

Indeed he seems to have been hypersensitive to the complexities of court intrigue and took pains to disassociate himself from any one party. Typical is the care he takes in *The Legend of Good Women* to emphasize that he is not of the 'leaf' nor the 'flower' – a reference to an apparently innocent court game which may, nevertheless, have had political overtones.[51] But if he did tend, prudently, to avoid particular issues in his poetry he was no quietist, and the political and social turmoil of the 1380s and 90s did impel him

F

to make some contribution to the debate on society and war. In *The Tale of Melibee*, *The Former Age* and *Lak of Stedfastnesse*, Chaucer reveals a consistent attitude to Richard's troubled reign. His opinions are even more discreetly generalized than Gower's – the commonplaces of the age in fact – but they are sufficient to align him with his friend and others whose disillusionment with the course of the war led them to advocate peace as the only sure basis for a stable society.

The Tale of Melibee is a prose translation of the *Livre de Melibée et de Dame Prudense* which is in turn a paraphrase of the *Liber Consolationis et Consilii* of Albertanus de Brescia.[52] The choice of this tale is typical of Chaucer's circumspection. It was originally written as a criticism of the power struggle in northern Italy in the thirteenth century; it is, however, so generalized as to be applicable to almost any kingdom at any period in the Middle Ages.[53] Without doubt this aspect of the tale recommended itself to Chaucer, and explains why he took the trouble to translate a rather unexceptional political allegory. *Melibee* is suggestive of several interpretations relevant to the politics of the 1380s,[54] but the general nature of the argument precludes any specific interpretation which might have brought the poet into disfavour. Also the translation is remarkably close to the French, a fact which may be of some significance. As a mere translator, Chaucer could disown responsibility for the allegory or for any interpretation which might be placed upon it. That he was aware of the tale's contemporary relevance is suggested by his suppression of a reference in his source to the misfortunes attendant on the succession of a boy king.[55]

Several passages in the tale are particularly apposite to conditions in the 1370s and 80s. Some of these may well have been intended by Chaucer as advice to Richard himself. There is, for example, the counsel of Dame Prudence to Melibeus that he look for three qualities when choosing advisers: 'that they be trewe, wise, and of oold experience' and that he avoid 'flatereres, swiche as enforcen hem rather to preise youre persone by flaterye than for to telle yow the soothfastnesse of thynges'. The advice of young men should especially be avoided 'for hir counseil is nat rype'. Complaints against Richard's choice of counsellors were commonly made on similar grounds, and the relevance of this passage cannot have escaped Chaucer.[56]

But the translation of the tale cannot be construed simply as an expression of dissatisfaction with Richard's government. It could equally have been translated in support of the 'court party' and Richard's policy of peace with France,[57] for *Melibee* reveals a profound distrust of war and the evils which stem from it. When Melibeus debates whether or not to declare war on his neighbour, an old man in his council argues in favour of peace in these words:

> Lordynges ... ther is ful many a man that crieth 'Werre! werre!' that woot ful litel what werre amounteth./ Werre at his bigynnyng hath so greet an entryng and so large, that every wight may entre whan hym liketh, and lightly fynde werre;/ but certes what ende that shal therof bifalle, it is nat light to knowe./ For soothly, whan that werre is ones bigonne, ther is ful many a child unborn of his mooder that shal sterve yong by cause of thilke werre, or elles lyve in sorwe and dye in wrecchednesse./ And therefore, er that any werre bigynne, men moste have greet conseil and greet deliberacion.[58]

This advice provides a remarkable parallel with the rise and fall of England's expectations in the Hundred Years War which must have been readily apparent to Chaucer's contemporaries.[59] Together with its insistence on the virtues of peace the tale mirrors the disillusionment with war experienced by many educated men in the late fourteenth century.[60] The counsel of Dame Prudence 'that ye accorde with youre adversaries and that ye have pees with hem', and again, that 'oon of the gretteste and moost sovereyn thyng that is in this world is unytee and pees', might have come from the pen of Gower or any one of a dozen contemporary poets and moralists.[61]

Lak of Stedfastnesse and *The Former Age* confirm the impression that Chaucer sympathized with the views set forth in the *Livre de Melibée*. *Lak of Stedfastnesse* is an unexceptional *balade* on the mutability of the world as a result of man's sinful nature, but in one respect it may be considered Chaucer's most outspoken poem, for he addressed an envoy to King Richard which comes close to criticizing him for the troubled state of the realm. The envoy opens with the appeal:

> O prince, desyre to be honourable,
> Cherish thy folk and hate extorcioun!

and is followed by the hope that Richard will institute a period of good government: 'Dred God, do law, love trouthe and

worthinesse'.[62] MS Harley 7333 records an interesting, but un-
verified, tradition that Chaucer presented the poem to Richard at
Windsor,[63] and it may be that he was prompted by his sense of
duty to advise the king so openly.

Even more than *Lak of Stedfastnesse*, *The Former Age* is wholly
conventional. Its theme – the contrast between the 'lambish peple'
of the Golden Age and the corrupt society of his own day – was
popular throughout antiquity and the Middle Ages, and Chaucer
drew heavily on the works of earlier poets.[64] The total effect is
nevertheless his own, and the poem's overwhelming sense of
melancholy suggests, at least, that Chaucer shared the disillusionment of the latter years of Richard's reign. Like Gower, he found
the cause of war in his own day in mankind's insatiable greed for
gain. He laments the passing of the Golden Age when 'No flesh ne
wiste offence of egge or spere'. In those happy times men had no
cause to make war until precious metals and gems were discovered
in the earth:

> Allas! than sprong up al the cursednesse
> Of coveytyse, that first our sorwe broghte!

The Former Age is a conventional lament, not a political pamph-
let, and Chaucer offers no solution for the ills of society. The tone
of the poem is consequently more pessimistic than almost anything
else he wrote. He looks back with longing to the age when
'Unforged was the hauberk and the plate', but the innocence of
life in the Golden Age merely serves as a foil to the wickedness of
men in his own day, and the poem ends on a stark, desponding
note:

> Allas, allas! now may men wepe and crye!
> For in oure dayes nis but covetyse,
> Doublenesse, and tresoun, and envye,
> Poysen, manslauhtre, and mordre in sondry wyse.[65]

In the summer of 1399 one of Richard's subjects living in the
Bristol area addressed a poem, *Mum and the Sothsegger*, to the king
on the subject of the governance of the realm. He was not a learned man, and he wrote in the alliterative style popular in the west
midlands.[66] He was, however, a loyal subject and considered it his
duty to counsel Richard in such troubled times. He had heard of

Bolingbroke's landing and realized that Richard's hold on the crown was precarious, but as a liegeman of the legitimate king he was resolved

> ... to written him a writte to wissen* him better,   *teach
> And to meuve* him of† mysserewle his mynde to reffresshe‡ . . .[67]
>   *move †from ‡strengthen

The author's name is unknown, for he prudently neglected to sign his poem, fearing the consequences of the king's anger, as he hints in the prologue. But it has been plausibly suggested that he was a member of the lesser gentry, in which case his poem provides a unique insight into the reactions of a member of this important social group to the last years of Richard's reign.[68]

In retrospect the poet found it difficult to account for the crisis of 1399, for no king had ascended the throne with a greater fund of popular good will than Richard:

> I not what you eylid but if it ese* were;   *idleness
> For frist* at youre anoyntynge alle were youre owen,   *first
> Bothe hertis and hyndis and helde of non other;
> No lede* of youre lond but as a liege aughte . . .   *man

There was, he asserts, no subject of the boy king who was not 'as redy to ride or renne at youre heste [command]', and in conformation of this one may recall the first version of the prologue to *Confessio Amantis* in which Gower declared his intention of writing a book 'for king Richardes sake':

> To whom belongeth my ligeance
> With al myn hertes obeissance
> In al that evere a liege man
> Unto his king may doon or can.[69]

Through his 'dulnesse', the author of *Mum and the Sothsegger* continues, Richard embarked on a reign of misrule which lost him the affection of his subjects. At first the poet, like Gower, was prepared to make allowances for the king's youthful inexperience, and blamed Richard's misplaced confidence in young counsellors who abused his trust to further their own ends.[70] In this he proved himself more generous than Walsingham who repeated rumours that Richard's dependence on favourites like de Vere was an unnatural one.[71] But as he witnessed the lamentable end of the reign, the poet was forced to conclude with many of his contemporaries that Richard was the author of his own downfall. The king's livery of the white hart, and the injustices and oppressions committed by those who wore it were, in his opinion, a major cause of Richard's unpopularity. Even worse was his unscrupulous imposition of taxes in time of peace, and the ruthlessness with which these were collected. As he reminds the king, allegiance is not confirmed

> By pillynge* of youre peple youre prynces to plese,   *robbery
> Or that youre wylle were wroughte though wisdom it nolde;
> Or be tallage* of youre townnes without ony werre,†   *tax †war
> By rewthles routus that ryffled* euere . . .[72]   *plundered

In the circumstances the poet might well have echoed his contemporary Adam of Usk in quoting Solomon: 'Wo to the kingdom whose king is a boy.'[73] *Mum and the Sothsegger* was never completed in its original form, however, for Richard was deposed while the poet was still writing, and he seems to have abandoned it for a time. But between 1402 and 1406 he conceived the idea of salvaging his poem by writing a continuation expressing his admiration and support for Henry iv.[74] He is indeed fulsome in his praise: the new king is generous, wise, noble of deeds, and fierce in battle – in short he is 'Ful of al vertue that to a king longeth'. Since Henry had first deposed and then murdered the poet's acknowledged sovereign-lord, such praise may well seem to suggest time-serving on his part. But on the testimony of his poem, he had remained loyal to Richard to the end, and he was not alone in seeing in the person of the new king those qualities which Richard had so regrettably lacked.[75]

John Gower evidently suffered a similar crisis of loyalty. As we have seen, he had been an enthusiastic supporter of Richard personally in the early years of the reign and had made allowances for the king's youth and inexperience. But by the 1390s such excuses were no longer possible and he clearly saw no hope for reform under Richard. The changes he made in the prologue to *Confessio Amantis* in 1393 reflect his despondency. The poem was no longer dedicated to Richard but to Henry of Derby and to an England whose future seemed at best uncertain, for 'What schal befalle hierafterward/ God wot [knows]'. In the circumstances, the only hope lay in the overthrow of Richard, but Gower was too much of a conservative ever to advocate open rebellion. If we may believe the testimony of the *Cronica Tripertita*, however, written two years after the event, he looked with a more than favourable eye on the earl of Derby at the time of his banishment; and in the revolution of 1399 he saw an answer to the kingdom's predicament: 'Then H., the glory of the English and the best of good men was chosen King, since it was fitting.'[76]

Gower became an enthusiastic supporter and advocate of the new king. In his desire to justify Henry, he circumvented the delicate issue of his usurpation by invoking the principle of *vox populi, vox dei* and by asserting that: 'It is a work done in Christ to depose haughty men from the throne and to exalt the humble. God did this. He cast the hateful Richard from his throne and He decided upon the glorious elevation of the pious Henry, who was a man most pleasing in the estimation of all.'[77] In this sense Henry was merely an instrument of God's justice. Chaucer, who may well have suffered a similar crisis of conscience in 1399, subtly combines Henry's threefold claim to the throne – by conquest, by popular acclaim, and by royal descent – in the envoy to his well-known begging poem *The Complaint of Chaucer to his Purse*:

> O conquerour of Brutes Albyon,
> Which that by lyne and free eleccion
> Been verray kyng, this song to yow I sende;
> And ye, that mowen alle oure harmes amende,
> Have mynde upon my supplicacion![78]

These lines may have been motivated by self-interest and nothing more. But it is not unlikely that Chaucer shared his friend's hopes for the new reign, especially in respect of peace and political stability.

In this context Gower foresaw and answered objections that Henry had obtained the crown by violent means. It is the king's duty, he argues, to defend his right with force especially (and here there is an obvious reference to Henry's declared aim in 1399):

> To cleime and axe his rightful heritage
> In alle places wher it is withholde.

If there is any choice, however, 'Betre is the pees, of which may no man lese', and it is the advantages of peace which the poet wishes to inculcate in the new king. Henry had already saved England from the miseries of Ricardian misrule: 'Through you, good king, we are set free who were before in servitude without cause.' He should now, as Gower is at pains to remind him, 'pourchas pes' and 'suffre noght thi poeple be devoured'. To this end he should put aside the 'cruel werreiour' who counsels war, and instead follow God's counsel of peace.[79]

In Praise of Peace contains nothing which Gower had not said elsewhere. But it is his finest and most sustained condemnation of war on Christian grounds, and its dedication to the 'worthi noble kyng, Henry the ferthe', suggests both the great hopes which he entertained for the new regime, and his relief at the despatch of the 'hateful Richard'. Certainly not everyone concurred in Gower's estimate of Henry's character or shared his enthusiasm for the new reign. The king was bitterly attacked in the poem, *The Six Kings to Follow King John*, in which amongst other things his death by drowning was predicted 'thurgh Vengance of God'. But even in this poem, written by a partisan of the Percy-Glendower faction, there is little praise for Richard, who is characterized as an ass with feet of lead and head of steel.[80]

Jean Froissart is one of the few who seems genuinely to have regretted the king's death, for he had looked to him for a more sympathetic policy towards France.[81] He was also motivated by personal considerations. Richard had received him well during his visit to England in 1395 and Froissart, always affected by the sight of lavish spectacle, had gained a most favourable impression of the royal court. It was therefore painful to him to record Richard's downfall and death, though true to his vocation as an historian he drew the appropriate moral from it – one with which even Richard's enemies and detractors would have concurred: 'Now lords consider; kings, dukes, counts, prelates, and all men of lineage and power, how dreadful and fickle are the fortunes of this world.'[82]

Appendices

Walsingham's Panegyric on Edward III

A

Fuerat nempe Rex iste inter omnes reges orbis et principes gloriosus, benignus, clemens, et magnificus, dictus autonomasice 'Gratiosus', propter gratiam singularem qua praecelluit; quia, virtute gratiae divinitus sibi concessae, universos praedecessores suos quadam excellentia gratiae praecellebat. Erat et corde magnanimus, qui licet aliquando infortunia diversa, aut incommoda emergentia, nosceret se passurum, nunquam expalluit aut mutavit vultum. Belliger quoque fuit insignis et fortunatus; qui de cunctis congressibus, in terra et in mari, semper triumphali gloria victoriam reportavit. Familiaris, humilis, et mansuetus erat omnibus, tam externis quam internis; subditos omnes suos fovens, diligens, promovens, et pie regens; Deo devotus extitit, peregrinationes saepe faciens, et ministros Ecclesiae venerans et honorans. In curis temporalibus providus et tractabilis, consilioque discretus; in eloquii suavitate mitis et affabilis, in gestu et moribus compositus et maturus. Orphanis erat quasi pater, afflictis compatiens, miseris condolens, oppressos relevans, et cunctis indigentibus impendens auxilia opportuna. Nempe in conferendis beneficiis ultra omnes viventes fuit semper profusus et promptus; in rerum modestus affluentia, non elatus aut superbus, sed se semper intra se continens, et inferioribus quasi parem se praebuit, et inter orbis primores et principes se dominum demonstravit. In aedificiis construendis curiosus et sollicitus, in regni sui locis diversis plura consummavit aedificia, arte exquisitissima, structura elegantissima, situ pulcherrima, et sumptibus pretiosa; moderate supportans gaudia, leviter ferens damna. Recreationum erant ei solatia aucupatio et venatio, quibus quotiens vacavit, prout tempus anni obtulit, multum indulsit. Largus erat in donis et hilaris, prodigus in expensis. Corpore fuit elegans, statura quae nec justum excederet, nec nimis depressioni succumberet; vultum habens humana mortalitate magis venerabilem, similem angelo; in quo relucebat tam mirifica gratia, ut si quis in ejus faciem palam respexisset, vel nocte de illo somniasset, eo proculdubio die sperabat sibi jocunda solatia proventura. Regnum vero suum usque in senium strenue, sapienter, et magnifice gubernavit. Et quia fuerat in universa morum honestate praeclarus, sub eo vivere regnare fuit, prout suis subditis videbatur. In tantum nempe ejus fama percrebruit apud nationes barbaras et remotas, ut aestimarent se felices, qui vel ejus erant dominio subditi; vel ei aliquatenus foederati. Nullum enim credebant fore sub coelo regnum, quod tam nobilem, tam generosum, et felicem produxit regem, aut, eo quoque extincto, in posterum suscitabit.

Luxus tamen et motus suae carnis lubricos, etiam in aestate senili, non cohibuit, alliciente eum satis inverecunde, ut fertur, dicta meretricula A.P.; unde citius, ut putatur, propter illius immoderantiam vitam finivit.

In hoc loco summe notandum est, quod sicut in ejus primordiis cuncta grata et prospera successive ipsum illustrem reddiderunt, et inclytum, ita, eo ad senilem aetatem vergente et ad occasum declinante, peccatis exigentibus, paulatim illa felicia decrescebant, et infortunia multa infausta et incommoda succrescebant; quae minuere, proh dolor! famam ejus (*Historia Anglicana*, I, 327f.).

Translation

Without doubt this king had been among all the kings and princes of the world renowned, beneficent, merciful, and august; given the epithet 'the Favoured One' on account of the remarkable favour through which he distinguished himself. Wherefore, by virtue of the grace granted him by divine providence, he excelled all his predecessors in a certain eminence of God-given talent. He was, besides, stout of heart and although sometimes unaware that he was about to experience diverse misfortunes or troublesome issues, never turned pale or changed his countenance. Waging war he was also distinguished and fortunate, who always brought back victory in triumphant glory from all encounters on land and sea. He was friendly, humble, and gentle to all, as much to foreigners as to his own; favouring, esteeming, advancing, and dutifully ruling all his subjects. He was outstanding in his devotion to God, often making pilgrimages, and venerating and honouring priests of the Church. In secular affairs he was prudent and yielding, and discreet in council; in the pleasantness of discourse gentle and courteous; in carriage and manners composed and mature. He was like a father to orphans, compassionate to the wretched, feeling for the afflicted, comforting the oppressed, and giving out seasonable help to all the poor. He was without doubt beyond all men living always lavish and prompt in conferring favours. Amidst the abundance of possessions he was moderate, not lofty or proud, but inwardly always temperate. He behaved almost like an equal to inferiors, and amongst men of the first rank and the princes of this world he showed himself a lord. He was assiduous and eager in the construction of buildings; in various parts of his kingdom he completed many buildings most excellent in craftsmanship, most elegant in design, most beautiful in location, and in costs of great value. Upholding pleasures with moderation, he sustained losses lightly. Hawking and hunting provided the relief of recreations for him; in which, as often as he was unoccupied, he greatly indulged himself according to the season of the year. He was liberal with gifts and good cheer; prodigal in expenses. He was elegant of body, as his height neither exceeded that which was seemly nor yielded overmuch to shortness. He had a countenance like an angel, the more venerable for its human mortality, in which shone forth such extraordinary beauty that if anyone had openly looked upon his countenance or dreamed of it by night, he would without doubt hope for delightful solaces to befall him that day. Assuredly, he ruled his kingdom actively, wisely, and nobly right up to the feebleness of old age. And because he had been distinguished by complete integrity of character, under him to live was to reign, as it seemed to his subjects. Certainly, his fame spread so far abroad amongst foreign and remote nations that they considered themselves fortunate who were either subject to his lordship or were partly allied with him. Indeed, they did not believe there could be any kingdom under the heavens which produced so noble, so high-minded, and so fortunate a king, or could in the future produce such another after his decease.

However, he could not repress debauchery and the transitory passions of his flesh even in the season of old age, through the said courtesan A [lice] P [errers] enticing him very shamelessly, as the report goes. Whence on account of his intempérance, as it is thought, he ended his life the sooner.

In this place it is particularly to be observed that, just as in his beginnings when all agreeable good fortune successively rendered him illustrious and renowned, so as he turned towards old age and declined towards death, little by little those good fortunes grew less for him through pressing sins. And many unpropitious and disagreeable misfortunes sprang up which, alas! have diminished his renown.

B

The Dangers of Political Comment
In Fourteenth-century England

During the Cambridge parliament of 1388 the Appellants enacted a statute which gave the council power to punish anyone who was 'so bold as to fabricate any further defamations or any such false things concerning the prelates, dukes, counts, barons etc.'. The statute gave legal sanction to the suppression of adverse criticism of the aristocracy: a practice which was in any case taken for granted by those who ruled fourteenth-century England. Political comment of any kind was fraught with danger, and the author of *Mum and the Sothsegger* was hardly exaggerating when he declared that:

> . . . yf a burne bolde hym to bable the sothe
> And mynne hym of mischief that misse-reule asketh,
> He may lose his life and laugh here no more,
> Or y-putte into prisone or y-pyned to deeth
> Or y-brent or y-shent or sum sorowe haue,
> That fro scorne other scathe scape shal he neure.[1]

An outstanding example of the dangers involved occurred during the events of 1377. At the height of John of Gaunt's unpopularity, the duke's arms were reversed (the sign of a traitor) by the hostile citizens of London, and lampoons were posted about the city.[2] These declared that the duke was not English but Flemish, the son of a butcher of Ghent: 'and that seemed plain enough for he loved the Flemmings twice as much as the English'. Walsingham says that the duke was 'most furiously angry' and took immediate steps to avenge his honour. He persuaded the Bishop of Bangor to excommunicate the authors of the 'verses', and had the refractory Londoners summoned before the king at Sheen. According to the *Anonimalle* chronicler the commons feared for their lives and only the more influential citizens dared accept the summons. In a scene calculated to intimidate them, Gaunt reminded the mayor and his officers that whatever was done in despite of himself was done in despite of the king, his sons, and all his lineage: 'for which it would be right to punish them so grievously that all the people of England might take example from them'. In response the citizens professed their innocence and begged on their knees for pardon. But this the duke, 'in his ferocity', refused until certain conditions were accepted. These were: that a pillar of marble be set up in Cheap, adorned with the duke's coat of arms; that a wax candle be carried in procession through Cheap to St Pauls and offered before the image of Our Lady; that the mayor, sheriffs, and aldermen be deposed; and finally, that those who reversed his arms and published the lampoons 'the same moment that they could be found by upright men who could swear that it was them, they should be sentenced to death or should await his pleasure.'[3]

Not all the duke's demands were met, but the marble pillar was set up in Cheap and the mayor deposed. Had the authors of the lampoons been taken there can have been little doubt as to their fate.[4] Lesser men provoked the wrath of the great to their cost. As the author of *Mum and the Sothsegger* observed with regard to a similar but unidentified incident:

> ... piez* with a papegeay† parlid of‡ oones,
>
> > *magpies †parrot
> > ‡spoke with
>
> And were y-plumed and y-pullid and put into a caige.
> Sith the briddes were y-bete the beke is vndre whinge
> But yf thay parle priuyly to thaire owen peeris.[5]

Such conditions explain certain features which recur in almost all the political literature of the period: the reluctance to name names or to be specific in any way; the preference for allegory, animal fable or pseudo-prophecy, and the all-pervading fear that too much has been said already. In fourteenth-century England, only the foolhardy were explicit. After narrating the political fable of the belling of the cat, Langland tells his readers to interpret it for themselves, 'for I ne dar bi dere god in heuene!' When Conscience is about to draw his deductions from the tale of Saul and Agog he refrains: 'An aunter it noiyide me non end wile I make'. Again and again the cautious Gower asserts that he writes in general condemnation of the age and not against individuals: 'I have not singled out anybody by a biting accusation, nor does my verse contain reproaches for anyone.' Elsewhere he exculpates himself on the grounds that he is merely the mouthpiece of the people or of divine inspiration.[6]

It was a device used by John Erghome, whose almost patholo-gical fear of detection is hardly surprising considering the enemies his work might be expected to make. Erghome had a powerful patron in Humphrey de Bohun, but in order to protect himself further he foisted the prophecy, as we have seen, on the 'divinely inspired' canon of Bridlington, reserving to himself the humbler role of commentator.[7] Nevertheless he preferred to remain anonymous, fearing, as he says in the prologue, the tongues of the envious, the power of the lords, and the angry displeasure of the wise and judicious. Moreover, at the end of the work Erghome appealed to Humphrey to keep the book away from the hands of the many and to conceal the author's name.[8]

But even these precautions failed to pacify Erghome's fear of reprisal. In his 'interpretation' he frequently feigned uncertainty as to the true meaning of the prophecy, a device which at once lent his commentary an air of learned disinterestedness, and pro-vided an ambiguity which might save him from the vengeance of those he attacked. It was a device which Erghome used to excess whenever he felt himself on really dangerous ground. Thus in his attack on those who plied the king with evil counsel, he identifies each courtier in terms of his individual physical peculiarity, but concludes that although eight such persons seem to be men-tioned in this way: 'either two or three names may designate one man who has the relevant conditions indicated by these names, but at least there are two such.'[9]

Erghome's circumspection should not be regarded as the product of a timorous spirit. His commentary on the prophecy contains most outspoken attacks on royal policy, on the king's mistress, and on the men who had Edward's ear. Erghome was acutely aware of the political realities of the society in which he lived. Had his authorship been made known to his enemies, the fate of the magpies in *Mum and the Sothsegger* was the best he could have hoped for. The protection of Humphrey de Bohun for an obscure Yorkshire friar could hardly be expected to extend so far as to oppose the vindictiveness of Alice Perrers as expressed through the will of the king. It is hardly surprising, therefore, that, like his contemporaries in the field of political comment, Erghome took every possible precaution to conceal his identity and, at times, his true meaning.

C

The Date of Composition of the Bridlington Prophecy
The terminal dates of the prophecy are established by Erghome's dedication to Humphrey de Bohun, who is styled earl of Hereford, Essex, and Northampton, constable of England, and lord of Brecknock. De Bohun did not succeed to all of these titles until 1361 and he died in 1372.[1] Most scholars who have studied the work favour an early date between 1362–4, only Wright hazarding a later date 'somewhere about the year 1370 or perhaps a little after'.[2]

The fullest study of the problem is that of Sister Peck who argues for a *terminus ad quem* of 1364 on the grounds that the author notes the arrival of King Peter of Cyprus in London in 1363 when he gained the support of de Bohun for a projected crusade, but makes no mention of the earl's presence at the fall of Alexandria two years later. Furthermore Erghome refers to John the Good as if he were still reigning, whereas he died on 8 August 1364. There are, claims Sister Peck, no events in the prophecy which can be substantiated from independent sources after 1364.[3]

In the absence of evidence to the contrary a date of composition shortly before 1364 would seem to be most likely. However, in common with Taylor and Gwynn, Sister Peck identifies the concubine who, according to Erghome, obstructed the king's prosecution of the siege of Calais (1347) with Alice Perrers. There can be little doubt that this identification is correct, but it makes a date of 1362–4 for the composition of the prophecy highly unlikely. Alice is not mentioned in any source before October 1366 when she appears as a lady of the bedchamber to Queen Philippa.

From then on there are numerous entries in the household accounts of grants made to her by the king,[4] and she may well have been his mistress before the death of Philippa in 1369. It is fairly certain, however, that their relationship did not become a public scandal until after the queen's death.[5] This is substantiated by Walsingham and Gower. Both were in at least as favourable a position as the Yorkshire friar to glean court gossip, and Walsing-ham would certainly have referred to the king's infatuation prior to 1369 if it had come to his notice. Erghome himself is manifestly writing about a scandal which had become a public – and extremely dangerous – talking point. Hence the allusiveness of his references, and the metamorphosis of Alice into a non-existent concubine who ensnared the king during the siege of Calais – Erghome is taking similar precautions to Gower in *Mirour de l'Omme.*

In a work such as Erghome's it is difficult to argue for a *terminus ad quem* on the identification of datable references to persons and events. The friar was not writing history, but propaganda, and in accordance with the nature of propaganda, he showed scant concern for historical accuracy when it suited his purpose. His devious attack on Alice is the most blatant example of this. Yet another may be found in his prediction of a great battle between the English, Scots, and French, in which the king of Denmark will send a fleet to the aid of the Scots. This has been dismissed as an example of the wild predictions which fill the closing pages of the prophecy. Certainly there was no such Dano-Scots alliance at this time (the battle is set in 1373), but there were rumours of such an alliance which John of Reading records under the year 1366.[6] It is likely that Erghome has taken an invasion scare of that year and characteristically transferred it to 1373 to give an air of greater probability to his prophecy. This in itself suggests a date of composition two years after the *terminus ad quem* of Sister Peck.

Apart from Erghome's violent outbursts against Edward's scandalous infatuation for Alice Perrers, his repeated references to the decline of England's military fortunes also point towards a date of about 1369–72. After the renewal of the war in 1369 it became clear that militarily England was no longer dominant, and to many educated men with conservative leanings the reason seemed to lie in the moral degeneracy of the kingdom's leaders.

Everything Erghome says is consistent with the attitudes of contemporaries such as Walsingham and Gower who, after the renewal of the war, looked to the king for the restoration of good government at home and an energetic prosecution of the war abroad.

D

Morte Arthure *and the Hundred Years War*

In his study of the alliterative *Morte Arthure*, W. Matthews examines the possible relationships between the poem and the Hundred Years War.[1] He argues that there is a close parallel between many aspects of Arthur's career and that of Edward III, and that the poet's criticism of Arthur's militarism was intended as a veiled attack on the Plantagenet's involvement in the war with France. In support of this Matthews adduces the similarity between the origins of the Hundred Years War and Arthur's war with Lucius; the close parallels between the Crécy campaign and Arthur's defeat of the Roman emperor; and between the sea battle off Southampton in the poem and the historical battle of Les Espagnols-Sur-Mer (1350).[2]

Matthews also points to what he feels to be the *Morte*'s consistently sympathetic attitude towards France; the intimate knowledge of French Arthurian romance displayed by the poet; and his fusion of motifs from the romances of Arthur and Alexander. Finally, he emphasizes the large number of French loan words to be found in the poem. On this basis he postulates a lost French romance inspired, like *Les Voeux du Héron*, by pacifist and anti-English feeling as a result of Edward's early campaigns in France. Such a romance, he considers, would have appealed to an English poet 'of courageous independence' during the last years of Edward III's reign. It would have presented 'a springboard from which to launch his own protest against the folly and unchristian cruelty of unjustified wars of the kind conducted by Alexander, Edward, and Arthur of Britain'.[3]

There can be no doubt that the *Morte* was intended, at least in part, as a criticism of Edward's war policy, or that it would have been so interpreted by a contemporary audience. In some respects, however, Matthews damages his case by overstatement. It is true that Arthur's battle with Lucius and the sea fight against Mordred bear some relation to Crécy and Les Espagnols-sur-Mer; but close parallels could also be found with Poitiers and Sluys and several other land and sea engagements. Matthews is on thinner ground still when he suggests that Arthur's campaign, culminating in a pitched battle with the emperor and the ensuing siege of Metz represent a detailed parallel with the Crécy campaign and the siege of Calais.[4]

The *Morte Arthure* is in a sense a more subtle work. The parallel between Arthur and Edward is achieved not by means of an exact identification of particular campaigns, but by the consistent description of Arthur and his conquests in terms of fourteenth-century English military practice. Through the steady accumulation of realistic detail the poem achieves an aura of contemporaneity quite unique in fourteenth-century English romance. This device enabled the author to criticize Arthur while leaving his audience to make the necessary inference concerning the morality and justice of Edward's war with France.

Some examples will make this clear. Throughout the poem, the diplomatic activity associated with war is kept quietly but consistently before the reader's attention. Imperial ambassadors come and go under carefully stipulated safe-conducts; messengers from the marshal of France keep Arthur informed of the emperor's latest moves; a herald brings news of Gawain's victory.[5] The most mundane aspects of military organization, most of which the chroniclers do not bother to mention, are presented in similar detail. After war has been declared, sergeants-of-arms are instructed to arrest ships and assemble a fleet at Sandwich, a favourite port of embarkation for English armies. Later the bustle and confusion of an army on the point of embarkation are described with a vigour and an accuracy quite unique in contemporary English literature. Sheriffs assign quarters to lords and their retinues and to the common soldiers, while other men load barges with all the paraphernalia of war:

> ... Bryngez blonkez* one bourde, and burlyche† helmes;
> *horses †tall
> Trussez in tristly* trappyde stedes,   *load confidently
> Tentez, and othire toylez*, and targez fulle ryche,   *equipment
> Cabanes,* and clathe-sekkes, and coferez fulle noble,   *cabins
> Hukes,* and haknays,† and horsez of armez ...[6]
> *horses †hackneys

Equal attention is paid to the aftermath of battle. Heralds search the battlefield for the bodies of prominent enemy dead; Lucius' camp is pillaged for booty; and there is much talk of ransom between the victors and their prisoners. At the diplomatic level, the lord of Milan tries to buy Arthur off; while the pope sends cardinals to seek terms, offering hostages in token of his good faith. When the conquest of Lorraine has been assured, the organization of government and the redistribution of estates by the conqueror are described at some length.[7]

But other aspects of contemporary warfare are introduced with a similar concern for accuracy: the brutality of soldiers as they ravage a city taken by storm where 'The pyne [suffering] of the pople was peté for to here'; and the cruelty and destructiveness characteristic of the *chevauchée*. As Arthur enters Tuscany:

> . . . Walles he welte downe,* wondyd knyghtez,   *overturned
> Towrres he turnes, and turmentez the pople,
> Wroghte* wedewes fulle wlonke,† wrotherayle‡ synges,
>   *made †proud ‡miserably
> Ofte wery* and wepe, and wryngene theire handis;   *lament
> And alle he wastys with werre, thare he awaye rydez,
> Thaire welthes and theire wonnynges,* wandrethe† he wroghte!
>   *dwellings †woe

As the poet observed of Arthur earlier, 'By conqueste fulle cruelle they knewe hym fore lorde'.[8]

By setting the legendary king's conquests in the context of contemporary English military practice, the poet had no need to make exact parallels between Arthur and Edward. The relevance of his criticism of Arthur's pride, covetousness, and cruelty to Edward III's militarism would not have been lost on a contemporary audience which was in any case used to hearing Edward compared with the British hero by admiring poets and chroniclers.

Moreover the author of the *Morte* was not alone in seizing the potentialities offered by Arthurian romance for political comment. Another English romance, *The Awntyrs of Arthure*,[9] may well date from the same period for, with pointed reference to the war with France, its author reveals an uncompromising attitude to those who live by the sword. When Sir Gawain meets the ghost of Guinevere's mother, he asks a strange question for a knight of romance:

> How shal we fare . . . that fondene* to fighte   *seek
> And thus defoulene the folke, one fele* kinges londes,   *many
> And riche [reymes* ouer rynnes]† with outene eny righte,
>   *realms †over-run
> Wynnene worshippe in werre thorghe wightnesse* of hondes?
>   *valour

The ghost's reply is not encouraging. She foretells the destruction
of the Round Table through the king's covetousness, prophesying
in particular the loss of France where Arthur is for the time being
acknowledged from Brittany to Burgundy and into Guienne,
whose inhabitants 'may grete [lament] the werre was bigonene'.
Again, an audience listening to these lines in the 1370s cannot but
have mused on the justice of Edward's cause and the wisdom of
his grandiose continental wars.[10]

In the *Morte*, however, there is an unresolved ambiguity in the
poet's attitude to Arthur which Matthews does not take into
sufficient consideration. Like his contemporary, Froissart, the
author of the *Morte* abhors the excesses of the military, especially
when committed against innocent civilians; but he is also sus-
ceptible to the chivalric ideal of warfare, which likewise finds a
prominent place in his poem.[11] This ambiguity centres on the
character of Arthur who is presented as a great chivalric and
national hero as well as a proud and avaricious tyrant. D. S.
Brewer is correct when he observes that 'the English audience
is expected to identify itself with Arthur and his men.'[12] The
Morte may well be based on an original sympathetic to 'douce
Fraunce', but it cannot be said that this spirit survives in anything
but a rudimentary way in the English romance. If the poet plays
upon contemporary dissatisfaction with Edward III's war policy,
he also reflects the patriotism of his audience who are asked to
admire 'our valyant biernez [warriors]' and 'oure cheualrous men'.
Arthur, like Edward, may be the subject of far-reaching criticism,
but he is still 'Sir Arthure of Inglande', 'owre wyese kyng'.[13]

Abbreviations

AHR   *American Historical Review*
ANTS   Anglo-Norman Text Society
BEC   Bibliothèque de l'École des Chartes
BIHR   *Bulletin of the Institute of Historical Research*
BJRL   *Bulletin of the John Rylands Library*
CS   Camden Society
DNB   *Dictionary of National Biography*
Econ. Hist. Rev.   *Economic History Review*
EETS   Early English Text Society
EHR   *English Historical Review*
ELH   *English Literary History*
ELN   *English Language Notes*
ES   *Essays and Studies*
JEGP   *Journal of English and Germanic Philology*
MAE   *Medium Aevum*
MLN   *Modern Language Notes*
MLQ   *Modern Language Quarterly*
MLR   *Modern Language Review*
MP   *Modern Philology*
MS   *Medieval Studies*
N&Q   *Notes and Queries*
PMLA   *Publications of the Modern Language Association of America*
PP   *Past and Present*
Rom. Rev.   *Romanic Review*
Rot. Parl.   *Rotuli Parliamentorum*
RS   Rolls Series
SATF   Société des Anciens Textes Français
SHF   Société de l'Histoire de France
STS   Scottish Text Society
TLS   *Times Literary Supplement*
TRHS   *Transactions of the Royal Historical Society*

Notes

Introduction

1 Manchester, 1966.
2 P. 154.

Chapter 1   Aspects of the War 1337–99

1 This chapter is concerned only with those aspects of the Hundred Years War which are particularly relevant to the main theme of the book. For a general narrative history of the war the reader is referred to E. Perroy, *The Hundred Years War*, Eng. trans. (1951, repr. 1965) and to other works cited in the Bibliography. I have attempted to indicate in the notes something of my debt to the researches of modern historians in this field.

2 Froissart, *Oeuvres*, ed. K. de Lettenhove, 25 vols (Brussels, 1867–77), II, 15.

3 E.g. *Chronica Monasterii de Melsa*, ed. E. A. Bond, 3 vols (1866–8), II, 355. The chronicler is following Ranulph Higden, *Polychronicon*, ed. J. R. Lumby and C. Babington, 9 vols (1865–86), VIII, 324–7 in his condemnation of the popular move to sanctify Edward.

4 *Melsa*, II, 355; M. McKisack, *The Fourteenth Century* (Oxford, 1959, repr. 1963), pp. 31, 95f.; H. Johnstone, 'Isabella, the She-Wolf of France', *History*, 21 (1936–7), p. 209.

5 C. W. C. Oman, *The Art of War in the Middle Ages*, rev. and ed. J. H. Beeler (New York, 1953, repr. 1960), pp. 122ff.; McKisack, pp. 32ff.

6 *Chronicon Henrici Knighton, Monachi Leycestrensis*, ed. J. R. Lumby, 2 vols (1889–95), I, 452.

7 Higden, VIII, 324; Adam Murimuth, *Continuatio Chronicarum*, ed. E. M. Thompson (1889), p. 53; Knighton, I, 445.

8 McKisack, pp. 98f.; R. Nicholson, *Edward III and the Scots*

(Oxford, 1965), ch. 4; *The Brut*, ed. F. W. D. Brie, 2 vols (1906–8), EETS OS 131, 136, p. 256.

9   Galfridus le Baker de Swynebroke, *Chronicon*, ed. E. M. Thompson (Oxford, 1889), p. 40; Knighton, I, 453.

10 Baker, p. 47.

11 Quoted by R. M. Wilson, *The Lost Literature of Medieval England* (1952), p. 197.

12 *Edward III and the Scots*, p. 106.

13 McKisack, pp. 115ff.; Nicholson, pp. 57ff.

14 Murimuth, p. 67; Baker, p. 50.

15 Laurence Minot, *Poems*, ed. J. Hall (Oxford, 1897), I, ll. 11–12. Roman numerals refer to the numbering of the poems in Hall's edition. See also McKisack, p. 117; Nicholson, pp. 107f.

16 *Chronicon de Lanercost*, ed. J. Stevenson (Edinburgh, 1839), p. 271.

17 *The Prophecies of John of Bridlington*, ed. T. Wright, *Political Poems and Songs*, 2 vols (1859–61), I, 142; *Lanercost*, pp. 269, 274.

18 Minot, II, 7–10, 1–4; Murimuth, p. 68; Andrew of Wyntoun, *The Original Chronicle*, ed. F. J. Amours, 6 vols (1903–14), STS, VI, Bk 8, ll. 3969–75; McKisack, p. 117; Nicholson, ch. 9.

19 See E. Perroy, *The Hundred Years War*, pt I, chs 3–4, esp. p. 69; McKisack, ch. 4. The tendency of historians to discount the importance of the dynastic issue is challenged in J. le Patourel, 'Edward III and the Kingdom of France', *History*, 43 (1958). See also his 'The Origins of the War' in *The Hundred Years War*, ed. K. Fowler (1971). The diplomatic history of the feudal and dynastic quarrel is covered by E. Déprez, *Les Préliminaires de la Guerre de Cent Ans* (Paris, 1902).

20 Froissart, II, 234; Nicholson, pp. 157f.; Knighton, I, 476f., II, I, 9. See also *Gesta Edwardi de Carnarvon*, ed. W. Stubbs in *Chronicles of the Reigns of Edward I and Edward II*, 2 vols (1882–3), II, 133; *The Kirkstall Abbey Chronicles*, ed. J. Taylor (Leeds, 1952), *Thoresby Soc. Publ.*, 42, p. 86.

21 Erghome, I, 144–5; see also Froissart, II, 321–3.

22 Murimuth, pp. 54, 56; Baker, p. 58.

23 *Melsa*, II, 383; Walsingham, *Chronicon Angliae*, ed. E. M. Thompson (1874), p. 6; *The Anonimalle Chronicle*, ed. V. H. Galbraith (Manchester, 1927), pp. 12f.; *Eulogium Historiarum*, ed. F. S. Haydon, 3 vols (1858–63), III, 203; Baker, p. 59; Higden VIII, 332–4; Knighton, I, 478; *Chroniques*

de London, ed. G. J. Aungier (1844), pp. 7of.; *Lanercost*, p. 293; Murimuth, p. 73.

24   McKisack, p. 131, n.1; Perroy, pt III, ch. 1.

25   Le Patourel, 'Edward III and the Kingdom of France', pp. 176–8; McKisack, pp. 140f.; Perroy, pp. 138f.

26   Quoted by Robert de Avesbury, *De Gestis Mirabilibus Regis Edwardi Tertii*, ed. E. M. Thompson (1889), p. 309. See also le Patourel, 'The Origins of the War', p. 45.

27   Murimuth, p. 103. See also Knighton, 11, 14; *Anonimalle*, p. 15; Froissart, 111, 66.

28   Froissart, 11, 317, IV, 160. This was also the opinion of the anonymous author of the anti-English satire, *Les Voeux du Héron*, ed. Wright, *Political Poems and Songs*, 1, 5f. and of Jean de Venette, *Chronicle*, ed. and trans. J. Birdsall and R. A. Newhall (New York, 1953), p. 33. See also le Patourel, 'The Origins of the War', pp. 28f.

29   See M. H. Keen, *The Laws of War in the Late Middle Ages* (1965), ch. 5.

30   Le Patourel, 'Edward III and the Kingdom of France', pp. 180f.; Hewitt, *The Organization of War under Edward III*, p. 159.

31   Included in many chronicles, e.g. Murimuth, pp. 91ff.; Avesbury, p. 303; Walsingham, *Historia Anglicana*, ed. H. T. Riley, 2 vols (1863–4), I, 201ff. For Henry of Grosmont's embassy see *Historia Anglicana*, I, 261; K. Fowler, *The King's Lieutenant* (1969), pp. 48f.

32   VII, 341. See Hewitt, *Organization of War*, pp. 158ff.

33   E.g. the manifesto of 1340 is quoted by Avesbury, pp. 308ff.; *Melsa*, III, 42; *Gesta Edwardi de Carnarvon*, 11, 148. Edward's letter to the College of Cardinals is quoted by Murimuth, Avesbury, and Walsingham (see above n. 31). Examples could be multiplied.

34   E.g. *Historia Anglicana*, 1, 215f.; Avesbury, pp. 302f.; Knighton 11, 10.

35   Murimuth, pp. 100f.; Perroy, pt 2, ch. 4. Murimuth even includes a detailed family tree to illustrate Edward's hereditary claim (facing p. 101).

36   Minot, 1, 31–2, 111, 7–10, IV, 7–9, 28–30, 51; *An Invective Against France*, ed. Wright, *Political Poems and Songs*, 1, 31, 35.

37   Erghome, p. 154; Lydgate, *The Fall of Princes*, ed. H. Bergen, 4 vols (1918–19), EETS ES 121–4, Bk IX, 3222–3.

38   See A. E. Prince, 'The Strength of English Armies in the Reign of Edward III', *EHR*, 46 (1931) and H. J. Hewitt, *The Black Prince's Expedition of 1355–7* (Manchester, 1958).

39   Jean de Venette, *Chronicle*, p. 94. See also pp. 84ff., 98ff., and *Récit des Tribulations d'un Religieux du Diocèse de Sens Pendant l'Invasion Anglaise de 1358*, ed. J. Quicherat, BEC, III, 4th ser. (Paris, 1857).

40   Minot, VII, 147f., XI, 1–3; Walter of Peterborough, *Prince Edward's Expedition into Spain and the Battle of Nájera*, ed. Wright, *Political Poems and Songs*, I, 94; Erghome, p. 213.

41   *Chronica Johannis de Reading et Anonymi Cantuariensis*, ed. J. Tait (Manchester, 1914), pp. 126f.; Froissart, v, 469; *Kirkstall Abbey Short Chronicle*, p. 107.

42   Minot, VIII, 1–24, X, 19–30, VII, 125–32.

43   Higden, I, 268; Richard de Bury, *Philobiblon*, ed. M. Maclagan (Oxford, 1960), p. 106. Bury's observation is interesting since it was made shortly before the period of England's greatest victories. He died 14 April 1345.

44   Minot, v, 11, IV, 90; *Invective Against France*, p. 28. See also Minot, IV, 55ff., VI, 19ff., VII, 139f. The author of the Anglo-Norman *Chroniques de London* shares many attitudes with Minot and seems to have written for a similar patriotic and unreflecting audience. He is equally contemptuous of Philip (see pp. 72, 81, 91, 92).

45   Knighton, II 39, 94. See also II, 18, 111; anonymous poem on Neville's Cross ed. Hall., *Poems of Laurence Minot*, Appendix IV, ll. 237ff.

46   *Chroniques de London*, p. 82; Froissart, VI, 298.

47   Ed. Wright, *Political Poems and Songs*, I. The titles are editorial.

48   *Invective*, p. 39; *On the Truce*, pp. 57, 54.

49   P. 49. See Erghome's objections to the truce of 1343, p. 150.

50   M. M. Postan, 'Some Social Consequences of the Hundred Years War', *Econ. Hist. Rev.*, 12 (1942), pp. 4f. See also his article, 'The Costs of the Hundred Years War', *PP*, 27 (1964), and for a contrary opinion, K. B. McFarlane, 'England and the Hundred Years War', *PP*, 22 (1962).

51   For a detailed account of this phase of the war see J. J. N. Palmer, *England, France, and Christendom 1377–99* (1972).

52   *Historia Anglicana*, I, 306f. See also *Anonimalle*, pp. 58f.; *The Sermons of Thomas Brinton, Bishop of Rochester, (1373–89)*, ed. Sister M. A. Devlin, 2 vols (1954), p. 54.

53   John of Reading, pp. 171, 180f.; Froissart, VII, 317, 415. See Tait's observations on the 'Danish raids', pp. 336ff.

54   Froissart, VII, 317f.; Perroy, pp. 152ff.; R. Delachenal, *Histoire de Charles V*, 5 vols (Paris, 1909–31), IV, 403ff.

55   *Chronicon Angliae*, p. 63.

56 *Chronicon Angliae*, pp. 65f.; *Historia Anglicana*, I, 315f.; *Chronique des Règnes de Jean II et de Charles V*, ed. R. Delachenal 3 vols (Paris, 1910–20), SHF, II, 172, 174. See also R. Delachenal, *Histoire de Charles V*, IV, 480ff.

57 Froissart, VII, 285f.; Chandos Herald, *The Life of the Black Prince*, ed. and trans. M. K. Pope, and E. C. Lodge (Oxford, 1910), ll. 3967ff., 3989ff.

58 Froissart, VIII, 5f., 201f., 207, 133ff.; *Chronique des Quatre Premiers Valois*, ed. S. Luce (Paris, 1862), SHF, p. 242; Chandos Herald, ll. 3963ff. See also J. W. Sherborne, 'The Battle of La Rochelle and the War at Sea, 1372–5', *BIHR*, 42 (1969).

59 Perroy, pp. 166ff.; P. E. Russell, *The English Intervention in Spain and Portugal in the Time of Edward III and Richard II* (Oxford, 1955), pp. 224f.; K. Fowler, 'Truces' in *The Hundred Years War*, pp. 194ff.

60 *Historia Anglicana*, I, 318f.; *Chronicon Angliae*, pp. 166f.; Froissart, VIII, 391ff.; Perroy, pp. 168f.; Russell, *English Intervention*, pp. 233f.; Delachenal, *Histoire de Charles V*, V, 17ff.

61 Froissart, VIII, 384, 388; *Rot. Parl.*, II, 361f.

62 *Brut*, p. 322. Cf. *Chronicon Angliae*, p. 65.

63 *Eulogium*, III, 336; *Anonimalle*, p. 79; *Historia Anglicana*, I, 318. See also Perroy, pp. 166f.; S. Armitage-Smith, *John of Gaunt* (1904, repr. 1964), pp. 118f.

64 *Anonimalle*, pp. 80f.; *Chronicon Angliae*, pp. 76ff. For a general account of the proceedings of the Good Parliament see McKisack, pp. 387ff. Latimer cannot be held personally responsible for the fall of St Sauveur-le-Vicomte and Becherel: see C. C. Bayley, 'The Campaign of 1375 and the Good Parliament', *EHR*, 55 (1940).

65 *Anonimalle*, pp. 92, 95; *Brut*, p. 330; *Chronicon Angliae*, pp. 60, 79f., 91f.; Erghome, pp. 204ff., 213; Capgrave, *The Chronical of England*, ed. F. C. Hingeston (1858), p. 231; *Historia Anglicana*, I, 305f.; *Kirkstall Abbey Short Chronicle*, p. 108. His final illness and death were widely lamented: Knighton, II, 124f.; *Brut*, p. 330; *Historia Anglicana*, I, 321; *Gesta Edwardi de Carnarvon*, p. 150; Froissart, VIII, 380; Brinton, pp. 75, 354ff.

66 *On the Death of Edward III*, ed. R. H. Robbins, *Historical Poems of the XIVth and XVth Centuries* (New York, 1959).

67 *Vox Clamantis*, ed. G. C. Macaulay in *Complete Works*, 4 vols (Oxford, 1899–1902), VI, 555* ff. The translation of this and all other quotations from Gower's Latin works is that of E. W. Stockton, *The Major Latin Works of John Gower* (Seattle, 1962). Line references are to Macaulay's text.

68 *Anonimalle*, p. 116; *Historia Anglicana*, I, 449; McKisack, pp. 402f., 406f.

69 *Brut*, p. 331f.; *Historia Anglicana*, II, 68ff., 153; R. H. Jones, *The Royal Policy of Richard II* (Oxford, 1968), p. 22.

70 *Chronicon Angliae*, p. 166f.

71 Knighton, II, 218f. For the proceedings of this parliament see McKisack pp. 442ff.; Jones, *Royal Policy of Richard II*, pp. 28ff. A. Steel, *Richard II* (Cambridge, 1941), pp. 120ff. is inclined to dismiss the report of Richard's threat to seek aid from France as the propaganda of his opponents.

72 See Jones, *Royal Policy of Richard II*, pp. 47ff.; McKisack, pp. 454ff.; A. Goodman, *The Loyal Conspiracy* (1971), ch. 2.

73 Knighton, II, 267ff.

74 Froissart, XVI, 200.

75 See Gaunt's conversations with Fogaça as reported by Froissart, XI, 298, 318. Also XII, 133f., 312; Perroy, p. 164; Armitage-Smith, *John of Gaunt*, pp. 310ff.

76 Armitage-Smith, *John of Gaunt*, pp. 232ff.; Goodman, *The Loyal Conspiracy*, p. 110; Palmer, *England, France and Christendom*, pp. 130ff.; *Brut*, pp. 325f.; *Anonimalle*, p. 131; *Historia Anglicana*, I, 418ff.; Gower, *Vox Clamantis*, VI, rubric to ll. 1271ff.

77 *Historia Anglicana*, I, 405, 406f.; Froissart, X, 249ff. Froissart's figures are certainly wrong here; French armies frequently exceeded 6,000.

78 Froissart, X, 296f. XI, 403; *Chronique des Règnes de Jean II et de Charles VI*, II, 183f. See also Wyntoun, IX, 1409ff.; Froissart, XII, 112, X, 269.

79 Brinton, p. 261; *Middle English Sermons*, ed. W. O. Ross (1940), EETS OS 209, p. 313. See also Brinton, pp. 258, 338f.; *On the Times*, ed. Wright, *Political Poems and Songs*, I, 270; *On the Death of Edward III*, ll. 17ff.; Erghome, pp. 181f., 206f.

80 See Delachenal, *Histoire de Charles V*, V, 17ff.; Russell, *The English Intervention in Spain and Portugal*, pp. 227ff.; Armitage-Smith, *John of Gaunt*, p. 70; Christine de Pisan, *Le Livre des Faits et Bonnes Meurs du Sage Roy Charles V*, ed. S. Solente, 2 vols (Paris, 1936–40), SHF, I, 239ff.

81 Froissart, IX, 278, also IX, 263. On the opposition of the French aristocracy to such a 'dishonourable' strategy see also *Chronique de Bertrand du Guesclin par Cuvelier*, ed. E. Charrière, 2 vols (Paris, 1839), II, 17557ff. Christine de Pisan felt it necessary to excuse Charles's failure to lead his troops in person on the grounds of an illness which overcame him at the time of his coronation: *Livre des Faits*, I, 131ff.

82   See Perroy, pp. 163f.; Froissart, VI, 224ff., VIII, 18ff., 291ff.
The long-term effectiveness of Charles's strategy has recently
been questioned by Palmer, *England, France, and Christendom*,
pp. 5ff.

83   Foissart, IX, 257, 330; Delachenal, *Histoire de Charles V*, v,
369ff.; Goodman, *The Loyal Conspiracy*, pp. 124ff.

84   Christine de Pisan, *The Book of Fayttes of Armes and of Chyualrye*, Caxton's trans., ed. A. T. P. Byles (1936), EETS OS 189,
pp. 128f., 16f., 20; *Quatre Premiers Valois*, p. 287; Froissart,
IX, 123. See also Eustache Deschamps, *Oeuvres Complètes*, ed.
Le Marquis de Queux de Saint-Hilaire and G. Raynaud, 11
vols (Paris, 1878–1903), SHF, balade no. 166 and *La Fiction
du Lion*, ll. 55–96.

85   *Historia Anglicana*, II, 198f. Froissart, XIV, 288, gives a similar
account of the negotiations.

86   The complex diplomatic activity of this period is narrated in
great detail by Palmer, *England, France and Christendom*.

Chapter 2   The Popular Response

1   See Hewitt, *The Organization of War*, ch. 7 and 'The Organization of War' in *The Hundred Years War*, ed. Fowler, pp. 91ff.

2   Walsingham, *Chronicon Angliae*, p. 6; Baker, p. 59; Murimuth,
p. 80.

3   *Lanercost*, p. 293; Knighton, II, 41.

4   Froissart, II, 471; *Chroniques de London*, pp. 74f.; Minot, III,
119f., 61f.; Baker, pp. 62f. See also *Melsa*, II, 383; Knighton, II,
3, 8; Murimuth, pp. 87ff.; *Rot. Parl.*, II, 104; Hewitt,
Organization of War, pp. 1f.

5   For the laws governing the division of spoils of war see D.
Hay, 'The Division of the Spoils of War in Fourteenth-Century
England', *TRHS*, 5th ser., vol. IV (1954); Keen, *The Laws of
War*, pt III, ch. 9; Hewitt, *Organization of War*, pp. 107ff.

6   See A. E. Prince, 'The Payment of Army Wages in Edward
III's Reign', *Speculum*, 19 (1944); McKisack, pp. 234ff.;
Hewitt, *Organization of War*, pp. 33ff.; Nicholson, *Edward III
and the Scots*, p. 115. On pardons to criminals see Hewitt, pp.
29ff.; E. L. G. Stones, 'The Folvilles of Ashby-Folville,
Leicestershire, and their Associates in Crime', *TRHS*, 5th
ser., vol. VII (1957). Pardons of this sort are occasionally
reported in the chronicles, e.g. *Eulogium Historiarum*, III, 204;
Knighton, II, 93.

7   G. A. Holmes, *The Estates of the Higher Nobility in Fourteenth-
Century England* (Cambridge, 1957) shows how conspicuous

war service in Scotland and France in the 1330s and 40s was largely instrumental is founding the fortunes of men like William de Bohun (p. 22) and William de Montague (p. 26).

8 Baker, p. 146; *Chroniques de London*, p. 76; Froissart, VI, 186f., 206, XI, 229.

9 Froissart, IV, 381, 386, 391. He emphasizes repeatedly the lack of opposition to the English army: IV, 381, 403, 409f.

10 Froissart, IV, 391, 404, 413; Murimuth, p. 248. See also *Les Grandes Chroniques de France*, ed. J. Viard, 10 vols (Paris, 1920–53), SHF, IX, 270ff.

11 See Walsingham, *Chronicon Angliae*, p. 25; *Historia Anglicana*, I, 270f.; Knighton, II, 32, 46; Froissart, IV, 180, 303f., V, 108ff.; *Acta Bellicosa*, printed as an appendix to J. Moisant, *Le Prince Noir en Aquitaine* (Paris, 1894), pp. 166f.; *Grandes Chroniques*, IX, 265ff., 287f.

12 V, 343ff., 459. See also *Chronicon Angliae*, p. 33; Chandos Herald, ll. 1394ff.

13 Froissart, IV, 390, 423, V, 346f., 459; Baker, p. 114.

14 Murimuth, p. 248; Froissart, IV, 304; Knighton, II, 99f.; *Historia Anglicana*, I, 286. See also Higden, VIII, 340; Knighton, II, 39.

15 The legend is reported by John Malvern, *Continuation of the Polychronicon* in Higden, *Polychronicon*, ed. J. R. Lumby, 9 vols (1865–86), IX, 282f. See also *DNB*.

16 Froissart, V, 469.

17 *Chronicon Angliae*, p. 26.

18 For the confirmation of the Sumptuary Laws and their failure see *Chronicon Angliae*, p. 53; Knighton, II, 298f.; Murimuth, p. 79; *Brut*, p. 293.

19 V, 223. See also Jean de Venette, p. 46.

20 Chandos Herald, ll. 1394ff.; Froissart, V, 452, 455, 458; *Kirkstall Abbey Short Chronicle*, p. 107. See Keen, *The Laws of War*, pt 3, ch. 10; McKisack, p. 247f. For an account of the ransoms gained during the Black Prince's *chevauchée* in Languedoc and Poitou see H. J. Hewitt, *The Black Prince's Expedition of 1355–57*, ch. 7; also D. M. Broome, 'The Ransom of John II, King of France, 1360–70', *Camden Misc.*, 14 (1926). The fortunes to be made as well as the great difficulties of finally realizing them are amply illustrated in an account of the aftermath of the battle of Nájera (1367) by A. Gutiérrez de Velasco, 'Los Ingleses en España (Siglo XIV)', *Estudios de la Edad Media de la Corona de Aragon* (Saragossa, 1950).

21 Knighton, II, 3, 15f.; *Brut*, p. 293f.; McKisack, pp. 162. For the

unpopularity of the taxes raised for the war in 1339–40 see
S. B. Terry, *The Financing of the Hundred Years War 1337–1360*
(1914), p. 56.

22   P. 294.

23   P. 295.

24   See McKisack, pp. 221, 242; Hewitt, *Organization of War*, pp.
169ff.; Nicholson, *Edward III and the Scots*, pp. 113ff.

25   P. 160.

26   Ed. J. Moisant (Paris, 1891). See also the complaints against
purveyors made by the shepherd in *King Edward and the
Shepherd*, ed. W. H. French and C. B. Hale, *Middle English
Metrical Romances*, 2 vols (New York, 1930, repr. 1964), ll.
31ff., 73ff., 146ff.

27   Pp. 86, 163f.

28   Murimuth, p. 244; John of Reading, p. 155; *Historia Anglicana*, I, 298; *Eulogium Historiarum*, III, 230; McKisack, p. 363.

29   Pp. 158, 178ff.

30   Some indication of the extent of the problem may be glimpsed
from Hewitt, pp. 173ff.; Stones, 'The Folvilles of Ashby-
Folville, Leicestershire, and Their Associates in Crime';
J. G. Bellamy, 'The Coterel Gang: an Anatomy of a Band of
Fourteenth-Century Criminals', *EHR*, 79 (1964); H. S.
Lucas, 'John Crabbe, Flemish Pirate, Merchant, and Adven-
turer', *Speculum*, 20 (1945).

31   *Melsa*, II, 380; Minot, I, 91f.

32   P. 78.

33   On this and the war with Scotland generally see Edward
Miller, *War in the North* (Hull, 1960) and Hewitt, *Organization
of War*, pp. 126ff.

34   *Rot. Parl.*, II, 345, III, 30, 42, 69, 80f.

35   *Rot. Parl.*, III, 161, 200, 213, 223, 251. Also III, 80f., 146.

36   *Rot. Parl.*, II, 345, III, 146.

37   *Rot. Parl.*, III, 138, 146.

38   See Hewitt, *Organization of War*, ch. 1.

39   A typical raid is described in an eye-witness account of the
expedition mounted by Pedro Niño, count of Buelna, and
Charles of Savoy at the turn of the century. It is written by
Gutierre Díez de Games who was Niño's standard-bearer.
See *El Victorial, Crónica de Don Pero Niño*, ed. J. de Mata
Carriazo (Madrid, 1940), pp. 193ff.

40   See Perroy, p. 190f.; J. J. N. Palmer, *England, France and
Christendom*, ch. 4.

41   *Historia Anglicana*, II, 127.

42   *Historia Anglicana*, II, 127, 145f. Also Froissart, XI, 368ff.

43 Knighton, II, 213ff.; *Historia Anglicana*, II, 148.
44 *Historia Anglicana*, I, 446f.
45 *Historia Anglicana*, I, 366f., 373, II, 127f. See also his accounts of the privateering of the men of Hull and Newcastle (I, 435ff.).
46 See Gower, *Mirour de l'Omme*, ll. 25429ff.; *Eulogium Historiarum*, III, 234; Reading, p. 161; Knighton, II, 105; *Anonimalle*, p. 13; *Historia Anglicana*, I, 253, 399, II, 97, 119; Erghome, pp. 147, 161.
47 Murimuth, p. 54 and again p. 56; Minot, III, 48; Knighton, II, 35. On the invasion plans of 1339 see *Rot. Parl.*, II, 158; Murimuth, pp. 205ff.; Avesbury, pp. 363ff.; Hewitt, *Organization of War*, p. 164.
48 P. 295. Similar tales were repeated under the years 1341 and 1343 in *Chronicon Angliae*, p. 12 and *Melsa*, III, 51f. where the necromancy is variously ascribed to Philip and his queen.
49 Knighton, I, 451f.; Minot, III, 53ff.
50 Baker, p. 58; *Lanercost*, p. 293.
51 *Chroniques de London*, pp. 91, 92, 71f.; Minot, VII, 91f., 139f. See also Minot, IV, 55ff., VI, 19ff.; *Historia Anglicana*, I, 269; *An Invective Against France*, p. 28.
52 *Chroniques de London*, pp. 71f.; Baker, p. 111; Erghome, p. 168.
53 *Melsa*, III, 45; Erghome, p. 177. The French joke is an old one; see P. Rickard, *Britain in Medieval French Literature, 1100–1500* (Cambridge, 1956), pp. 165f.
54 Ed. Wright, *Pol. Poems and Songs*, I, 91ff. and entitled by him *Dispute between the Englishman and the Frenchman*.
55 Pp. 91–3.
56 P. 26.
57 XI, 6. The anonymous continuator of Reading's chronicle is exceptional in his sympathetic account of King John's death in 1364 (pp. 215ff.).
58 Knighton, II, 109; *Chronicon Angliae*, pp. 40f.
59 *Historia Anglicana*, II, 81f., 107, 120.
60 Knighton, II, 119f.; *Anonimalle*, pp. 58f.; *Historia Anglicana*, I, 306f., 318; Brinton, p. 54.
61 Knighton, I, 452; Miller, pp. 6f.
62 See e.g. *Brut*, p. 256; Avesbury, pp. 286ff. The *Brut* bases England's claim to overlordship on Brutus's supposed conquest of Scotland; Avesbury (who claims to have culled his evidence from 'ancient chronicles') goes back to biblical times and makes Arthur one of the 'English' kings who have ruled over Scotland.
63 Higden, I, 386ff.; Froissart, X, 402, V, 120. See also X, 335f.

Minot makes the distinction between 'wild Scottes and . . .
tame' (1, 60) meaning highlanders and English-speaking low-
landers respectively.
64 Froissart, III, 444; Knighton, II, 308f. See also the poem from
MS Harley 4843 printed as an appendix to Hall's edition of
Minot, ll. 37ff.; *Melsa*, III, 61; *Lanercost*, pp. 344ff.
65 Murimuth, p. 68; Minot, I, 63f.; *Gesta Edwardi*, p. 127f.; *The
Battle of Neville's Cross*, ed. Wright, *Pol. Poems*, I, 42.
66 *Of Prelates* in John Wyclif, *The English Works*, ed. F. D.
Matthew (1880), EETS OS 74, p. 99; *Morte Arthure*, ed. E.
Brock (1871, repr. 1961), EETS OS 8, l. 32. See also *Rot.
Parl.*, III, 354; Murimuth, p. 67; Knighton, I, 475; *Historia
Anglicana*, I, 446; Reading, p. 180; *Melsa*, II, 379; Minot, II,
where each stanza ends with a warning against the guile of the
Scots.
67 *Historia Anglicana*, I, 387, 446; *Brut*, p. 191; *Lanercost*, p. 344;
Reading, p. 180; Minot, II, 19f.; MS Harley 4843, l. 15.
68 *Lanercost*, p. 346; Erghome, p. 143. See also *Melsa*, II, 361;
The Battle of Neville's Cross, l. 46f. On his sexual excess see
Melsa, II, 361; Erghome, p. 143.
69 See e.g. *Historia Anglicana*, I, 269f.; *Anonimalle*, pp. 27f.;
Minot, IX, 49ff.; MS Harley 4843, ll. 201ff. Also Nicholson,
Edward III and the Scots, pp. 235f.
70 See G. Mollat, *Les Papes d'Avignon (1305–1378)* (Paris, 1964),
pp. 424ff.; McKisack, pp. 272ff.
71 See e.g. *Winner and Waster*, ed. I. Gollancz (1930), ll. 143ff.,
156ff., 169ff.; *Piers Plowman B-Text*, ed. W. W. Skeat (1869,
repr. 1950), EETS OS 38, passus 19, 407ff.; Gower, *Mirour de
l'Omme*, ll. 7357ff., 18433ff., 18517ff., 18577ff., 18895ff.
72 See Perroy, pp. 90ff., 115ff., 129f., 166ff., and his 'Franco–
English Relations, 1350–1400', *History*, 21 (1936), pp. 148f.
73 See Knighton, II, 28f., 31; Murimuth, p. 138; *Historia
Anglicana*, I, 452.
74 Knighton, II, 98; Murimuth, p. 173ff. The belief was firmly
established amongst the Wyclifites in the 1370s and 80s. See
Of the Leaven of the Pharisees, pp. 22f.; *Of Prelates*, pp. 66, 92;
The Office of Curates, p. 144, all ed. F. D. Matthew, *The
English Works of John Wyclif*. See also Mollat, *Les Papes d'Avignon*, p. 432.
75 P. 175.
76 Knighton, II, 28f.; Erghome, pp. 155; Murimuth, p. 162f. See
also Murimuth, p. 148; Erghome, pp. 151, 164f.; *Anonimalle*,
p. 39; Froissart, VIII, 55; Mollat, *Les Papes d'Avignon*, p. 432f.
77 See Mollat, *Les Papes d'Avignon*, p. 90.

78 See *Historia Anglicana*, I, 1271; *Melsa*, III, 56; *Lanercost*, p. 335; *Brut*, pp. 304f.; Avesbury, p. 424.

79 See Hewitt, *The Black Prince's Expedition*, pp. 110ff.

80 *Eulogium Historiarum*, III, 223; Froissart, V, 441. See also Lettenhove's comments in XXI, 119.

81 Chandos Herald, ll. 773ff., 922ff.; Sir Thomas Gray, *Scalacronica*, ed. J. Stevenson (Edinburgh, 1836), p. 174. The author of *Chronique Normande du XIVe Siècle*, ed. A. and É. Molinier (Paris, 1882), SHF, p. 113, believed that the Black Prince used Talleyrand in an attempt to persuade John to grant a truce.

82 *Anonimalle*, p. 39. See also Knighton, II, 94; Erghome, pp. 164f.

83 Ll. 18697ff. See also *Anonimalle*, p. 70, where the chronicler expresses doubts about the motives of Cardinal Langham's visit to England in 1371.

84 P. 54.

Chapter 3   Aristocracy, Knighthood and Chivalry

1 Raimundo Lullio, *Libro del Orden de Caballería*, Spanish trans. (Buenos Aires, 1949). References are to this edition. It was translated in the fifteenth century by Caxton from an expanded French version of the original. See *The Book of the Ordre of Chyualry*, ed. A. T. P. Byles (1926), EETS OS 168.

2 R. L. Kilgour, *The Decline of Chivalry as Shown in the French Literature of the Late Middle Ages* (Cambridge, Mass., 1937), p. 8. See also p. 4.

3 Hewitt, *Organization of War*, pp. 131f. Hewitt makes a distinction between battle and war. Only in battle is the chivalric ideal given the opportunity of expressing itself in action. In war (the major form of conflict in the fourteenth century) the brutality and mercenary motives common to the *chevauchée* predominate. Battles were few and of short duration, while war was 'military pressure exerted day after day for weeks or months' (pp. 135f.).

4 Kilgour, p. 66. See also Hewitt's adverse comments on the military value of the Order of the Star, *Black Prince's Expedition*, pp. 96f. Huizinga, while recognizing the importance of chivalric ideas, feels that their influence on politics was an adverse one. See *The Waning of the Middle Ages*, Eng. trans. (1924, repr. 1952), p. 82. See also F. J. C. Hearnshaw, 'Chivalry and its Place in History', *Chivalry*, ed. E. Prestage (1928), p. 25.

o

5   Hewitt, *Organization of War*, p. 135; Huizinga, pp. 69, 84; Kilgour, pp. 4, 8, 66. This attitude now seems to be accepted as axiomatic. See e.g. the statements by K. Fowler and M. Powicke in *The Hundred Years War*, ed. Fowler, pp. 7f., 122ff.

6   See S. Runciman, *A History of the Crusades*, 3 vols (Cambridge, 1951), I, 83ff. Also E. R. Curtius, *European Literature and the Latin Middle Ages*, Eng. trans. (New York, 1953), p. 536.

7   See Runciman, I, passim.

8   Sidney Painter is one of the few historians of chivalry to question the validity of using the ideal of religious chivalry as a yardstick in judging the behaviour of knights at any period. See *French Chivalry* (Baltimore, 1940), p. 92.

9   See e.g. Fowler, *The King's Lieutenant* (1969).

10   *Les Voeux du Héron*, ed. Wright, *Pol. Poems and Songs*, I, 15f.; Wyntoun, VI, B.8, ll. 5134ff. See also B. J. Whiting, 'The Vows of the Heron', *Speculum*, 20 (1945), p. 271.

11   VI, B.8, l. 5133. See also ll. 5226ff.

12   Erghome, p. 163; J. Capgrave, *Liber de Illustribus Henricis*, ed. F. C. Hingeston (1858), p. 162. On contemporary justification for the sacking of cities taken by storm see M. H. Keen, *The Laws of War in the Late Middle Ages* (1965), pp. 121ff. Froissart reports that Henry's threat to put all to the sword at Monségur in 1345 was enough to cause the citizens to imprison their garrison commander and surrender (IV, 279). That Henry was in earnest is shown by his sack of Poitiers, when men, women and children were slaughtered.

13   *Chronicon Angliae*, p. 19; Christine de Pisan, *The Book of Fayttes of Armes and of Chyualrye*, Caxton's trans. ed. A. T. P. Byles (1936), EETS OS 189, p. 77; Capgrave, p. 161.

14   Fowler, *The King's Lieutenant*, pp. 136f.; Knighton, II, 78f.; Froissart, IV, 240.

15   Capgrave, pp. 161, 163; Knighton, II, 115f.; Fowler, *The King's Lieutenant*, pp. 187ff.

16   Capgrave, p. 163; Hoccleve, *The Regement of Princes*, ed. F. J. Furnivall (1897), EETS ES 72, ll. 2647ff.

17   *Le Livre de Seyntz Medicines*, ed. E. J. Arnould (Oxford, 1940), ANTS 2, pp. 240f. See also Fowler, *The King's Lieutenant*, pp. 193ff.

18   *Scalacronica*, p. 200.

19   *Livre*, pp. 10, 13, 47, 48, 49, 76.

20   *Livre*, pp. 21f., 22, 69, 77, 179.

21 *Livre*, p. 27.
22 *Livre*, pp. 16, 66f. See also pp. 24, 71ff.
23 *Livre*, pp. 72f. See also J. Pitt-Rivers, 'Honour and Social Status', in *Honour and Shame* ed. J. G. Peristiany (1965), pp. 21ff.
24 *Livre*, pp. 17, 67.
25 See G. R. Owst, *Literature and Pulpit in Medieval England* (Oxford, 1961), pp. 77ff.
26 *Livre*, pp. 65, 71, 81, 82f.
27 *Livre*, pp. 18f., 43ff., 68.
28 *Livre*, pp. 44, 61.
29 E.g. Froissart's account of the colourful career of Eustace d'Aubrecicourt (VI, 154).
30 See R. Cline, 'The Influence of Romances on Tournaments of the Middle Ages', *Speculum*, 20 (1945); R. S. Loomis, 'Chivalric and Dramatic Imitations of Arthurian Romance', *Medieval Studies in Memory of A. Kingsley Porter*, ed. W. R. W. Koehler, 2 vols (Cambridge, Mass., 1939) and his 'Edward I, Arthurian Enthusiast', *Speculum*, 28 (1953).
31 See Huizinga, *Waning of the Middle Ages*, ch. 9. A. Borst argues that there was no 'general, binding ideal of chivalry' in the later Middle Ages. He sees the troubadour ideal as a 'pleasing game' and little else ('Knighthood in the High Middle Ages: Ideal and Reality' in *Lordship and Community in Medieval Europe*, ed. F. R. Cheyette (New York, 1968), pp. 183, 185).
32 Murimuth, pp. 155f., 232; Froissart, IV, 204. See also N. Harris Nicolas, *History of the Orders of Knighthood of the British Empire*, 4 vols (1842), I, 8ff.; Cline, p. 207; Loomis, 'Chivalric and Dramatic Imitations of Arthurian Romance', p. 82. The 'round table' at Windsor caused a great stir and is widely reported by the English chroniclers: *Anonimalle* p. 18; *Historia Anglicana*, I, 263; Murimuth, pp. 155f.; *Melsa*, III, 52; *Lanercost*, p. 341.
33 M. McKisack, 'Edward III and the Historians', *History*, 45 (1960), pp. 7f. See also A. B. Ferguson, *The Indian Summer of English Chivalry* (Durham, N. Carolina, 1960), pp. 128f.; M. Bloch, *Feudal Society*, Eng. trans. (1962), p. 449: ' . . . in a society which continued to be beset with many disorders, the needs which had given rise to the ancient practice of companionage, and then to vassalage, had not ceased to be felt. Among the various reasons which led to the creation of the orders of chivalry which were founded in such great numbers in the fourteenth and fifteenth centuries, one of the

most decisive was undoubtedly the desire of princes to attach to themselves a group of highly-placed retainers by an especially compelling bond.'

34   Discussion is based on Bonet, *L'Arbre des Batailles*, ed. N. Nys (Brussels, 1883). It has been translated and edited by G. W. Coopland (Liverpool, 1949). Quotations are from Coopland's translation with page references to the edition of Nys. The introduction to Coopland's edition contains an important discussion of Bonet's sources and the significance of his personal contribution. Caxton's translation of Christine's book has been used throughout: *The Book of Fayttes of Armes and of Chyualrye*, ed. A. T. P. Byles (1936), EETS OS 189. Bonet is heavily indebted to the *De Bello, de Represaliis et de Duello* of John of Legnano. Christine draws on Bonet, the *Strategemata* of Frontinus, and the *Epitoma Rei Militaris* of Vegetius. In Book II she also uses the 'counseyll of the wyse knyghtes that be expert in the sayde thynges of armes'. Who they were it is unfortunately impossible to say since 'it pleaseth not to theyre humylyte to be aledged nor named' (p. 153). Keen, *The Laws of War* is an indispensable secondary source.

35   See Bonet, pp. 41ff., 80ff., 83ff., 105ff., 126ff.; Christine, pp. 9ff., 20ff., 104ff., 189ff., 199ff., 218ff., 284ff.

36   See e.g. Gower, *Mirour de l'Omme*, ll. 23893ff., 24013ff.; *Vox Clamantis*, V, 535ff., VII, 263ff.

37   Pp. 139f. See also Christine, pp. 223ff. The payment of wages is similarly discussed without any sense that it is contrary to chivalry: Bonet, pp. 126ff.; Christine, pp. 199ff.

38   Pp. 80, 153. See also Bonet, pp. 94, 138.

39   See also Bonet, pp. 75ff., 95f.

40   Pp. 18f., 128f.

41   One of the few scholars to suggest this is Curtius, *European Literature and the Latin Middle Ages*, p. 535.

42   Hewitt, *Organization of War*, pp. 131ff.; Huizinga, *Waning of the Middle Ages*, p. 57. For a view much closer to my own see McKisack, pp. 249ff.

43   Froissart, IV, 412, 413, 416f., 417f. Chandos is said by Froissart to have saved the daughters of the comte de Poix 'pour la cause de gentillèce' from some archers who would otherwise have raped them (IV, 433). *Les Grandes Chroniques de France*, IX, 262, comments on the difficulties of punishing malefactors after the siege of La Roche Derrien in 1345. See also Hewitt *Organization of War*, pp. 93ff., 120ff.; K. Fowler, 'Les Finances et la Discipline dans les Armées Anglaises en

France au XIVe Siècle', *Les Cahiers Vernonnais*, 4 (Caen, 1964), pp. 74f., 77.

44 For a common modern response see M. Powicke, 'The English Aristocracy and the War', *The Hundred Years War*, ed. Fowler, pp. 126ff. Professor Powicke's attitude is both unsympathetic and, it may be argued, somewhat anachronistic. On William Marshal see S. Painter, *William Marshal, Knight-Errant, Baron, and Regent of England* (Baltimore, 1933, repr. 1967), passim.

45 *Quatre Premiers Valois*, p. 241.

46 Jean de Venette, p. 92. This is confirmed by the *Chronique Normande du XIVe Siècle*, p. 147f. See also the disdain of the French knights for their Genoese archers at Crécy (Froissart, v, 49); and the statement by Cuvelier that the English knights on the Black Prince's expedition to Spain were eager for chivalric encounters 'without foot-soldiers and bourgeois' (*Chronique de Bertrand du Guesclin*, I, 11072–6). A classic encounter of this kind is described in *La Bataille de Trente Anglois et de Trente Bretons*, ed. H. R. Brush, 2 pts, *MP*, 9, 10 (1911–13). The difference in attitude between the French aristocracy and the common soldier is admirably illustrated in Philippe Contamine, *Guerre, État et Société à la Fin du Moyen Âge* (Paris, 1972), ch. 7, 'Service du Roy et Conception de la Guerre', esp. pp. 185f., 193.

47 v, 444. See also his judgement of the battle of Otterburn in 1388 (XIII, 214ff.).

48 Chandos Herald, ll. 984ff.; Froissart, v, 185, VI, 222, X, 249. Also Chandos Herald, ll. 1055ff., 602ff., 2592ff., 3013ff.; Froissart, III, 43, V, 409, VII, 198f., VIII, 139; *Quatre Premiers Valois*, pp. 15, 179; Cuvelier, *Chronique de Bertrand du Guesclin*, I, 10752ff., 10985f., 11023ff.

49 v, 417f. Froissart describes the way in which the French nobles vied with one another in painting and fitting out their vessels in preparation for the invasion of England in 1386 (XI, 367).

50 *Quatre Premiers Valois*, p. 54; Froissart, VII, 218. See also Chandos Herald, ll. 3262ff., 305f., 984ff., 1055ff., 1180f., 1222ff., 3262ff., 3335ff., 3390ff., 3445ff.

51 *Le Livre Messire Geoffroi de Charny*, selections ed. A. Piaget, *Romania*, 26 (Paris, 1897).

52 See Piaget, ed., p. 394f.; R. Barber, *The Knight and Chivalry* (1970), pp. 146f.; Philippe Contamine, *Guerre, État et Société à la Fin du Moyen Âge*, pp. 184ff.

53 Pp. 401f. Exactly the same attitude is taken by Gutierre Díez

de Games in *El Victorial*, pp. 42f., and with satiric intent in the anti-English poem, *Les Voeux du Héron*, p. 21.

54 'Honour and Social Status', p. 21.

55 'Honour and Social Status', p. 29.

56 VI, 943ff.

57 Bertrand du Guesclin was similarly admired. According to Cuvelier his name was used by nurses in France to scare little children into keeping quiet (*Chronique de Bertrand du Guesclin*, I, 44–6).

58 Knighton, II, 124f.; *Chronicon Angliae*, p. 91; Froissart, v, 454. See also Baker, p. 151; *Kirkstall Abbey Short Chronicle*, p. 108; John of Reading, p. 123; *Brut*, p. 330; *Chronicon Angliae*, pp. 88, 91; *On the Death of Edward III*, ed. Wright, *Pol. Poems and Songs*, p. 220; Brinton, p. 355.

59 See rubric, p. 257.

60 Baker, p. 133; Froissart, VII, 292.

61 E.g. G. P. R. James, *A History of the Life of Edward the Black Prince*, 2 vols (1836), II, 470f.; McKisack, p. 145; P. Shaw, 'The Black Prince', *History*, 24 (1939), p. 10; Armitage-Smith, *John of Gaunt*, pp. 81ff.; Kilgour, p. 66f.

62 For a detailed account of events see Armitage-Smith, pp. 80ff.

63 VIII, 41f. I quote from the translation of G. Brereton in Froissart, *Chronicles* (Penguin, 1968), p. 178.

64 In 1346 Caen was sacked by Edward III and Poitiers by Henry of Grosmont with equal brutality. See A. H. Burne, *The Crécy War* (1955), pp. 126, 147; Hewitt, *Organization of War*, pp. 120ff.; Froissart, III, 444, IV, 180, v, 5.

65 *Chronicon Angliae*, p. 67. See also *Brut*, pp. 323f.

66 See Keen, *Laws of War*, pp. 119ff.

67 *Chronicon Angliae*, p. 67; Chandos Herald, ll. 4049ff.

68 See e.g. Kilgour, pp. 66f.

69 *A Chronicle of the Kings of England* (1643), p. Y^v.

70 The point about the collective responsibility of honour is important. See Pitt-Rivers, 'Honour and Social Status', pp. 35ff.; and Julio Caro Baroja, 'Honour and Shame: A Historical Account of Several Conflicts', pp. 89ff. both in *Honour and Shame*, ed. Peristiany. Caro Baroja is concerned with collective honour within kinship networks in medieval Spain, but his observations are apposite to feudal relations too.

71 Froissart, VII, 246; Cuvelier, II, 13378ff.

72 Froissart, VII, 245; Cuvelier, II, 13654. See also Delachenal, *Histoire de Charles V*, III, 451ff. On the importance of the

concept of the 'word of honour' see Pitt-Rivers, pp. 34f., and Keen, *Laws of War*, p. 242.

73 v, 463. See also Chandos Herald, ll, 1411ff.

74 D. M. Broome, 'The Ransom of John II, King of France, 1360–1370', p. xxiv.

75 Kilgour, p. 4.

76 See Huizinga, *Waning of the Middle Ages*, pp. 31ff.

77 v, 463. On Edward's courtesy towards noble prisoners captured at the battle of Nájera, see Froissart, vii, 221f.; Chandos Herald, ll. 3521ff.; Russell, *English Intervention in Spain and Portugal*, pp. 105f.

78 Froissart, viii, 42f.

79 *Quatre Premiers Valois*, pp. 143, 257; Jean de Venette, pp. 119f.; Froissart, viii, 381.

80 Froissart, v, 77. The blind king deliberately sought death in battle rather than flight, whatever the consequences for his kingdom. It is yet another example of the relentless pursuit of personal honour. See *Une Poème Tchèque sur la Bataille de Crécy*, ed. and trans. L. Leger, *Journal des Savants* (Paris, 1902), pp. 323ff.

81 Froissart, vii, 458ff. There is interesting corroboration of Froissart in *Chronicon Angliae*, p. 68.

82 Harris Nicolas, *History of the Orders of Knighthood of the British Empire*, i, 27f.

83 Froissart, iv, 213f.; Harris Nicolas, i, 32ff.

84 John of Reading, p. 152; *Eulogium Historiarum*, iii, 227; Knighton, ii, 98f. See also *Chroniques de London*, p. 62; Murimuth, pp. 63, 123f., 146, 159; Avesbury, 285f.

85 Murimuth, p. 123; John of Reading, p. 131f.

86 *Melsa*, iii, 49, 52, 69; Knighton, ii, 57f.; *Anonimalle*, p. 18; *Lanercost*, p. 341.

87 Baker, pp. 112ff.; John of Reading, p. 112.

88 Froissart, viii, 381; Chandos Herald, ll. 938ff.; Pedro Lopez de Ayala, *Crónicas de los Reyes de Castilla*, ed. E. de Llaguno Amirola, 2 vols (Madrid, 1779–80), i, 443. See also Ayala, i, 442; Cuvelier, i, 1065ff.; Jean de Venette, pp. 38, 109, 138 for admiring comments on English knights.

89 *Quatre Premiers Valois*, p. 173; Chandos Herald, ll. 1966ff.; A. Gutiérrez de Velasco, 'Los Ingleses en España (Siglo xiv)', p. 221.

90 The most infamous example of this in the fourteenth century was the Norwich Crusade of 1383. For the decline of the ideal in the later Middle Ages see Runciman, *History of the Crusades*, iii, 469ff.

91   The lull in the war after the Treaty of Bretigny led to a number of crusades. English and Gascon soldiers fought under the king of Cyprus at Alexandria in 1365 and Thomas Beauchamp, earl of Warwick, led an expedition against the pagan Lithuanians (*Chronicon Angliae*, p. 56; John of Reading, p. 172.)

92   *Chronicon Angliae*, p. 56; *Historia Anglicana*, I, 304.

93   Froissart, VII, 145.

94   *Chronicon Angliae*, p. 56.

95   Froissart, VII, 420.

96   Froissart, VI, 371ff.; Murimuth, pp. 73, 78; Knighton, I, 476; *Anonimalle*, p. 12.

97   *Laws of War*, p. 242.

98   P. 242f.

99   Froissart, IV, 433, V, 417, VII, 459.

100   V, 436, 447, 454, VII, 215.

101   VII, 39. Chandos was less successful with the earl of Pembroke who refused to serve under him in 1369 because it was beneath his dignity to take orders from a simple knight. Pembroke made a *chevauchée* of his own, was captured, and suffered the indignity of being rescued by Chandos (Froissart, VII, 389ff.) See Contamine, *Guerre, État et Société*, pp. 196f., and more generally, ch. 7. He stresses the individualistic attitude to war of the French nobility.

102   Chandos Herald, ll. 2725ff. Sir Walter Manny was another prominent captain in Edward's allegiance who was well known for his chivalric foolhardiness (see Froissart, II, 489, IV, 46).

103   His appointment as one of seven men commissioned to supervise the transfer of French territory in Gascony to Edward III after the Treaty of Bretigny was a signal mark of favour (Froissart, VI, 326; Hewitt, *Organization of War*, pp. 143f.).

104   Je Jehan Chandault, des anglois capitaine,
                    Fort chevalier, de Poictou sénéschal
                    Après avoir fait guerre tres lointaine
                    Au rois francois, tant à pied qu'â cheval
                    Et pris Bertrand de Guesclin en un val,
                    Les Poitevins prés Lussac, me diffirent,
                    A Mortemer, mon corps enterrer firent,
                    En un cercueil elevé tout de neuf,
                    L'an mil trois cens avec seixante neuf.

      (Quoted in Froissart, *Chronicles*, trans. T. Johnes, 12 vols (1808), IV, 50n).

105 Froissart, VI, 326.
106 *DNB.*
107 It is discussed briefly by M. D. Legge, *Anglo-Norman Literature and its Background* (Oxford, 1963), pp. 283ff.
108 *Scalacronica*, pp. 190f. Gray's objectivity in his account of Cardinal Talleyrand's attempt to negotiate a truce before Poitiers has already been discussed. See *Scalacronica*, p. 174.
109 *Scalacronica*, pp. 180, 190, 192.
110 *Scalacronica*, pp. 145f. My italics.
111 'Honour and Social Status', p. 39.
112 Ll. 1623ff.

Chapter 4   Patriots and Patriotism

1 No distinction is made between nationalism and patriotism in this chapter. For a discussion of the concepts with relation to the Middle Ages see E. H. Kantorowicz, 'Pro Patria Mori in Medieval Political Thought', *AHR*, 56 (1951), pp. 474ff.; J. Huizinga, 'Patriotism and Nationalism in European History' in *Men and Ideas*, Eng. trans. (1960), p. 97; V. H. Galbraith, 'Nationality and Language in Medieval England', *TRHS*, 4th ser. 23 (1941), p. 113.
2 See P. S. Lewis, 'War Propaganda and Historiography in Fifteenth-Century France and England', *TRHS*, 5th ser., 15 (1965), p. 21; Hewitt, *Organization of War*, p. 177. The conscious articulation of patriotic sentiment in the fifteenth century emerges clearly in V. J. Scattergood, *Politics and Poetry in the Fifteenth Century* (1971), esp. chs 1–6.
3 H. J. Chaytor, *From Script to Print* (1945, repr. 1966), p. 22. See more generally his important chapter, 'Language and Nationality', pp. 22–47.
4 XV, 167. Edward III seems nevertheless to have spoken English. See O. F. Emerson, 'English or French in the Time of Edward III?', *Rom. Rev.*, 7 (1916), pp. 130ff.; M. D. Legge, 'Anglo-Norman and the Historian', *History*, 26 (1941–2), p. 169. Miss Legge suggests that Richard II was probably the first king since the Conquest to have English as his mother tongue (p. 170). R. M. Wilson has calculated that with the possible exception of Henry I and II, English kings before Edward I could neither speak nor understand English with any degree of fluency. See 'English and French in England, 1100–1300', *History*, 28 (1943), pp. 44f.
5 *Chronicon Angliae*, p. 52. See also *Eulogium Historiarum*, III, 230; *Chronica Johannis de Reading et Anonymi Cantuariensis*, p.

214. On the ineffectiveness of the Act see M. D. Legge, 'Anglo-Norman and the Historian', p. 167.

6   See M. K. Pope and E. C. Lodge, *The Life of the Black Prince*, intro. pp. xxix, xxxi; *Un traitié selonc les auctours pour essampler les amantz marietz*, XVIII, 4.

7   *Livre de Seyntz Medicines*, p. 239.

8   II, 419. This statement is given support by the conclusions of W. Rothwell, 'The Teaching of French in Medieval England', *MLR*, 63 (1968), passim. Rothwell's examination of a number of teaching manuals leads him to the conclusion that French was already an acquired language by the late thirteenth century.

9   William of Palerne, ed. W. W. Skeat (1867), EETS ES 1, ll. 161ff., 5521ff., 5533; *The Gest Hystoriale of the Destruction of Troy*, ed. G. A. Panton and D. Donaldson, 2 vols (1869–74), EETS OS 39, 56, pp. vi ff.; Higden, *Polychronicon*, VIII, 352; D. Mehl, *The Middle English Romances of the Thirteenth and Fourteenth Centuries* (1968), p. 247; Holmes, *Estates of the Higher Nobility*, p. 20f.; M. V. Clarke, *Fourteenth-Century Studies* (Oxford, 1937), pp. 120f.

10 Higden, II, 161.

11 Froissart, XV, 114f.

12 See P. Rickard, *Britain in Medieval French Literature*, pp. 170ff.

13 Chaucer, *Canterbury Tales*, prologue, ll. 124ff. All references to Chaucer are to *Complete Works*, ed. F. N. Robinson, 2nd edn (1957); *Piers Plowman*, B-Text, V, 239.

14 See e.g. Robert Manning, *Handlyng Synne*, ed. F. J. Furnivall, 2 vols (1901–3), EETS OS 119, 123, ll. 41ff.; Dan Michel, *Ayenbite of Inwyt*, ed. R. Morris, rev. P. Gradon (1965), EETS OS 23, p. 5.

15 *Troilus and Criseyde*, V, 1793ff.; *Parson's Prologue*, ll. 42ff.; Higden, II, 158ff. See also Chaytor, *From Script to Print*, pp. 30ff.

16 See Goodman, *The Loyal Conspiracy*, p. 139; Holmes, *Estates of the Higher Nobility*, p. 20.

17 *Cursor Mundi*, ed. R. Morris, 6 vols (1874–93), EETS, ll. 231ff., 241ff.

18 *Rot. Parl.*, II, 147, my italics. See also II, 158; Knighton, II, 280; Rickard, *Britain in Medieval French Literature*, p. 40.

19 See Scattergood, *Politics and Poetry in the Fifteenth Century*, esp. pp. 41ff.

20 V. H. Galbraith, 'Nationality and Language in Medieval England', *TRHS* 4th ser. 23(1941), pp. 22f.

21 *Rot. Parl.*, II, 362.

22 See e.g. *Historia Anglicana*, I, 372, 397ff.; Knighton, II, 18; *Chronicon Anonymi Cantuariensis*, p. 218; Erghome, p. 158.

23 The idea is also expressed by Erghome, pp. 195ff. 204ff. It is implicit in several of Brinton's sermons, e.g. pp. 61f., 216; and is the theme of the macaronic poem, *On the Times*, ed. Wright, *Pol. Poems and Songs*.

24 *The Romance and Prophecies of Thomas of Erceldoune*, ed. J. A. H. Murray (1875), EETS OS 61, ll. 23f.; also ll. 13f.; Minot, III, 125f.; also I, 11f., IV, 43ff.

25 *Acta Bellicosa*, p. 159; Wyntoun, VI, B.8, ll. 6595ff.; Baker, *Chronicle of the Kings of England*, p. Y6ᵛ. Baker is reiterating a commonplace of the fifteenth century on. See Lydgate, *The Fall of Princes*, IX, 3150ff.; Hoccleve, *The Regement of Princes*, ed. F. J. Furnivall (1897), EETS ES 72, ll. 869ff.; Caxton, *The Book of the Ordre of Chyualry*, p. 123.

26 Knighton, II, 35; *Eulogium Historiarum*, III, 211; Avesbury, p. 428; *Kirkstall Abbey Long Chronicle*, p. 96. See also Knighton, II, 102f.

27 Ayala, p. 444; Froissart, VII, 183, XII, 133. See also Chandos Herald, ll. 2973ff.; Cuvelier, I, 10976ff., 11370ff. The author of the *Quatre Premiers Valois* continually praises the prowess and military experience of Edward III and his armies, e.g. pp. 114, 201, 204, 215, 242.

28 Chandos Herald, ll. 2794ff., 3378f.; Froissart, II, 21; *The Battle of Nevilles Cross*, ed. Wright, *Pol. Poems and Songs*, I, 45. The Lanercost chronicler speaks highly of Percy and compares him to Judas Maccabeus (p. 350). See also Froissart, V, 293f.; Chandos Herald, ll. 161ff.

29 Knighton, II, 42; *Lanercost*, p. 350f.; *Pol. Poems and Songs*, I, 45f. See also Baker, p. 146.

30 A similar identification of chivalry with patriotism is made with reference to Poitiers by Reading, p. 126. He is echoed by the *Brut*, p. 308.

31 Knighton, II, 72. For a circumstantial account of the duel see Fowler, *The King's Lieutenant*, pp. 106ff.

32 *Historia Anglicana*, II, 127f.

33 *Canterbury Tales*, prologue, ll. 398ff.; *El Victorial*, p. 206.

34 *Anonimalle*, p. 136. On the concept and organization of the garde de la mer, see Hewitt, *Organization of War*, pp. 9ff., and 'The Organization of War', in *The Hundred Years War*, ed. Fowler, p. 77.

35 P. 135. See also *Historia Anglicana*, I, 288. Minot says of the men of Durham and Carlisle in 1346 that they would never cease 'the wirschip of Ingland with wappen to win' (IX, 31f.).

36 See Sylvia Thrupp, *The Merchant Class of Medieval London* (Ann Arbor, 1948, repr. 1962), p. 360.

37 *Chronicon Angliae*, pp. 198ff.; *Historia Anglicana*, I, 370; McKisack, p. 403. See also C. F. Richmond, 'The War at Sea', in *The Hundred Years War*, ed. Fowler, p. 110.

38 *Historia Anglicana*, I, 371, II, 115. The Abbot of Battle (d. 1382) provides a clerical parallel to Philipot. He was active in the defence of Winchelsea during the raids of 1377 and was something of a local hero. See *Chronicon Angliae*, p. 167; John of Malvern, IX, 17.

39 *Vox Clamantis*, VII, 1289ff. Similar sentiments are scattered throughout Gower's works although nowhere are they expressed with such evident emotion. See *Vox Clamantis*, I, 1963ff., VII, 1367ff.; *Cronica Tripertita*, III, 77ff.

40 *Vox Clamantis*, I, 1963ff.

41 Baker, *Chronicle of the Kings of England*, p. Y6^v; Joshua Barnes, *The History of that Most Victorious Monarch Edward III* (Cambridge, 1688), p. 5Z$_4$^{r}.

42 J. Mackinnon, *The History of Edward III* (1900). Professor McKisack's sympathetic reassessment of Edward is exceptional. See *The Fourteenth Century*, pp. 270f., and 'Edward III and the Historians', passim.

43 *The History of Edward III*, pp. 606f.

44 Chandos Herald, ll. 1513ff.; *Eulogium Historiarum*, III, 233; Froissart, VIII, 389. See also Chandos Herald, ll. 1837ff.; *Invective Against France*, pp. 30f. Such romantic associations may explain the curious anecdote concerning Edward's love for the countess of Salisbury. In his first account of the affair Froissart ascribed to the king all the passions and conflicts associated with the literary conventions of *fine amour* (III, 455 ff., 467). It is probable that the story was invented and attributed to Edward because of its appropriateness in one who lived the noble life so ostentatiously. Later, after extensive enquiries in England, Froissart rejected the tale as untrue (IV, 273). The author of the *Chronique Normande* ungenerously says that Edward raped the countess (pp. 54, 59f.).

45 See Knighton, II, 57f.; Erghome, p. 150; *Melsa*, III, 49, 52; *Anonimalle*, p. 18.

46 *Quatre Premiers Valois*, p. 114; Knighton, II, 55. See also *Quatre Premiers Valois*, pp. 24, 31, 201; Froissart, II, 99; Chandos Herald, ll. 57f.; Erghome, p. 139.

47 V, 34. See also Minot, V, 77ff.; *Quatre Premiers Valois*, p. 106.

48 Froissart, III, 197. See also Baker, p. 106; Avesbury, p. 410; Higden, VIII, 340ff.

49 E.g. *Rot. Parl.*, II, 103, 117.
50 *Rot. Parl.*, II, 361ff.
51 *Melsa*, III, 45. This coin was not in fact struck until four years after the battle in 1344. The image has been variously interpreted. Sir J. E. Evans, 'The First Gold Coins of England', *The Numismatic Chronicle*, 20 (1900), pp. 245–8, expressed doubt as to the striking of the coin being connected with Sluys. But W. J. W. Potter, 'The Gold Coinages of Edward III, pt I The Early and Pre-Treaty Coinages', *The Numismatic Chronicle*, 7th ser., vol. III (1963), p. 110f., while seeing the image as being essentially an allegory of the king guiding the ship of state, does definitely regard it as referring back to the victory at Sluys. The noble is reproduced by Potter, plates 8–10; by J. J. North, *English Hammered Coinage* vol. 2, *Edward I – Charles II, 1272–1662* (1960), plate 1; and by G. C. Brooke, *English Coins from the Seventh Century to the Present Day* (1932, 3rd edn 1950), plate xxv, 14.
52 Froissart, v, 34; *Rot. Parl.*, II, 264f., 103.
53 P. 30f. As we have seen, the same concept of war as an enterprise undertaken by the king and his people for their mutual benefit, underlies the Middle English poem, *On the Death of Edward III*.
54 See Curtius, *European Literature and the Latin Middle Ages*, pp. 154ff., 176ff.
55 See Cicero, *De Inventione*, ed. and trans. H. M. Hubbell (1949, repr. 1960), pp. 70ff.; *Rhetorica ad Herennium*, ed. and trans. H. Caplan (1954, repr. 1964), pp. 172ff. On their influence in the Middle Ages see Curtius, p. 66; R. R. Bolgar, *The Classical Heritage* (1954, repr. New York 1964), pp. 37, 420.
56 *De Inventione*, pp. 70ff.
57 See Appendix A for text and translation.
58 See *Ad Herennium*, p. 250.
59 See Curtius, pp. 180f.; *De Inventione*, pp. 70f.; *Ad Herennium*, p. 174; Aristotle, *The Art of Rhetoric*, ed. and trans. J. H. Freese (1926, repr. 1967), pp. 55f.
60 'Waging war he was also distinguished and fortunate, who always brought back victory in triumphant glory from all encounters on land and sea.' 'Assuredly, he ruled his kingdom actively, wisely, and nobly right up to the feebleness of old age.'
61 Curtius, pp. 159ff.
62 Walsingham also employs the topic at the beginning of his panegyric when he declares: 'Without doubt this king had been among all the kings and princes of the world renowned,

beneficent, merciful, and august; given the epithet "the Favoured One" on account of the remarkable favour through which he distinguished himself. Wherefore, by virtue of the grace granted him by divine providence, he excelled all his predecessors in a certain eminence of God-given talent.'

63   See e.g. Lull, *Libro del Orden de Caballería*, pp. 38f.; and more generally the debate on chivalry and war discussed in ch. 5.

64   *On the Death of Edward III*, ed. Wright, p. 219. The topic of 'outdoing' (Curtius, pp. 162ff.) was a cliché of vernacular literature and was used, e.g. by the Chandos Herald when he claimed that 'since the time of King Arthur there was no king of such power' (l. 1840f.). See also *An Invective Against France*, p. 30; *Rot. Parl.*, II, 361f.; the *proemium* to Walter of Peterborough's poem on the battle of Nájera (p. 99). For other conventional catalogues of Edward's virtues see *On the Truce of 1347*, p. 56; and the Latin *On the Death of Edward III*, pp. 223f.

Chapter 5   Conservatives and Intellectuals: The Debate on War

1   Gower, *Mirour de l'Omme*, ll. 26557ff., Brinton, pp. 338f., 216f., 356, 62. See also pp. 47f.

2   E.g. the suggestion that Gaunt may have been in league with the French, and the repetition of the rumour that he was a changeling (*Chronicon Angliae*, pp. 106f., 168).

3   *Chronicon Angliae*, pp. 168f., 205, 196. When he revised his chronicle Walsingham relented somewhat in his personal attack on the duke; nevertheless, his criticism of the government in the person of Gaunt remained (see *Historia Anglicana*, I, 367f., 374). The reasons for these alterations are uncertain. The traditional view has been that his original comments were too outspoken and that the changes were felt to be politic. J. Taylor has plausibly suggested, however, that they may reflect a genuine change in the chronicler's opinion of Gaunt (*The Universal Chronicle of Ranulph Higden* (Oxford, 1966), p. 126). For the duke's part in the defence of the realm in these years see Armitage-Smith, *John of Gaunt*, pp. 230ff.

4   *Chronicon Angliae*, pp. 103f., 64, 105f.; J. Capgrave, *The Chronicle of England*, ed. F. C. Hingeston (1858), p. 232. On Queen Philippa see also Chandos Herald, ll. 59ff.; Froissart, VII, 428f.

5   *Mirour de l'Omme*, ll. 22813ff. For a detailed study of the contemporary significance of this section of the poem see G. Stillwell, 'John Gower and the Last Years of Edward III',

SP, 45 (1948). It is possible that an even more veiled attack on the evil consequences for England of Edward's infatuation with Alice is contained in the description of Lady Mede in *Piers Plowman*. See the A-Text, ed. G. Kane (1960), passus 3, ll. 174ff., where there is a specific reference to the failure of the war effort. The exact campaign referred to is in dispute, but see B. F. Huppé, '*Piers Plowman* and the Norman Wars', *PMLA*, 54 (1939), where the author argues convincingly in favour of the 1373 campaign of John of Gaunt rather than that of 1359 as hazarded by Skeat.

6 Most scholars who have studied the prophecies are agreed on this point. See Wright, ed., p. 123, n.1; A. Gwynn, *The English Austin Friars in the Time of Wyclif* (1940), pp. 137f.; Sister H. M. Peck, 'The Prophecy of John of Bridlington', unpublished doctoral diss., University of Chicago (1930), pp. 4ff. R. Taylor, *The Political Prophecy in England* (New York, 1911), p. 52 is sceptical about the attribution to Erghome, believing that the author is in fact unknown.

7 See Peck, pp. 102ff.

8 Pp. 184, 160. See also pp. 159f.; and Appendix B.

9 P. 160. See also Appendix C.

10 Pp. 184, 160, 173, 162, 172f., 193.

11 *Piers Plowman* A-Text, I, 96ff., 103ff.; Brinton, pp. 167f. Brinton is probably following John of Salisbury (see Painter, *French Chivalry*, pp. 68f.).

12 P. 167.

13 v, 1ff. Langland's concept of the obligations of knighthood is similar (A-Text, VII, 23ff.). See also Chaucer's portrait of the knight in the prologue to the *Canterbury Tales*, ll. 43ff.

14 Brinton, p. 168; *Mirour de l'Omme*, ll. 24169ff. See also *Vox Clamantis*, v, 469ff.; Brinton, p. 48.

15 *Mirour de l'Omme*, ll. 23608ff. See also *Confessio Amantis*, III, 2230ff., VII, 3594ff.

16 See ll. 2137ff.

17 See ll. 23269ff., 24013ff., 24049ff., 24145ff.

18 *Vox Clamantis*, v, 251ff. See also Brinton, p. 48.

19 VII, 33ff. See also v, 536ff. where he attacks knights who engage in war for the sake of personal gain, and also the knight who refuses to take up arms, preferring to stay at home despoiling the poor.

20 *Vox Clamantis*, VII, 263ff. The greed of the English was proverbial amongst their French and Spanish enemies. See Froissart, x, 203f., 205f.; *El Victorial*, p. 142; Philippe de

Mézières, *Le Songe du Vieil Pelerin*, ed. G. W. Coopland, 2 vols (Cambridge, 1969), 1, 397.

21   *Vox Clamantis*, III, 343ff., 631ff.; *Confessio Amantis*, prologue, ll. 212ff. Later in a damning piece of self-revelation, Gower makes the pope expatiate cynically on his worldly and martial pretensions (*Vox Clamantis*, III, 817ff.). See also *Piers Plowman*, C-Text, XVIII, 233ff.

22   *The Office of Curates*, p. 152; *Of Prelates*, p. 100. See also pp. 59, 73. All ed. Matthew, *The English Works of John Wyclif*. Matthew considers these two tracts to be the work of disciples of Wyclif. See also Mézières, *Songe*, 1, 402.

23   On Mézières and the crusading propaganda of the late fourteenth century see G. W. Coopland, intro. to *Songe*; J. J. N. Palmer, *England, France and Christendom 1377–99*, pp. 186ff.; Runciman, *A History of the Crusades*, III, 427ff.

24   See *Vox Clamantis*, III, 651ff.; *In Praise of Peace*, ll. 246ff.

25   III, 2490ff.

26   XIV, 384.

27   Froissart, XIV, 384; *Piers Plowman* C-Text, IV, 236ff.

28   Froissart, XV, 140ff.; *Complainte sur la Bataille de Poitiers*, ed. Ch. de Beaurepaire, BEC, II, 3rd ser. (Paris, 1851), ll. 41ff.; *El Victorial*, pp. 182f. See also Mézières, *Songe*, III, 373ff.

29   XIV, 314, 384, XVI, 3.

30   XIV, 383.

31   XV, 108f.

32   See Froissart, XIV, 314, 384; *Continuatio Eulogii Historiarum*, III, 369; Mézières, *Songe*, III, 375f.; Steel, *Richard II*, pp. 165, 189; Armitage-Smith, *John of Gaunt*, pp. 394f.; McKisack, pp. 151, 248.

33   In a letter to *TLS*, 3480 (7 November 1968), p. 1251.

34   Díez de Games thought so, too. See *El Victorial*, p. 182.

35   Froissart, XVI, 2ff.

36   See, however, Goodman, *The Loyal Conspiracy*, ch. 4, for a more detailed and in many ways more sympathetic interpretation of Gloucester's character.

37   Thomas Hoccleve, *The Regement of Princes*, ed. F. J. Furnivall (1897), EETS ES 72, l. 5340f.

38   *Regement*, ll. 5307ff., 5321ff., 5335ff., 5342ff., 5370ff. Some of these attitudes to war even find a reflection in romance in the late fourteenth and early fifteenth centuries. See Appendix D.

39   *Historia Anglicana*, 1, 311, II, 117, 198ff.

40   IX, 56. Malvern says that the duke urged an invasion of France, but in view of his involvement in Peninsular politics

at this time, this must either be a slip of the pen or Malvern was misinformed. Gaunt took an active part in the peace negotiations with France, for a continuation of the war was against his interests in Castile. Almost certainly the duke urged the invasion of Castile at this meeting. See Armitage-Smith, *John of Gaunt*, pp. 297ff.

41 Malvern, IX, 56; *Historia Anglicana*, II, 110. See also Malvern, IX, 103.

42 *Tractatus de Ecclesia*, ed. J. Loserth (1886), p. 427; *The Order of Priesthood*, p. 176. See also *Of Prelates*, pp. 90f.; *Of Clerks Possessioners*, pp. 132ff.; *The Office of Curates*, p. 147, all ed. Matthew, *The English Works of John Wyclif*.

43 *Mirour de l'Omme*, ll. 24097ff.; *Confessio Amantis*, prologue, 892ff., 970ff.

44 *Confessio Amantis*, III, 2251ff., 2260ff., 2267ff.

45 By implication in III, 2332ff.

46 *Confessio Amantis*, III, 2633ff., 2352ff., prologue, 189ff.

47 *The Curial Made by Maystere Alain Charretier*, trans. Caxton, ed. F. J. Furnivall and P. Meyer (1888, repr. 1965), EETS ES 54, p. 13.

48 See D. S. Brewer, *Chaucer*, 2nd edn (1960, repr. 1961), pp. 61f.; Steel, *Richard II*, p. 126.

49 *The Book of the Duchess* was probably composed as a consolation to John of Gaunt on the death of his wife, Blanche, in 1369 (Robinson, ed., p. 773); *The Legend of Good Women* may have been commissioned by Queen Anne and certainly contains flattering references to her (Robinson, pp. 839f.); *The Knight's Tale* may have been 'written, or adapted, to celebrate the royal wedding' of Richard and Anne (Robinson, p. 669); *The Parlement of Fowls* and *The Complaint of Mars* were composed for St Valentine's Day celebrations at court (D. S. Brewer, ed., *The Parlement of Foulys* (1960), p. 5); *Lak of Stedfastnesse* was addressed to Richard II (Robinson, p. 862); and *The Complaint of Chaucer to his Purse* to Henry IV. Attempts to identify specific occasions for other poems are discussed by Robinson in his notes.

50 Corpus Christi MS 61. It is reproduced as a frontispiece in D. S. Brewer, *Chaucer in his Time* (1963) and in Matthew, *The Court of Richard II*, facing p. 76.

51 F. 188ff., G. 71ff. See Brewer, *Chaucer in his Time*, p. 185.

52 See J. B. Severs, 'The Source of Chaucer's *Melibeus*', *PMLA*, 50 (1935), passim; Robinson, pp. 740f.

53 See G. Stillwell, 'The Political Meaning of Chaucer's *Tale of Melibee*', *Speculum*, 19 (1944), pp. 434f.

54   A date somewhere in the mid-1380s is generally accepted by critics. See Stillwell, pp. 441f.; Robinson, p. 741.

55   See Stillwell, p. 433; Severs, p. 92; J. S. P. Tatlock, *The Development and Chronology of Chaucer's Works* (1907), *Chaucer Soc.*, 2nd ser., no. 37, pp. 188ff.; Robinson, p. 741.

56   *Melibee*, VII, 1168, 1174, 1198. See *Mum and the Sothsegger*, eds M. Day and R. Steele (1936), EETS OS 199, I, 80ff.; Gower, *Vox Clamantis*, VI, 550*ff.; Froissart, X, 395ff.; *Historia Anglicana*, II, 97.

57   See Stillwell, p. 438.

58   *Melibee*, VII, 1038ff.

59   The advice of Dame Prudence that 'ye bigynne no werre in trust of youre richesses, for they ne suffisen noght werres to mayntene' provides another obvious parallel (VII, 1647ff.).

60   On the Continent war was condemned in similar terms by Lopez de Ayala, *Rimado de Palacio*, ed. F. Janer (Madrid, 1864), *Biblioteca de Autores Españoles*, 57, stanza 502ff.; Mézières, *Songe*, III, 373ff.; Eustache Deschamps, *Oeuvres Complètes*, ed. Le Marquis de Queux de Saint-Hilaire and G. Raynaud, 11 vols (Paris, 1878–1903), SATF, *Le Lay des Douze Estas du Monde*, ll. 119ff., and *balades* nos 48, 64, 65, 66, 93, 394, 883, 1148, 1171.

61   *Melibee*, VII, 1674ff.

62   Ll. 22f., 27.

63   Robinson, p. 862.

64   Notably Boethius and to a lesser extent Ovid and the *Roman de la Rose* (Robinson, p. 859).

65   Ll. 19, 31f., 49, 60ff.

66   On his learning see Day and Steele, eds, pp. xxivf.

67   Prologue, ll. 19ff.

68   Prologue, ll. 76ff. On his social status see Day and Steele, p. xvii.

69   *Mum and the Sothsegger*, II, 46ff.; *Confessio Amantis*, prologue, ll. 24*ff. See also Adam of Usk, *Chronicon*, ed. and trans. E. M. Thompson (2nd edn, 1904), p. 1.

70   I, 80ff. See also Gower, *Vox Clamantis*, VI, 550*ff. Froissart clearly disapproved of Richard's dependence on Michael de la Pole (x, 395ff.).

71   *Historia Anglicana*, II, 148.

72   II, 1ff., I, 13ff. The author makes the same point later (IV, 46ff.) in a reference to the parliament of January 1398. He repeats a speech allegedly made by some members who opposed the granting of taxes except in time of war. Did the

poet perhaps attend this parliament? See also Knighton, II, 218ff.; *Historia Anglicana*, II, 229.

73 *Chronicon*, p. 3.
74 See Day and Steele, pp. xixff.
75 M, 211ff.
76 *Confessio Amantis*, prologue, ll. 24ff.; *Cronica Tripertita*, III, 77ff., 298f.
77 *In Praise of Peace*, ll. 1ff.; *Cronica Tripertita*, marginal note to preface. See also Stockton, *The Major Latin Works*, pp. 18ff.
78 Ll. 22ff.
79 *In Praise of Peace*, ll. 5off., 69f., 120ff., 127ff.; *Cinkante Balades*, I, 1ff.
80 *The Six Kings to Follow King John*, ed. J. Hall in Minot, *Poems*, appendix 2, ll. 269f., 189ff. See also Scattergood, *Politics and Poetry in the Fifteenth Century*, ch. 4.
81 Froissart is expressing the view commonly held in France. See e.g. Christine de Pisan, *Le Livre des Faits et Bonnes Meurs du Sage Roy Charles V*, I, 147f.; Deschamps, *balade* no. 1200. See also *El Victorial*, p. 182f.
82 XVI, 233f.

Appendices

B *The Dangers of Political Comment in Fourteenth-Century England*
1 Knighton, II, 306; *Mum and the Sothsegger*, M. 165ff.
2 *Anonimalle*, p. 104; *Chronicon Angliae*, p. 129.
3 *Anonimalle*, pp. 104f.; *Chronicon Angliae*, pp. 129f.
4 See McKisack, pp. 396f.; Armitage-Smith, *John of Gaunt*, pp. 154ff.
5 M, 152ff. The arbitrary suppression of criticism and advice is revealed in an anecdote in the *Continuatio Eulogii Historiarum*, III, 380. A north-country hermit is said to have approached the archbishop of Canterbury with the information that God had revealed to him that Richard should restore the possessions of the disinherited lords. The archbishop sent the hermit on to the king who promptly gaoled him in the Tower. Death sentences were passed on political pamphleteers in the fifteenth century. See Scattergood, *Politics and Poetry in the Fifteenth Century*, pp. 21f.
6 *Piers Plowman*, B-Text, prologue, 208f.; A-Text, III, 259; *Vox Clamantis*, VII, 1459f. See also *Vox Clamantis*, III, prologue, 9ff., 23ff.; *Mirour de l'Omme*, ll. 18445ff.
7 See Sister Peck, pp. 4, 18ff.

8 Pp. 124, 215. He did, however, reveal his name in a crypto-graph. See Gwynn, *The English Austin Friars in the Time of Wyclif*, p. 135.

9 Pp. 185f. His use of the device in his attack on Alice Perrers has already been discussed in chapter 5.

C The Date of Composition of the Bridlington Prophecy

1 P. 123; Peck, pp. 43ff.

2 Gwynn, p. 138, 'soon after 1362' (no reason stated); Taylor, p. 52, 1364; Peck, pp. 43ff., between 13 November 1362 (possibly November–December 1363) and 8 April 1364; Wright, *Pol. Poems*, i, xxix.

3 See Peck, pp. 43ff.

4 See *N&Q*, 7th ser. vol. 7, p. 449; *DNB*, p. 898.

5 See McKisack, pp. 384, 390; Armitage-Smith, *John of Gaunt*, p. 76.

6 Erghome, pp. 195ff.; John of Reading, pp. 171, 336ff.

D Morte Arthure *and the Hundred Years War*

1 W. Matthews, *The Tragedy of Arthur* (Berkeley and Los Angeles, 1960), pp. 178ff.

2 Matthews points to other minor similarities, although not all of them are convincing: e.g. the parallel he makes between the characters of Arthur and Edward is based upon conventional descriptive epithets commonly associated with kingship (p. 187).

3 P. 191.

4 Pp. 185f.

5 Ll. 443ff., 1232ff., 3013ff.

6 Ll. 632ff., 725ff. The activities involved in setting sail are described with equal attention to detail (736ff.).

7 Ll. 2294ff., 2282ff., 3134ff., 3176ff., 3084ff., 1502ff., 1527f., 1549ff.

8 Ll. 3032ff., 3150ff., 43.

9 *The Awntyrs of Arthure at the Terne Wathelyne*, ed. F. J. Amours, in *Scottish Alliterative Poems* (Edinburgh, 1897), STS. The poem is now generally accepted as English and not Scottish. On internal evidence J. P. Oakden places it 'near Carlisle, or at least the county of Cumberland' and assigns it to 'the latter part of the fourteenth century' (*Alliterative Poetry in Middle English*, 2 vols (1930–5, repr. New York, 1968), i,

113f.). See also H. N. McCracken, 'Concerning Huchown', *PMLA*, 18 (1910), pp. 507ff., 528.

10 Ll. 261ff. In the *Bruce* Barbour makes the dying Scots hero repent of his warlike career in very similar terms:

> For throu me and my warraying
> Of blud thar has beyne gret spilling,
> Quhar mony sakles* man wes slayne.   *innocent
>   (xx, 173 ff.)

The hardships suffered by the English under a martial king like Arthur and the need to establish peace provide a minor theme which runs throughout *Le Mort Arthur*, ed. J. D. Bruce (1903, repr. 1959), EETS ES 88, ll. 2248f., 2260f., 2273, 2301, 2962ff., 3032f., 3662ff.

11 See e.g. the *melée* fought between Sir Cador and the Romans (ll. 1617ff.).

12 *The Morte Darthur, Parts Seven and Eight*, ed. D. S. Brewer (1968), p. 7.

13 Ll. 1251, 1958, 2989, 3500, 1973.

Bibliography

I *Primary Sources*

(a) Chronicles

Acta Bellicosa, printed as an appendix to J. Moisant, *Le Prince Noir en Aquitaine* (Paris, 1894).

Adam of Usk, *Chronicon*, ed. and trans. E. M. Thompson (2nd edn, 1904).

Annales Prioratus de Wigornia, ed. H. R. Luard (1869).

Anonimalle Chronicle, ed. V. H. Galbraith (Manchester, 1927).

Avesbury, Robert de, *De Gestis Mirabilibus Regis Edwardi Tertii*, ed. E. M. Thompson (1889).

Baker, Geoffrey, *Chronicon*, ed. E. M. Thompson (Oxford, 1889).

Barbour, John, *The Bruce*, ed. W. W. Skeat, 2 vols (1894), STS.

Brut, The, ed. F. W. D. Brie, 2 vols (1906–8), EETS OS 131, 136.

Capgrave, John, *The Chronicle of England*, ed. F. C. Hingeston (1858).

Crónicas de los Reyes de Castilla, ed. C. Rosell (Madrid, 1875), *Biblioteca de Autores Españoles*, 66.

Chronicle of Lanercost, The, ed. and trans. H. Maxwell (Glasgow, 1913).

Chronicon de Lanercost, ed. J. Stevenson (Edinburgh, 1839).

Chroniques de London, ed. G. J. Aungier (1844).

Chronique du Mont-Saint Michel, ed. S. Luce, 2 vols (Paris, 1879–83), SATF.

Chronique Normande du XIVᵉ Siècle, ed. A. and É. Molinier (Paris, 1882), SHF.

Chronique des Quatre Premiers Valois, ed. S. Luce (Paris, 1862), SHF.

Chronique des Règnes de Jean II et de Charles V, ed. R. Delachenal, 3 vols (Paris, 1910–20), SHF.

Díez de Games, Gutierre, *El Victorial, Crónica de Don Pero Niño*, ed. J. de Mata Carriazo (Madrid, 1940).

Eulogium Historiarum, ed. F. S. Haydon, 3 vols (1858–63).
Froissart, Jean, *Chroniques*, ed. K. de Lettenhove, 25 vols (Brussels, 1867–77).
——, *Chronicles*, ed. and trans. Thomas Johnes, 12 vols (1808).
——, *Chronicles*, selection trans. G. Brereton (Penguin, 1968).
Gesta Edwardi de Carnarvon, Auctore Canonico Bridlingtoniensi, cum Continuatione ad A.D. 1377, ed. W. Stubbs (1883), in vol. 2 of *Chronicles of the Reigns of Edward I and Edward II*, RS.
Grandes Chroniques de France, Les, ed. J. Viard, 10 vols (Paris, 1920–53), SHF.
Gray, Sir Thomas, *Scalacronica*, ed. J. Stevenson (Edinburgh, 1836).
Higden, Ranulph, *Polychronicon*, eds J. R. Lumby and C. Babington, 9 vols (1865–86).
Kirkstall Abbey Chronicles, The, ed. J. Taylor (Leeds, 1952), *Thoresby Soc. Publications*, 42.
Knighton, Henry, *Chronicon Henrici Knighton, Monachi Leycestrensis*, ed. J. R. Lumby, 2 vols (1889–95).
Lopez de Ayala, Pedro, *Crónicas de los Reyes de Castilla*, ed. E. de Llaguno Amirola, 2 vols (Madrid, 1779–80).
Malvern, John, *Continuation of the Polychronicon*, ed. J. R. Lumby, printed as an appendix to *Polychronicon*, VIII.
Manning of Brunne, Robert, *Chronicle*, ed. F. J. Furnivall, 2 vols (1887).
Melsa, Chronica Monasterii de, ed. E. A. Bond, 3 vols (1866–8).
Murimuth, Adam, *Continuatio Chronicarum*, ed. E. M. Thompson (1889).
Reading, *Chronica Johannis de Reading et Anonymi Cantuariensis*, ed. J. Tait (Manchester, 1914).
Venette, Jean de, *Chronicle*, ed. and trans. J. Birdsall and R. A. Newhall (New York, 1953).
Walsingham, Thomas, *Chronicon Angliae*, ed. E. M. Thompson (1874).
——, *Historia Anglicana*, ed. H. T. Riley, 2 vols (1863–4).
——, *The St Albans Chronicle 1406–1420*, ed. V. H. Galbraith (Oxford, 1937).
Wyntoun, Andrew of, *The Original Chronicle*, ed. F. J. Amours, 6 vols (1903–14), STS.

(b)   Poetry, Sermons, Biographies, Political and Religious Tracts, etc.

'Anciens Proverbes Français', ed. E. Langlois, BEC, 60 (Paris, 1899).

Anglo-Norman Political Songs, ed. I. S. T. Aspin (Oxford, 1953), ANTS 11.

Arderne, John, *Treatises of Fistula in Ano*, ed. D'Arcy Power (1910), EETS OS 139.

Aristotle, *The Art of Rhetoric*, ed. and trans. J. H. Freese (1926 repr. 1967).

Awntyrs of Arthure at the Terne Wathelyne, ed. F. J. Amours in *Scottish Alliterative Poems* (Edinburgh, 1897), STS.

Bataille de Trente Anglois et de Trente Bretons, La, ed. H. R. Brush, 2 pts, MP, 9–10 (1911–13).

Bernadus de Cura Rei Famuliaris with some Early Scottish Prophecies, ed. J. R. Lumby (1870, repr. 1965), EETS OS 42.

Bonet, Honoré, *L'Arbre des Batailles*, ed. E. Nys (Brussels, 1883).

——, *The Tree of Battles*, ed. and trans. G. W. Coopland (Liverpool, 1949).

Brinton, *The Sermons of Thomas Brinton, Bishop of Rochester, (1373–89)*, ed. Sister M. A. Devlin, 2 vols (1954).

Capgrave, John, *Liber de Illustribus Henricis*, ed. F. C. Hingeston (1858).

Chandos Herald, *The Life of the Black Prince*, ed. and trans. M. K. Pope and E. C. Lodge (Oxford, 1910).

Chartier, Alain, *Le Quadrilogue Invectif*, ed. E. Droz, 2nd edn (Paris, 1950), *Les Classiques Français du Moyen Âge*.

——, *The Curial Made by Maystere Alain Charretier*, Caxton's trans., ed. P. Meyer and F. J. Furnivall (1888, repr. 1965), EETS ES 54.

Chaucer, Geoffrey, *The Canterbury Tales*, ed. J. M. Manly (1940).

——, *Complete Works*, ed. W. W. Skeat, 7 vols (Oxford, 1894–7).

——, *Works*, ed. F. N. Robinson (2nd edn, 1957).

——, *The Parlement of Foulys*, ed. D. S. Brewer (1960).

Chaucer's World, compiled E. Rickert, ed. C. C. Olson and M. M. Crow (New York, 1948, repr. 1962).

Christine de Pisan, *The Book of Fayttes of Armes and of Chyualrye*, Caxton's trans., ed. A. T. P. Byles (1936), EETS OS 189.

——, *Le Livre des Faits et Bonnes Meurs du Sage Roy Charles V*, ed. S. Solente, 2 vols (Paris, 1936–40), SHF.

Cicero, *De Inventione*, ed. and trans. H. M. Hubbell (1949, repr. 1960).

Complainte sur la Bataille de Poitiers, ed. Ch. de Beaurepaire, BEC, 11, 3rd ser. (Paris, 1851).

Cursor Mundi, ed. R. Morris, 6 vols (1874–93), EETS OS 57, 59, 62, 66, 68, 101.

Cuvelier, *Chronique de Bertrand du Guesclin par Cuvelier*, ed. E.

Charrière 2 vols (Paris, 1839), *Collection de Documents Inédits sur l'Histoire de France.*
Deschamps, Eustache, *Oeuvres Complètes*, ed. Le Marquis de Queux de Saint-Hilaire and Gaston Raynaud, 11 vols (Paris, 1878–1903), SATF.
Erceldoune, Thomas of, *Romance and Prophecies of Thomas of Erceldoune*, ed. J. A. H. Murray (1875), EETS OS 61.
Geoffroi de Charny, *Le Livre Messire Geoffroi de Charny*, ed. A. Piaget, *Romania*, 26 (Paris, 1897).
Gest Hystoriale of the Destruction of Troy, ed. G. A. Panton and D. Donaldson, 2 vols (1869–74), EETS OS 39, 56.
Gower, John, *Complete Works*, ed. G. C. Macaulay, 4 vols (Oxford, 1899–1902).
——, *The Major Latin Works*, ed. and trans. E. W. Stockton (Seattle, 1962).
Henry of Grosmont, Duke of Lancaster, *Le Livre de Seyntz Medicines*, ed. E. J. Arnould (Oxford, 1940), ANTS 2.
Historical Poems of the XIVth and XVth Centuries, ed. R. H. Robbins (New York, 1959).
Hoccleve, Thomas, *The Regement of Princes*, ed. F. J. Furnivall (1897) EETS ES 72.
Langland, William, *Piers Plowman, A-Text*, ed. G. Kane (1960).
——, *Piers Plowman*, Texts A, B, & C, ed. W. W. Skeat (1867–73, repr. 1950–9), EETS OS 28, 38, 54.
Lopez de Ayala, Pedro, *Rimado de Palacio*, ed. F. Janer (Madrid, 1864), *Biblioteca de Autores Españoles*, 57.
Lulio, Raimundo, *The Book of the Ordre of Chyualry*, Caxton's trans., ed. A. T. P. Byles (1926), EETS OS 168.
——, *Libro del Orden de Caballería*, Spanish trans. (Buenos Aires, 1949).
Lydgate, John, *Fall of Princes*, ed. H. Bergen, 4 vols (1918–19), EETS ES 121–4.
Malory, Sir Thomas, *Morte Darthur, Parts Seven and Eight*, ed. D. S. Brewer (1968).
Mandeville's Travels, ed. P. Hamelius, 2 vols (1919–23, repr. 1960–1), EETS OS 153–4.
Manning of Brunne, Robert, *Handlyng Synne*, ed. F. J. Furnivall, 2 vols (1901–3), EETS OS 119, 123.
Mézières, Philippe, de, *Le Songe du Vieil Pelerin*, ed. G. W. Coopland, 2 vols (Cambridge, 1969).
Michel, Dan, *Ayenbite of Inwyt*, ed. R. Morris, revised P. Gradon (1866, corrected edn 1965), EETS OS 23.
Middle English Metrical Romances, ed. W. H. French and C. B. Hale (New York, 1930, repr. 1964).

Middle English Sermons, ed. W. O. Ross (1940), EETS OS 209.
Minot, Laurence, *Poems*, ed. J. Hall (Oxford, 1897).
Mort Arthur, Le, ed. J. D. Bruce (1903, repr. 1959), EETS ES 88.
Morte Arthure, ed. E. Brock (1871, repr. 1961), EETS OS 8.
Mum and the Sothsegger, ed. M. Day and R. Steele (1936), EETS OS 199.
Parlement of the Thre Ages, ed. M. Y. Offord (1959), EETS OS 246.
Petrarch, F., *Epistolae de Rebus Familiaribus et Variae*, ed. J. Fracassetti, 3 vols (Florence, 1859–63).
Poème Tchèque sur la Bataille de Crécy, Un, ed. and trans. L. Leger, *Journal des Savants* (Paris, 1902).
Political Poems and Songs, ed. T. Wright, 2 vols (1859–61).
Récit des Tribulations d'un Religieux du Diocèse de Sens Pendant l'Invasion Anglaise de 1358, ed. J. Quicherat, BEC, III, 4th ser. (Paris, 1857).
Rhetorica ad Herennium, ed. H. Caplan (1954, repr. 1964).
Richard de Bury, *Philobiblon*, ed. M. Maclagan (Oxford, 1960).
Richard Coer de Lion, ed. H. Weber, *Metrical Romances*, 3 vols (Edinburgh, 1810).
Sege of Melayne, The, ed. S. J. Herrtage (1880), EETS ES 34.
Somer Soneday, ed. Carleton Brown in *Studies in English Philology in Honour of Frederick Klaeber*, ed. Kemp Malone (Minneapolis, 1929).
Speculum Regis Edwardi III, ed. J. Moisant (Paris, 1891).
Tour-Landry, *The Book of the Knight of the Tower*, trans. Caxton, ed. M.Y. Offord (1971), EETS SS 2.
——, *Le Livre du Chevalier de la Tour Landry*, ed. A. de Montaiglon (Paris, 1854).
William of Palerne, ed W. W. Skeat (1867), EETS ES 1.
Winner and Waster, ed. I. Gollancz (1930).
Wyclif, John, *The English Works*, ed. F. D. Matthew (1880), EETS OS 74.
——, *Tractatus de Ecclesia*, ed. J. Loserth (1886).

(c)   Public Records

Rotuli Parliamentorum, ut et Petitiones et Placita in Parliamento, vols 2 and 3, *Record Commission* (1783).

11   *Secondary Sources*

Ackerman, R. W., 'The Knighting Ceremonies in the Middle English Romances', *Speculum*, 19 (1944).

Allmand, C. T., 'Historians Reconsidered: Froissart', *History Today*, 16 (1966).
——, 'War and Profit in the Late Middle Ages', *History Today*, 15 (1965).
Armitage-Smith, S., *John of Gaunt* (1904, repr. 1964).
Ascoli, G., *La Grande-Bretagne Devant l'Opinion Française* (Paris, 1927).
Baker, Sir Richard, *A Chronicle of the Kings of England* (1643).
Barber, R., *The Knight and Chivalry* (1970).
Barnes, Joshua, *The History of that Most Victorious Monarch Edward III* (Cambridge, 1688).
Bayley, C. C., 'The Campaign of 1375 and the Good Parliament', *EHR*, 55 (1940).
Bellamy, J. G., 'The Coterel Gang: an Anatomy of a Band of Fourteenth-Century Criminals', *EHR*, 79 (1964).
Bennett, J. A. W., 'The Date of the B-Text of *Piers Plowman*', *MAE*, 12 (1943).
Bloch, M., *Feudal Society*, Eng. trans. (1962).
Bolgar, R. R., *The Classical Heritage and its Beneficiaries from the Carolingian Age to the End of the Renaissance* (1954, repr. 1964, Harper Torchbook).
Borst, A., 'Knighthood in the High Middle Ages: Ideal and Reality', edited Eng. trans., in *Lordship and Community in Medieval Europe*, ed. F. R. Cheyette (New York, 1968).
Braddy, H., 'Chaucer's Don Pedro and the Purpose of the *Monk's Tale*', *MLQ*, 13 (1952).
——, 'The Two Petros in the *Monkes Tale*', *PMLA*, 50 (1935).
Brewer, D. S., *Chaucer* (2nd edn 1960, repr. 1961).
——, *Chaucer in his Time* (1963).
——, ed., *Chaucer and the Chaucerians: Critical Studies in Middle English Literature* (1966).
Brooke, G. C., *English Coins from the Seventh Century to the Present Day* (1932, 3rd edn 1950).
Broome, D. M., 'The Ransom of John 11, King of France, 1360–1370', *Camden Miscellany*, 14 (1926).
Burne, A. H., *The Agincourt War* (1956).
——, *The Crécy War* (1955).
Chaplais, P., 'English Arguments Concerning the Feudal Status of Aquitaine in the Fourteenth Century', *BIHR*, 21 (1946–8).
Chaytor, H. J., *From Script to Print* (1945, repr. 1966).
Chew, H. M., 'Scutage in the Fourteenth Century', *EHR*, 38 (1923).
Clarke, M. V., *Fourteenth Century Studies* (Oxford, 1937). Contains

'The Kirkstall Chronicle, 1355–1400', and 'Henry Knighton and the Library Catalogue of Leicester Abbey'.

Cline, R., 'The Influence of Romances on Tournaments of the Middle Ages', *Speculum*, 20 (1945).

Coffman, G. R., 'John Gower in his Most Significant Role', *Elizabethan Studies and Other Essays in Honour of George F. Reynolds* (Boulder, Colorado, 1945).

——, 'John Gower, Mentor for Royalty: Richard II', *PMLA*, 69 (1954).

Contamine, P., *Guerre, État et Société à la Fin du Moyen Âge* (Paris, 1972).

Crow, M. M. and Olson, C. C., eds, *Chaucer Life-Records* (Oxford, 1966).

Curtius, E. R., *European Literature and the Latin Middle Ages*, Eng. trans. (New York, 1953).

Daly, L. J., *The Political Theory of John Wyclif* (Chicago, 1962).

Delachenal, R., *Histoire de Charles V*, 5 vols (Paris, 1909–31).

Denholm-Young, N., *History and Heraldry 1254–1310* (Oxford, 1965).

Déprez, E., *Les Préliminaires de la Guerre de Cent Ans* (Paris, 1902).

Edwards, J. G., 'Ranulph, Monk of Chester', *EHR*, 47 (1932).

——, 'Some Common Petitions in Richard II's First Parliament', *BIHR*, 26 (1953).

Emerson, O. F., 'English or French in the Time of Edward III?', *Rom. Rev.*, 7 (1916).

Evans, J. E., 'The First Gold Coins of England', *The Numismatic Chronicle*, 20 (1900).

Ferguson, A. B., *The Indian Summer of English Chivalry* (Durham, N. Carolina, 1960).

Fisher, J. H., *John Gower, Moral Philosopher and Friend of Chaucer* (1965).

Fowler, D. C., 'New Light on John Trevisa', *Traditio*, 18 (1962).

Fowler, K., *The Age of Plantagenet and Valois* (1967).

——, 'Les Finances et la discipline dans les armées anglaises en France au XIVᵉ siècle', *Les Cahiers Vernonnais*, 4 (Caen, 1964).

——, ed., *The Hundred Years War* (1971).

——, *The King's Lieutenant, Henry of Grosmont, First Duke of Lancaster, 1310–1361* (1969).

Galbraith, V. H., 'The Battle of Poitiers', *EHR*, 54 (1939).

——, 'The Chronicle of Henry Knighton', in *Fritz Saxl Memorial Lectures*, ed. D. J. Gordon (1957).

——, 'Nationality and Language in Medieval England', *TRHS*, 4th ser., 23 (1941).

———, 'Thomas Walsingham and the Saint Albans Chronicle, 1272–1422', *EHR*, 47 (1932).
Garbaty, T. J., 'Chaucer in Spain, 1366: Soldier of Fortune or Agent of the Crown?', *ELN*, 5 (1967).
Gaylord, A., 'A85–88: Chaucer's Squire and the Glorious Campaign', in *Papers of the Michigan Academy of Science, Arts, and Letters*, 44 (1960).
Giffin, M. E., 'Cadwalader, Arthur, and Brutus in the Wigmore Manuscript', *Speculum*, 16 (1941).
Gollancz, I., *Ich Dene* (1921).
Goodman, A., *The Loyal Conspiracy: The Lords Appellant under Richard II* (1971).
Grosjean, G., *Le Sentiment National dans la Guerre de Cent Ans* (Paris, 1927).
Gutiérrez de Velasco, A., 'Los Ingleses en España (Siglo XIV)', *Estudios de la Edad Media de la Corona de Aragon* (Saragossa, 1950).
Gwynn, A., *The English Austin Friars in the Time of Wyclif* (1940).
Hale, J. R., Highfield, J. R. L., Smalley, B., eds, *Europe in the Late Middle Ages* (1965),. Contains 'The Crusade in the Fourteenth Century' by A. Luttrell, and 'England, Scotland and the Hundred Years War in the Fourteenth Century' by J. Campbell.
Harris Nicholas, Sir N., *History of the Orders of Knighthood of the British Empire*, 4 vols (1842).
Hay, D., 'The Division of the Spoils of War in Fourteenth-century England', *TRHS*, 5th ser., 4 (1954).
Heers, M. J., 'Difficultés économiques et troubles sociaux en France et en Angleterre pendant la guerre de cent ans: le problème des origines', *Les Cahiers Vernonnais*, 4 (Caen, 1964).
Herben, S. J., 'Arms and Armour in Chaucer', *Speculum*, 12 (1937).
Hewitt, H. J., *The Black Prince's Expedition of 1355–7* (Manchester, 1958).
———, *The Organization of War Under Edward III, 1338–62* (Manchester, 1966).
Holmes, G. A., *The Estates of the Higher Nobility in Fourteenth-Century England* (Cambridge, 1957).
Huizinga, J., *Men and Ideas*, Eng. trans. (1960). Contains 'Patriotism and Nationalism in European History' and 'The Political and Military Significance of Chivalric Ideas in the Late Middle Ages'.
———, *The Waning of the Middle Ages*, Eng. trans. (1924, repr. 1952).
Huppé, B. F., '*Piers Plowman* and the Norman Wars', *PMLA*, 54 (1939).

James, G. P. R., *A History of the Life of Edward the Black Prince*, 2 vols (1836).

Jenkins, C., *The Monastic Chronicler and the Early School of St. Albans* (1922).

Johnstone, H., 'Isabella, the She-Wolf of France', *History*, 21 (1936).

Jones, R. H., *The Royal Policy of Richard II: Absolutism in the Later Middle Ages* (Oxford, 1968).

Kantorowicz, E. H., 'Pro Patria Mori in Medieval Political Thought', *AHR*, 56 (1951).

Keeler, L., *Geoffrey of Monmouth and the Late Latin Chroniclers 1300–1500* (Berkeley and Los Angeles, 1946).

Keen, M. H., 'Brotherhood in Arms', *History*, 47 (1962).

——, *The Laws of War in the Late Middle Ages* (1965).

Kellog, E. H., 'Bishop Brunton and the Fable of the Rats', *PMLA*, 50 (1935).

Kilgour, R. L., *The Decline of Chivalry as Shown in the French Literature of the Late Middle Ages* (Cambridge, Mass., 1937).

——, 'Honoré Bonet: a Fourteenth-Century Critic of Chivalry', *PMLA*, 50 (1935).

Kuhl, E. P., 'Chaucer the Patriot', *PQ*, 25 (1946).

Langenfelt, G., *Select Studies in Colloquial English of the Late Middle Ages* (Lund, 1933).

Lapsley, G., 'Archbishop Stratford and the Parliamentary Crisis of 1341', *EHR*, 30 (1915).

Lawrence, W. W., 'The Tale of Melibeus', *Essays and Studies in Honor of Carleton Brown* (New York, 1940).

Legge, M. D., 'Anglo-Norman and the Historian', *History*, 26 (1941–2).

——, *Anglo-Norman Literature and its Background* (Oxford, 1963).

Lewis, N. B., 'The Last Medieval Summons of the English Feudal Levy, 13th June 1385', *EHR*, 73 (1958).

Lewis, P. S., *Later Medieval France, the Polity* (1968).

——, 'War Propaganda and Historiography in Fifteenth-Century France and England', *TRHS*, 5th ser., 15 (1965).

Loomis, R. S., 'Chivalric and Dramatic Imitations of Arthurian Romance', *Medieval Studies in Memory of A. Kingsley Porter*, ed. W. R. W. Koehler, 2 vols (Cambridge, Mass., 1939).

——, 'Edward I, Arthurian Enthusiast', *Speculum*, 28 (1953).

——, 'Was Chaucer a Laodicean?', *Essays and Studies in Honor of Carleton Brown* (New York, 1940).

Lourie, E., 'A Society Organized for War: Medieval Spain', *PP*, 35 (1966).

Lucas, H. S., 'Edward III and John Boendale', *Speculum*, 12 (1937).

——, 'John Crabbe, Flemish Pirate, Merchant, and Adventurer', *Speculum*, 20 (1945).

McCracken, H. N., 'Concerning Huchown', *PMLA*, 18 (1910).

McFarlane, K. B., 'England and the Hundred Years War', *PP*, 22 (1962).

Mackinnon, J., *The History of Edward III* (1900).

McKisack, M., 'Edward III and the Historians', *History*, 45 (1960).

——, *The Fourteenth Century, 1307–1399* (Oxford, 1959, repr. 1963).

Macray, W. D., 'Robert Baston's Poem on the Battle of Bannockburn', *EHR*, 19 (1904).

Manly, J. M., *Some New Light on Chaucer* (1926).

Mathew, G., *The Court of Richard II* (1968).

——, 'Ideals of Knighthood in Late Fourteenth-Century England', *Studies in Medieval History Presented to Frederick Maurice Powicke* (Oxford, 1948).

Matthews, W., *The Tragedy of Arthur* (Berkeley and Los Angeles, 1960).

Mehl, D., *The Middle English Romances of the Thirteenth and Fourteenth Centuries* (1968).

Miller, E., *War in the North* (Hull, 1960).

Mirot, L. and Déprez, E., 'Les Ambassades anglaises pendant la guerre de cent ans', BEC, 60 (Paris, 1899).

Moisant, J., *Le Prince Noir en Aquitaine* (Paris, 1894).

Mollat, G., *Les Papes d'Avignon (1305–1378)* (Paris, 1964).

Moorman, C., *A Knyght There Was* (Lexington, Kentucky, 1967).

Morris, J. E., 'Mounted Infantry in Medieval Warfare', *TRHS*, 3rd ser., 8 (1914).

Nicholson, R., *Edward III and the Scots* (Oxford, 1965).

North, J. J., *English Hammered Coinage*, vol. 2, *Edward I – Charles II, 1272–1662* (1960).

Oakden, J. P., *Alliterative Poetry in Middle English*, 2 vols (1930–5, repr. New York 1968).

Offler, H. S., 'England and Germany at the Beginning of the Hundred Years War', *EHR*, 54 (1939).

O'Loughlin, J. L. N., 'The Middle English Alliterative *Morte Arthure*', *MAE*, 4 (1935).

Oman, C. W. C., *The Art of War in the Middle Ages*, rev. and ed. J. H. Beeler (New York, 1953, repr. 1960).

Owst, G. R., 'The "Angel" and the "Goliardeys" of Langland's Prologue', *MLR*, 20 (1925).

——, *Literature and Pulpit in Medieval England* (Oxford, 1933, 2nd rev. edn 1961).

Painter, S., *French Chivalry* (Baltimore, 1940).

——, *William Marshal, Knight-Errant, Baron, and Regent of England* (Baltimore, 1933, repr. 1966).

Palmer, J. J. N., 'The Impeachment of Michael de la Pole in 1386', *BIHR*, 42 (1969).

——, *England, France and Christendom, 1377–99* (1972).

Parks, G. B., *The English Traveller to Italy*, vol. 1, *The Middle Ages (to 1525)* (Rome, 1954).

——, 'King Arthur and the Roads to Rome', *JEGP*, 45 (1946).

——, 'The Route of Chaucer's First Journey to Italy', *ELH*, 16 (1949).

Patourel, J. le, 'Edward III and the Kingdom of France', *History*, 43 (1958).

——, 'The Treaty of Brétigny, 1360', *TRHS*, 5th ser., 10 (1960).

Peck, Sister H. M., 'The Prophecy of John of Bridlington' (unpublished doctoral dissertation, University of Chicago, 1930).

Peristiany, J. G., ed., *Honour and Shame, The Values of Mediterranean Society* (1965).

Perroy, E., *The Hundred Years War*, Eng. trans. (1951, repr. 1965).

——, 'Franco-English Relations, 1350–1400', *History*, 21 (1936).

Post, G., 'Two Notes on Nationalism in the Middle Ages', *Traditio*, 9 (1953).

Postan, M. M., 'The Costs of the Hundred Years War', *PP*, 27 (1964).

——, 'Some Social Consequences of the Hundred Years War', *Econ. Hist. Rev.*, 12 (1942).

Potter, W. J. W., 'Gold Coinages of Edward III, pt 1, The Early and Pre-Treaty Coinages', *The Numismatic Chronicle*, 7th ser., III (1963).

Power, E., *The Wool Trade in English Medieval History* (Oxford, 1941, repr. 1965).

Powicke, Michael, *Military Obligation in Medieval England* (Oxford, 1962).

Pratt, R. A., 'Chaucer's Use of the *Teseida*', *PMLA*, 62 (1947).

——, 'Geoffrey Chaucer, Esq., and Sir John Hawkwood', *ELH*, 16 (1949).

Prestage, E., ed., *Chivalry* (1928).

Prince, A. E., 'The Payment of Army Wages in Edward III's Reign', *Speculum*, 19 (1944).

——, 'The Strength of English Armies in the Reign of Edward III', *EHR*, 46 (1931).

Richardson, H. G. and Sayles, G., 'The Parliaments of Edward III', 2 pts, *BIHR*, 8, 9 (1930–2).

Rickard, P., *Britain in Medieval French Literature, 1100–1500* (Cambridge, 1956).

Robertson, S., 'Elements of Realism in the *Knight's Tale*', *JEGP*, 14 (1915).
Rothwell, W., 'The Teaching of French in Medieval England', *MLR*, 63 (1968).
Runciman, S., *A History of the Crusades*, 3 vols (Cambridge, 1951).
Russell, P. E., *The English Intervention in Spain and Portugal in the Time of Edward III and Richard II* (Oxford, 1955).
Savage, H., 'Chaucer and the "Pitous Deeth" of "Petro, Glorie of Spayne"', *Speculum*, 24 (1949).
——, '*Sir Gawain* and the Order of the Garter', *ELH*, 5 (1938).
Sayles, G., 'The "English Company" of 1343', *Speculum*, 6 (1931).
Scattergood, V. J., *Politics and Poetry in the Fifteenth Century* (1971).
Schirmer, W. F., *John Lydgate*, Eng. trans. (1961).
Seidlmayer, M., *Currents of Medieval Thought*, Eng. trans. (Oxford, 1960).
Severs, J. B., 'The Source of Chaucer's Melibeus', *PMLA*, 50 (1935).
Shaw, P., 'The Black Prince', *History*, 24 (1939).
Shears, F. S., *Froissart, Chronicler and Poet* (1930).
Sherborne, J. W., 'The Battle of La Rochelle and the War at Sea 1372–5', *BIHR*, 42 (1969).
——, 'The English Navy: Shipping and Manpower 1369–1389', *PP*, 37 (1967).
——, 'Indentured Retinues and English Expeditions to France, 1369–1380', *EHR*, 79 (1964).
Smalley, B., *English Friars and Antiquity in the Early Fourteenth Century* (Oxford, 1960).
Steadman, J. M., 'The Date of *Winnere and Wastoure*', *MP*, 19 (1921).
Steel, A., *Richard II* (Cambridge, 1941).
Stillwell, G., 'John Gower and the Last Years of Edward III', *Studies in Philology*, 45 (1948).
——, 'The Political Meaning of Chaucer's *Tale of Melibee*', *Speculum*, 19 (1944).
——, '*Wynnere and Wastoure* and the Hundred Years War', *ELH*, 8 (1941).
Stillwell, G. and Webb, H. J., 'Chaucer's Knight and the Hundred Years War', *MLN*, 59 (1944).
Stones, E. L. G., 'The Folvilles of Ashby-Folville, Leicestershire, and Their Associates in Crime', *TRHS*, 5th ser., VII (1957).
Tait, J., 'The Date and Authorship of the *Speculum Regis Edwardi*', *EHR*, 16 (1901).
Tatlock, J. S. P., *The Development and Chronology of Chaucer's Works* (1907).

H

Taylor, J., *The Universal Chronicle of Ranulf Higden* (Oxford, 1966).
Taylor, R., *The Political Prophecy in England* (New York, 1911).
Terry, S. B., *The Financing of the Hundred Years' War 1337–1360* (1914).
Thrupp, S. L., *The Merchant Class of Medieval London* (Ann Arbor, 1948, repr. 1962).
Tout, T. F. and Broome, D. M., 'A National Balance Sheet for 1362–3', *EHR*, 39 (1924).
Tout, T. F., *Edward I* (1893, repr. 1896).
——, 'Firearms in England in the Fourteenth Century', *EHR*, 26 (1911).
——, 'Some Neglected Fights Between Crécy and Poitiers', *EHR*, 20 (1905).
——, 'The Study of Medieval Chronicles', *BJRL*, 6 (1922).
Vising, J., *Anglo-Norman Language and Literature* (1923).
Wagner, A. R., *Heralds and Heraldry in the Middle Ages* (1939).
Whiting, B. J., 'The Vows of the Heron', *Speculum*, 20 (1945).
Wilson, R. M., 'English and French in England, 1100–1300', *History*, 28 (1943).
——, *The Lost Literature of Medieval England* (1952).

Index